ULTIMATE GALACTUS
ULTIMATE
NIGHTMARE

WRITER: WARREN ELLIS
PENCILS: TREVOR HAIRSINE
WITH STEVE EPTING FOR CHAPTER 3

INKS: NELSON DeCASTRO AND SIMON COLEBY
WITH TOM PALMER, MARK MORALES AND RODNEY RAMOS
COLORS: FRANK D'ARMATA
LETTERS: CHRIS ELIOPOULOS

ASSISTANT EDITOR: NICK LOWE
EDITOR: RALPH MACCHIO
BASED ON AN IDEA BY JOE QUESADA

COLLECTIONS EDITOR: JEFF YOUNGQUIST
ASSISTANT EDITOR: JENNIFER GRÜNWALD
DIRECTOR OF SALES: DAVID GABRIEL
PRODUCTION: LORETTA KROL
BOOK DESIGNER: JEOF VITA
CREATIVE DIRECTOR: TOM MARVELLI

EDITOR IN CHIEF: JOE QUESADA
PUBLISHER: DAN BUCKLEY

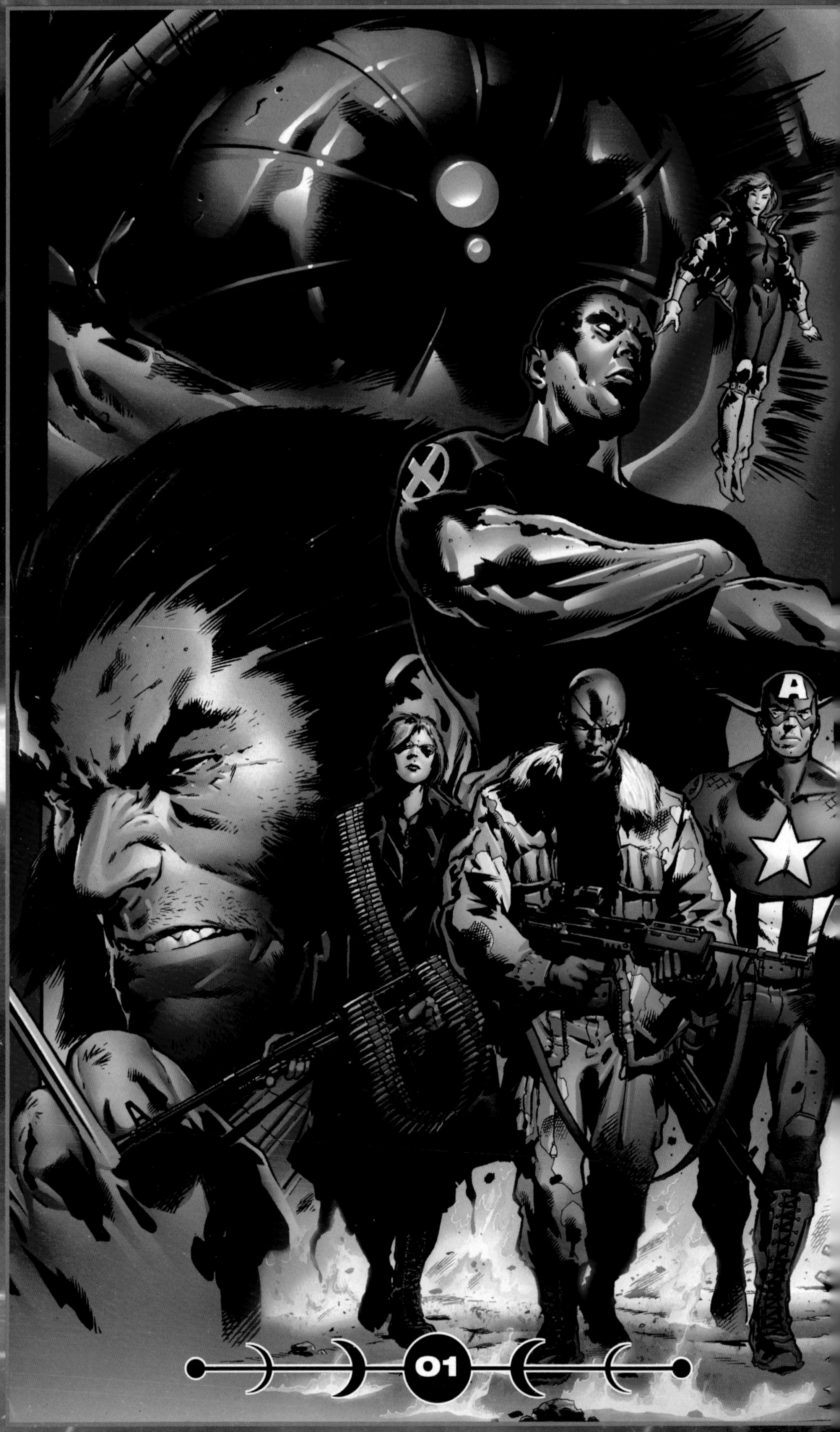

01

Gathered by mutant psychic Professor Charles Xavier, THE X-MEN are soldiers for his dream of coexistence between normal humans and mutants like them.

Formed by General Nick Fury and led by Captain America, THE ULTIMATES are a small but lethal army created to protect humanity against all the new rising threats to the world.

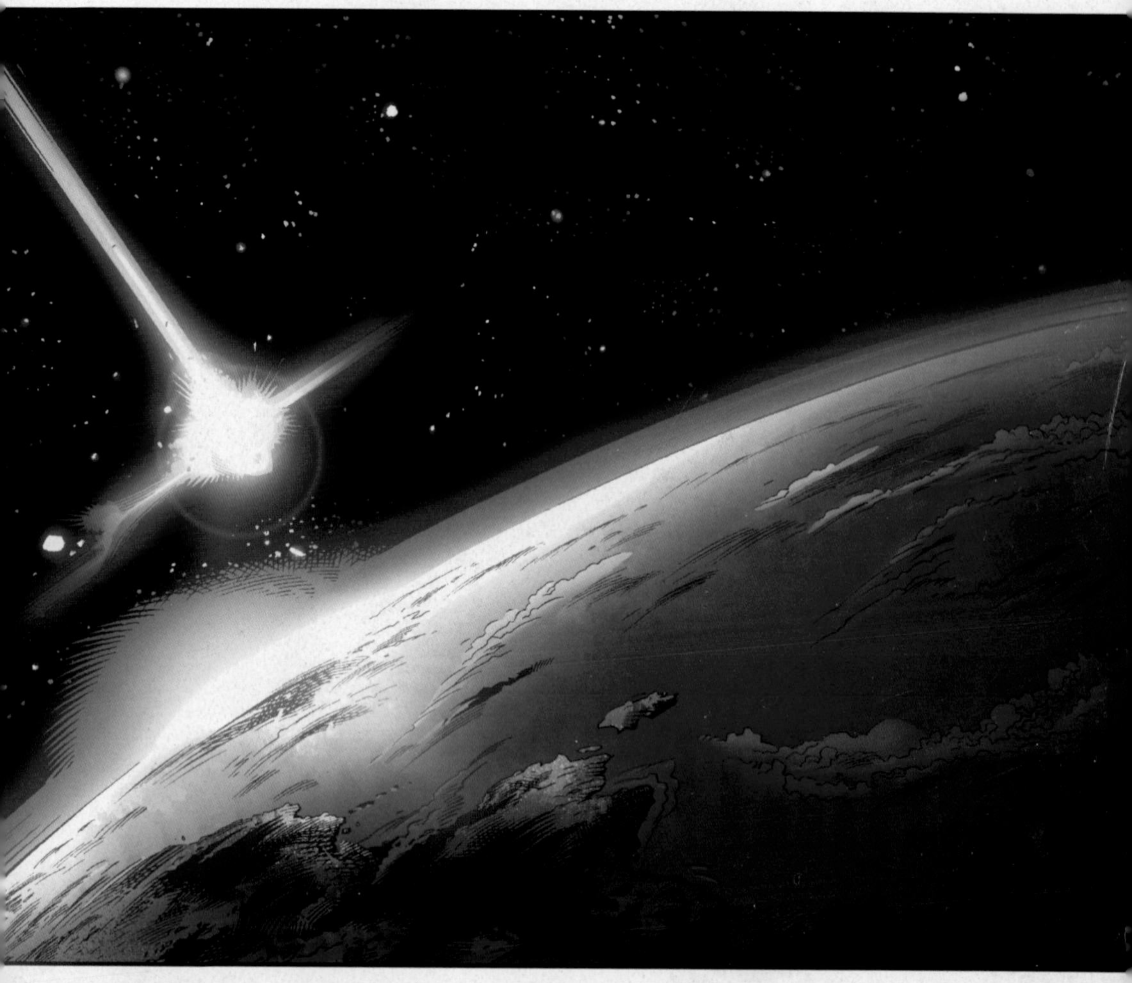

tan Lee presents:

ULTIMATE NIGHTMARE

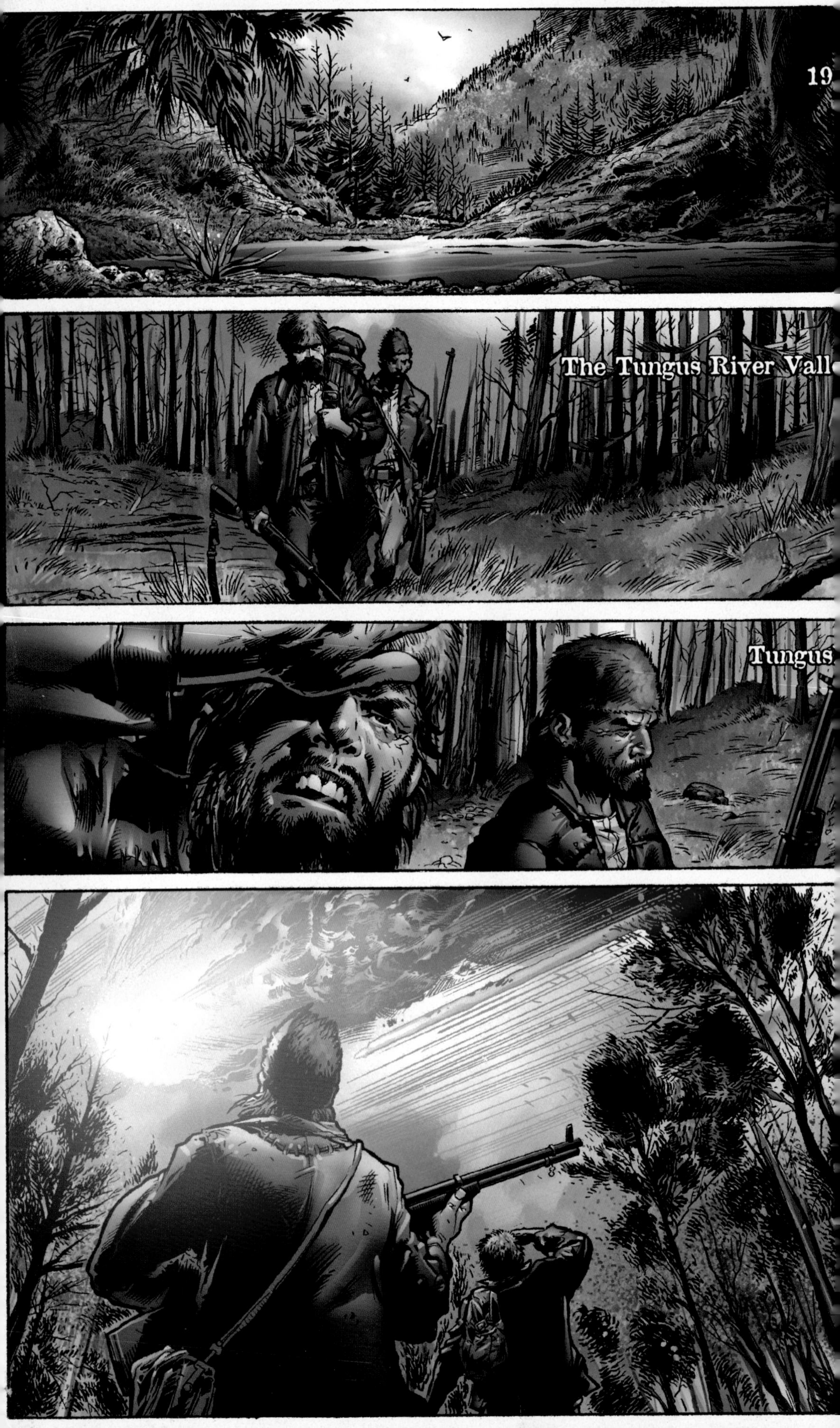
The Tungus River Vall
Tungus

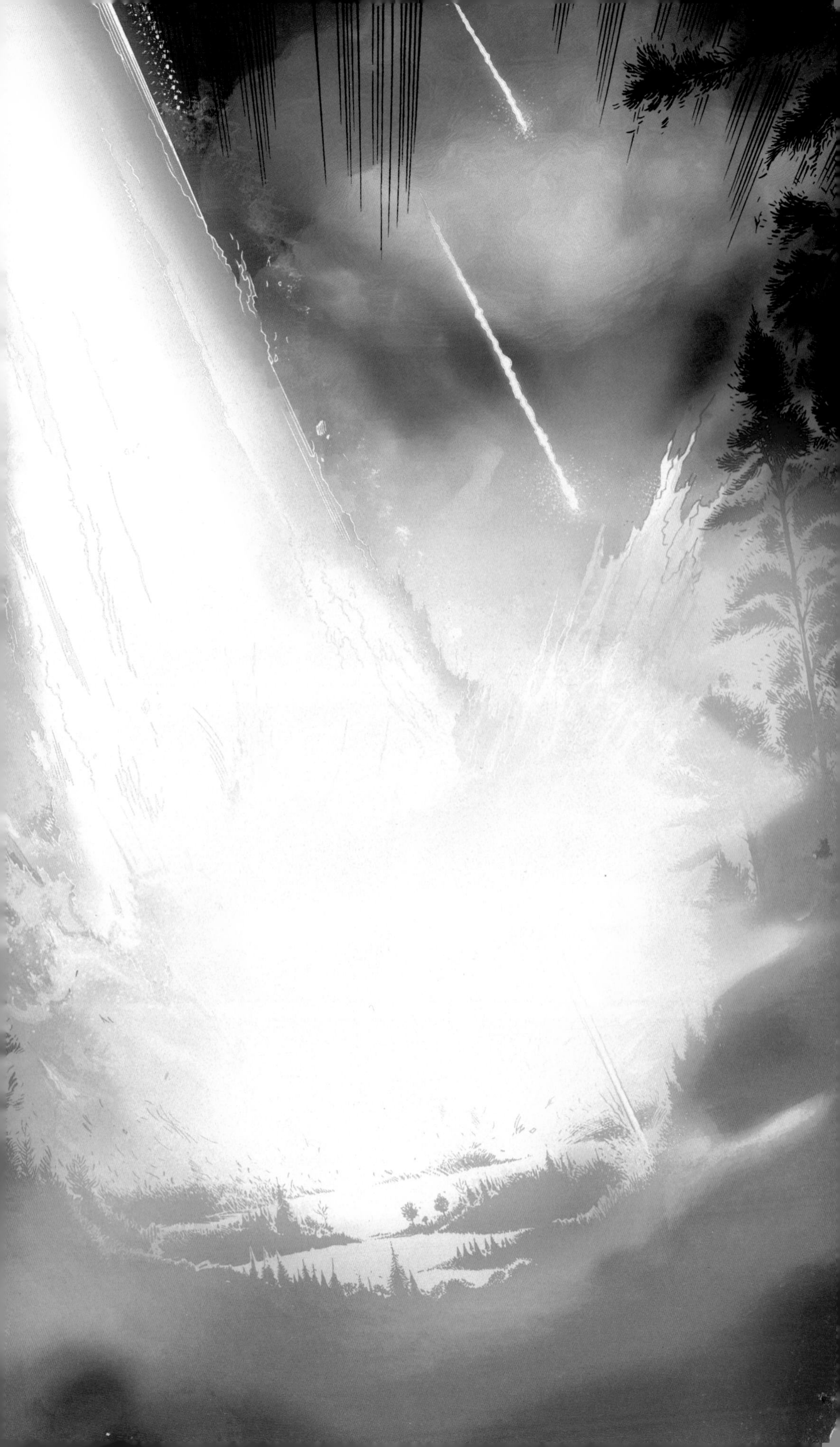

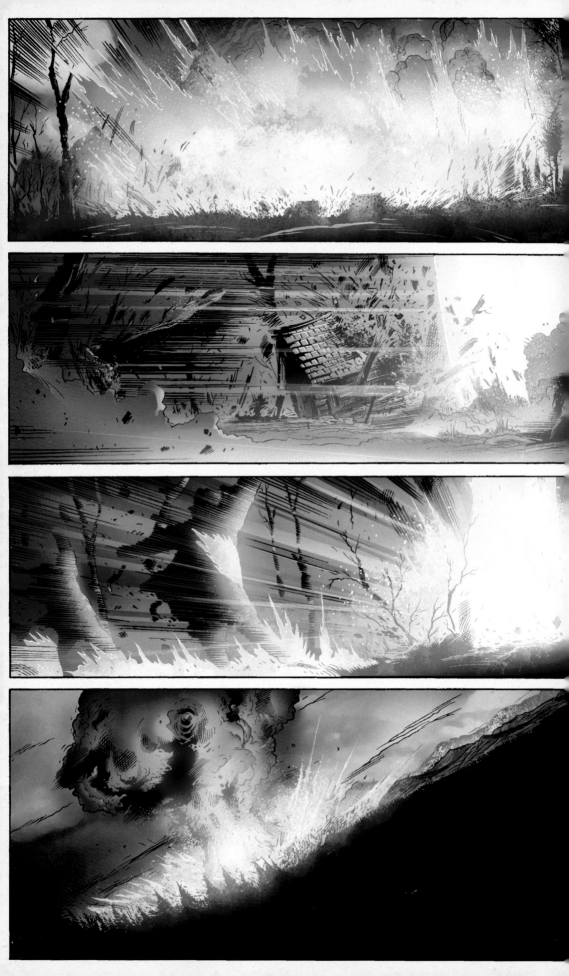

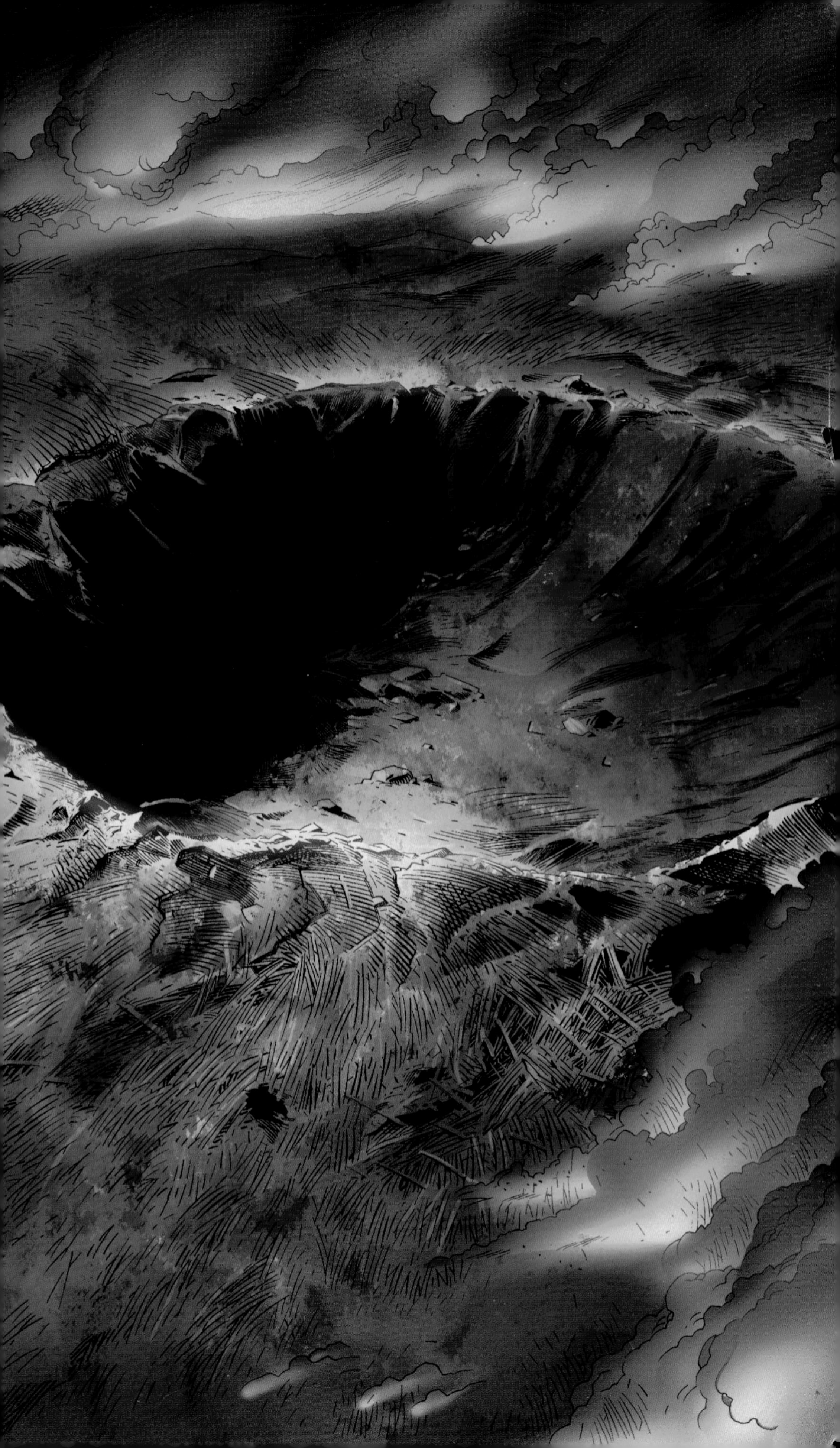

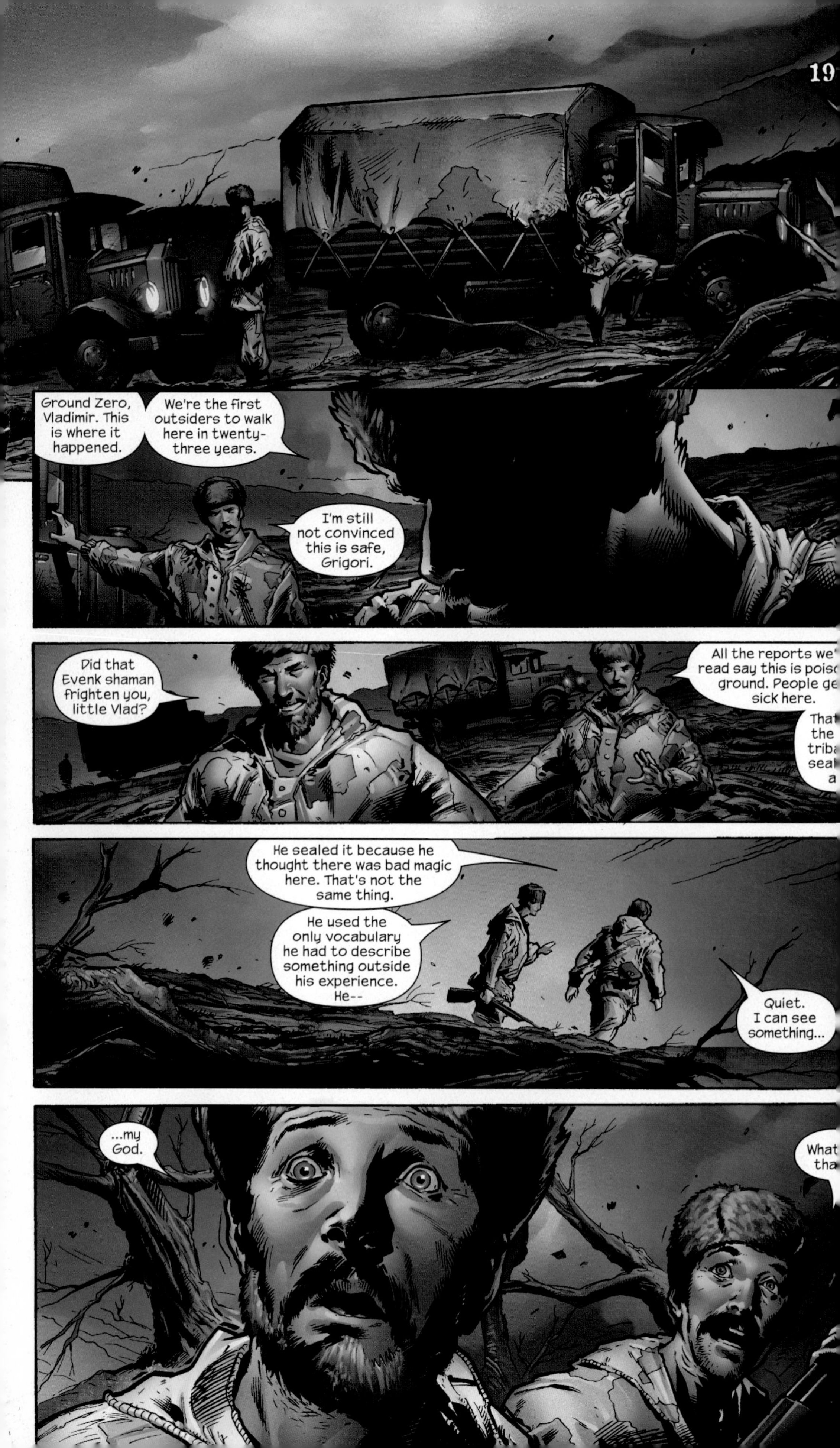
Ground Zero, Vladimir. This is where it happened.
We're the first outsiders to walk here in twenty-three years.
I'm still not convinced this is safe, Grigori.
Did that Evenk shaman frighten you, little Vlad?
All the reports we' read say this is poiso ground. People ge sick here.
He sealed it because he thought there was bad magic here. That's not the same thing.
He used the only vocabulary he had to describe something outside his experience. He--
Quiet. I can see something...
...my God.

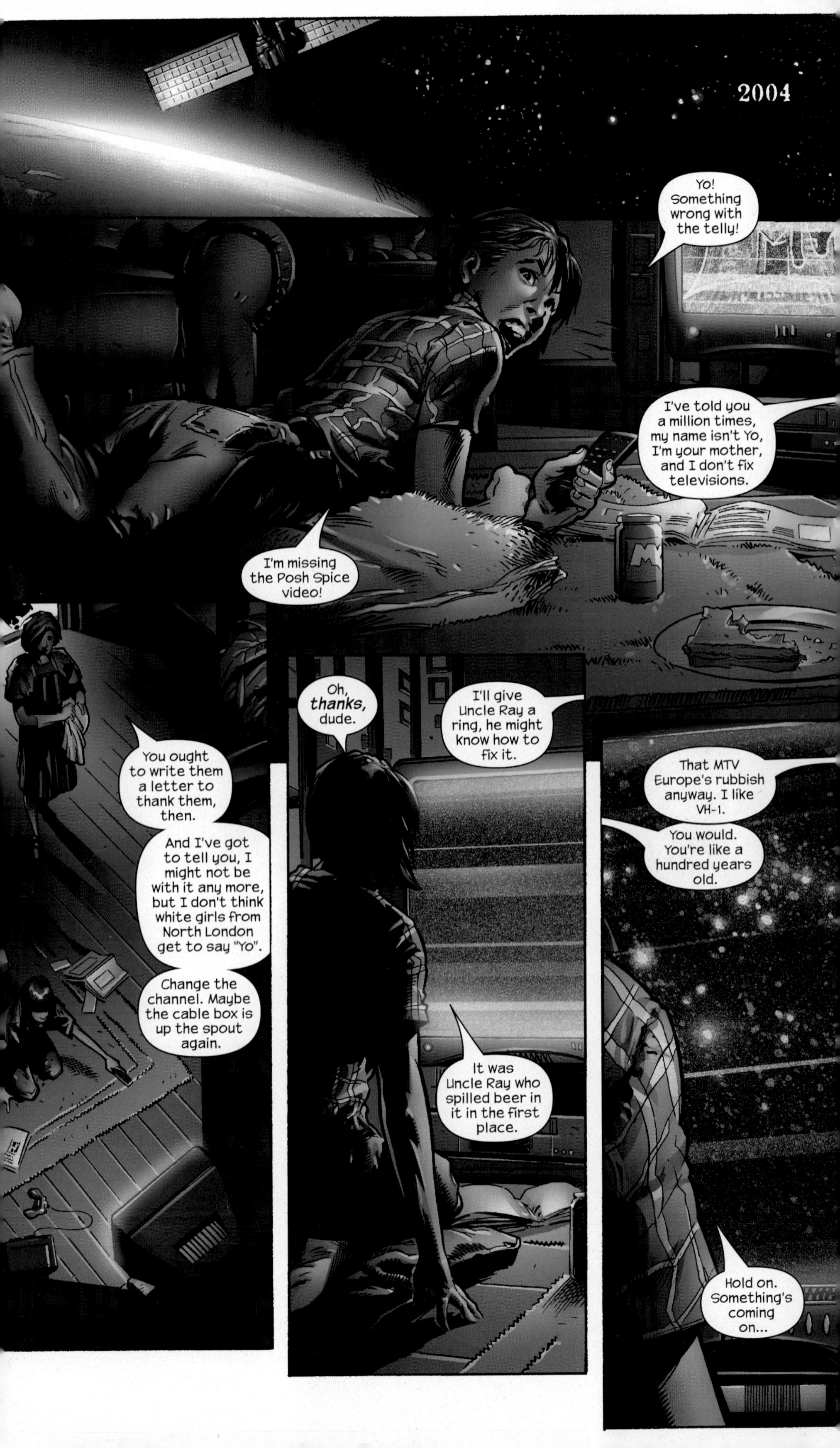
2004
Yo! Something wrong with the telly!
I've told you a million times, my name isn't Yo, I'm your mother, and I don't fix televisions.
I'm missing the Posh Spice video!
You ought to write them a letter to thank them, then.
And I've got to tell you, I might not be with it any more, but I don't think white girls from North London get to say "Yo".
Change the channel. Maybe the cable box is up the spout again.
Oh, *thanks,* dude.
I'll give Uncle Ray a ring, he might know how to fix it.
It was Uncle Ray who spilled beer in it in the first place.
That MTV Europe's rubbish anyway. I like VH-1.
You would. You're like a hundred years old.
Hold on. Something's coming on...

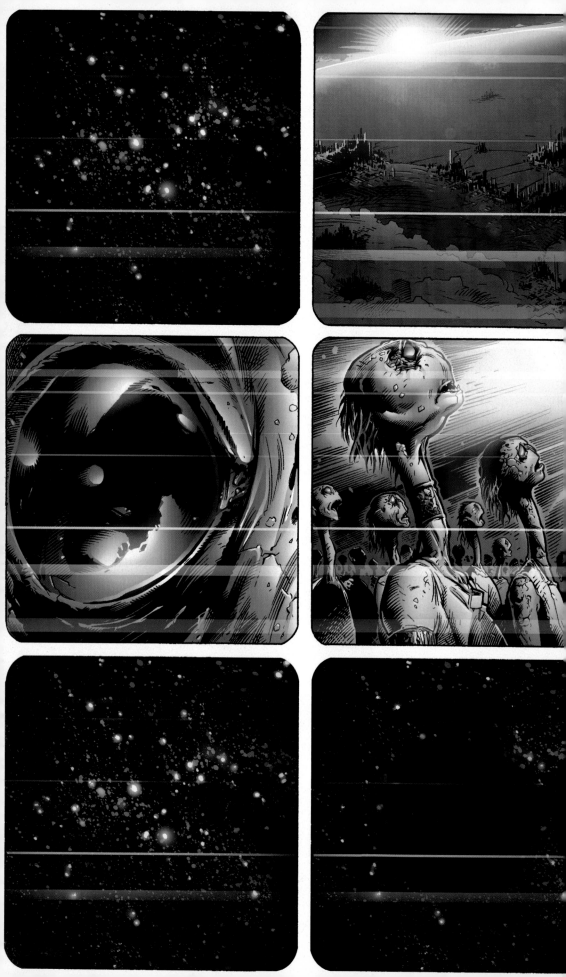

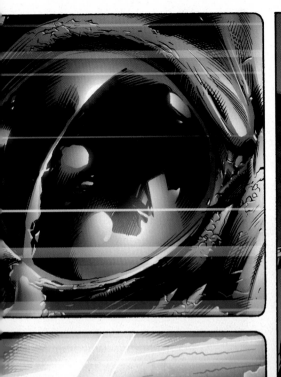

Urrr! Mum, that's horrible--

Must be that heavy-metal music channel-- they shouldn't show things like that in the middle of the day.

EEEEEEEEEEEEEEEEEEEEEE

EEEEEEEEEEEEEEEEEEEEEEEE
It's horrible! They sound like babies! Mum, make it stop!
I can't!
God, it's like the sour of babies dying!

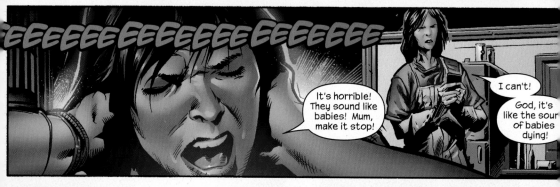

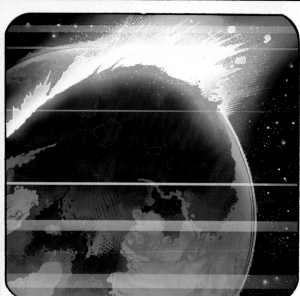

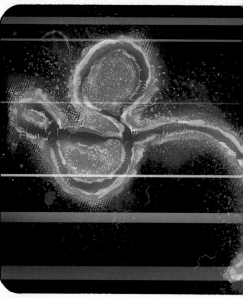

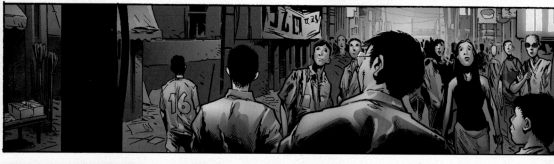

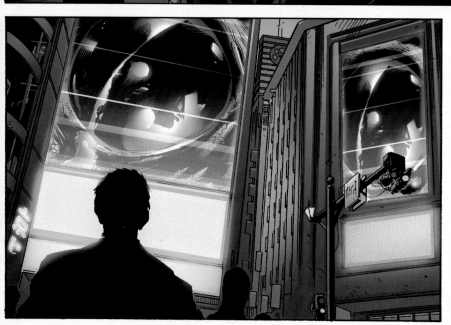

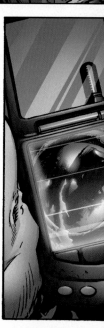

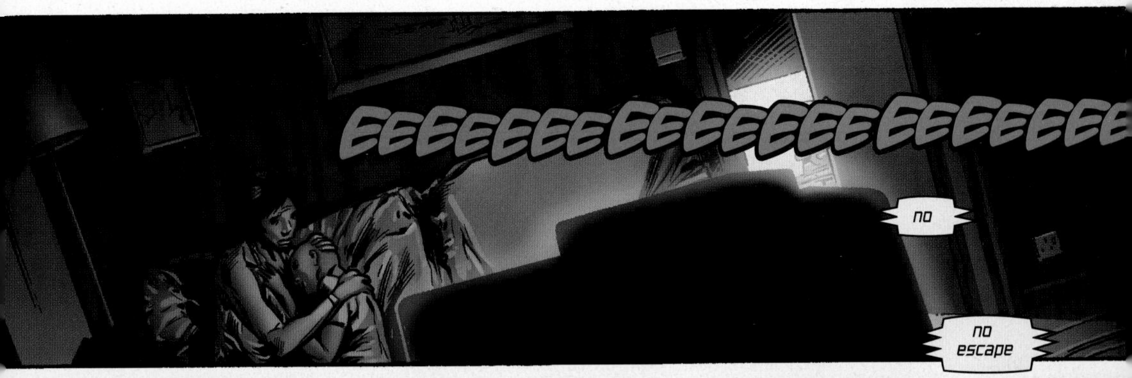
EEEEEEEEEEEEEEEEEEEEEEEEE
no
no escape

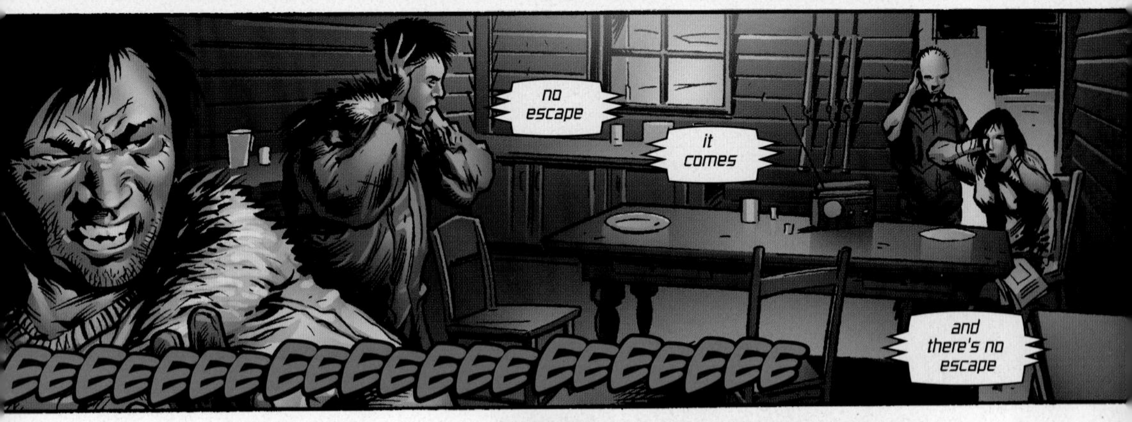
no escape
it comes
EEEEEEEEEEEEEEEEEEEEEEEEE
and there's no escape

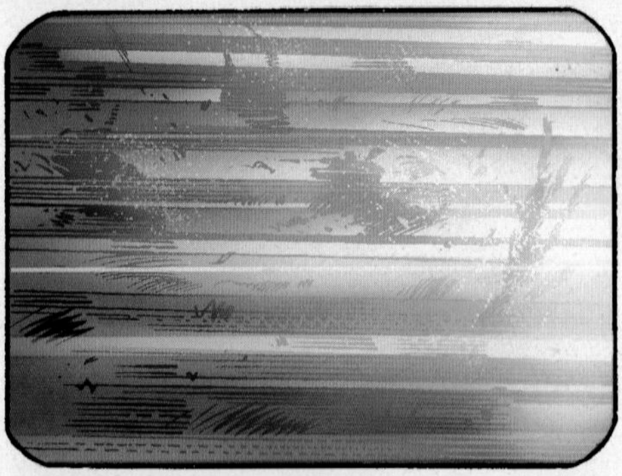

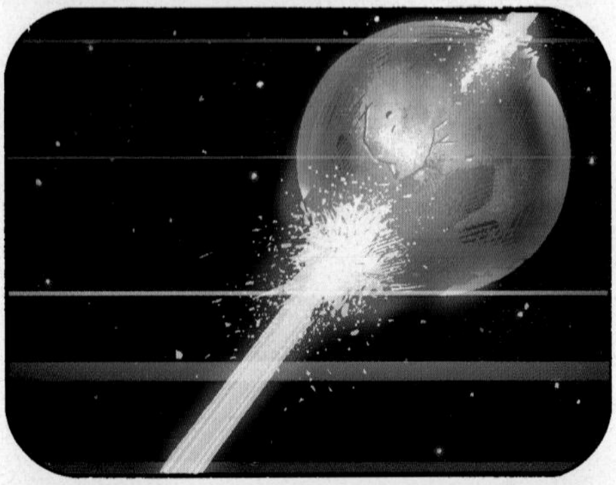

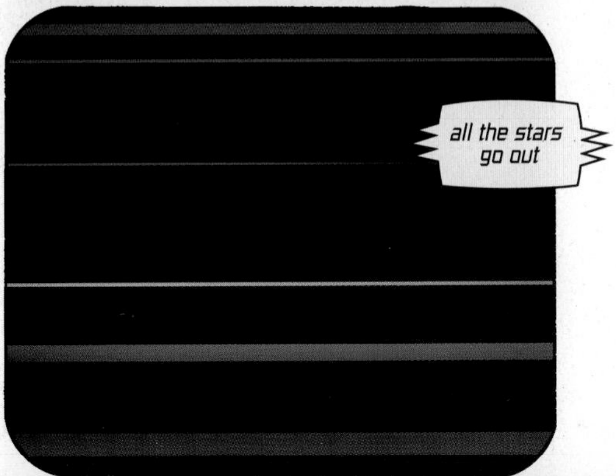
all the stars go out

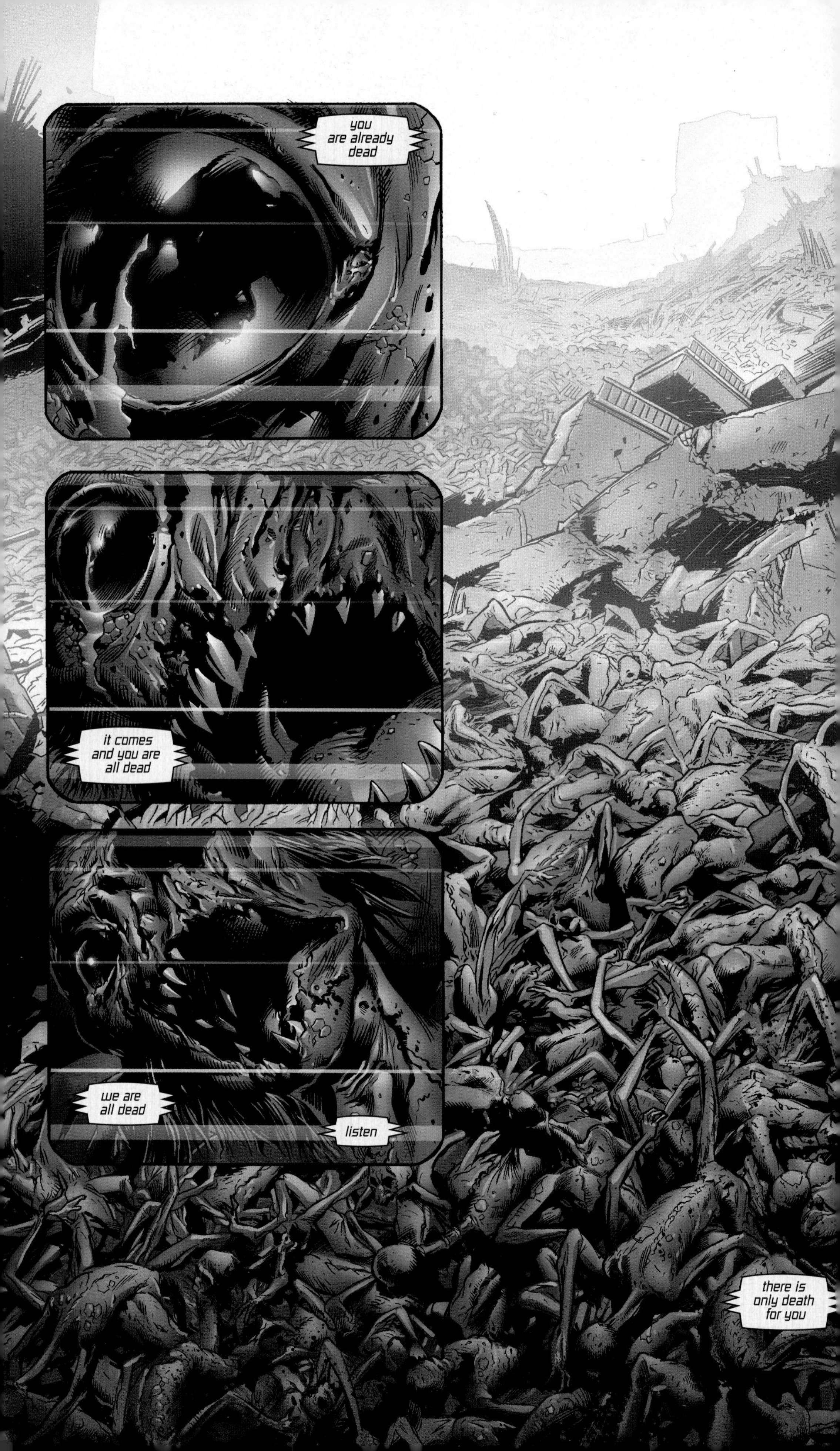
you are already dead
it comes and you are all dead
we are all dead
listen
there is only death for you

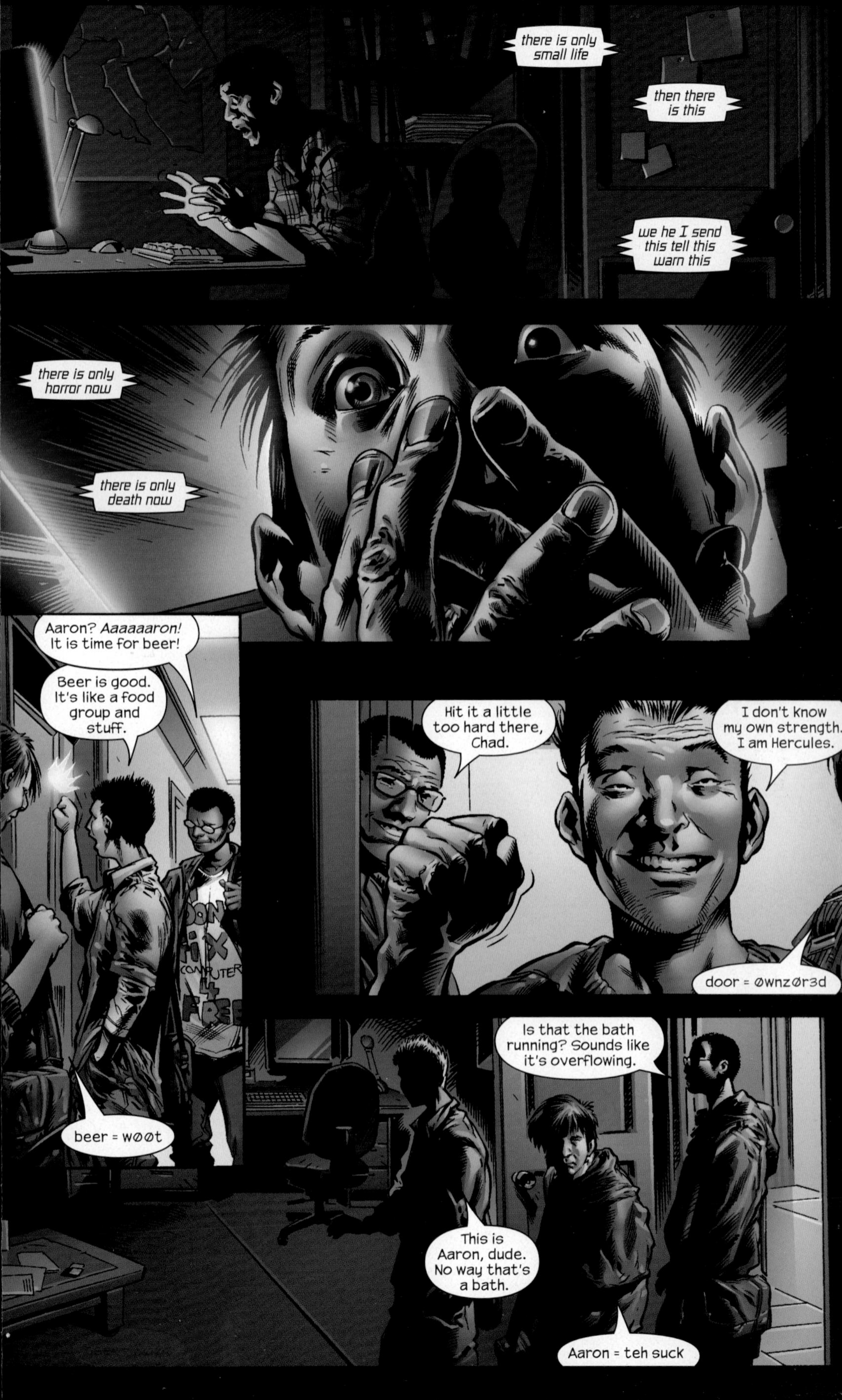
there is only
small life
then there
is this
we he I send
this tell this
warn this
there is only
horror now
there is only
death now
Aaron? Aaaaaaron!
It is time for beer!
Beer is good.
It's like a food
group and
stuff.
beer = wØØt
Hit it a little
too hard there,
Chad.
I don't know
my own strength.
I am Hercules.
door = Øwnz0r3d
Is that the bath
running? Sounds like
it's overflowing.
This is
Aaron, dude.
No way that's
a bath.
Aaron = teh suck

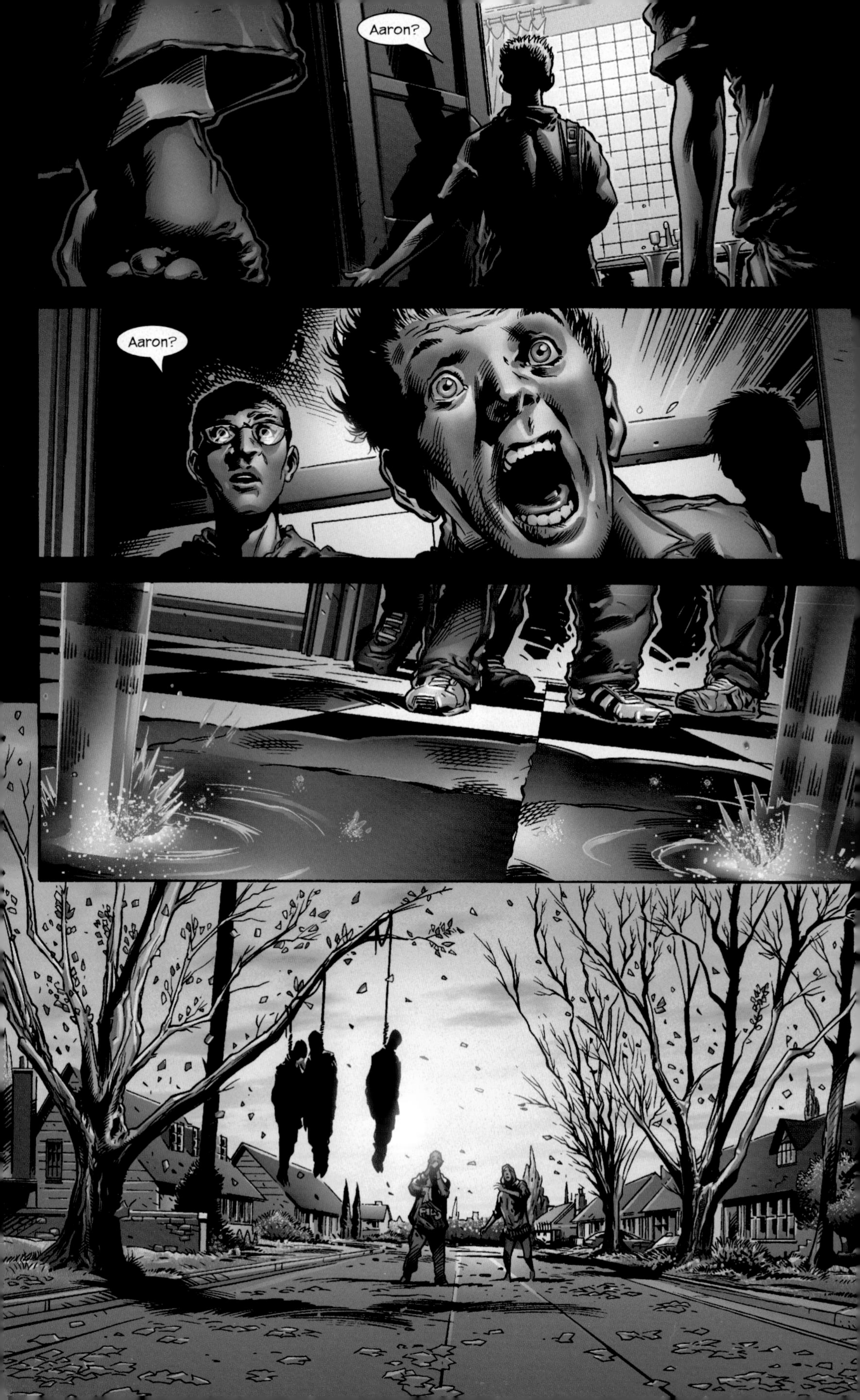
Aaron?
Aaron?

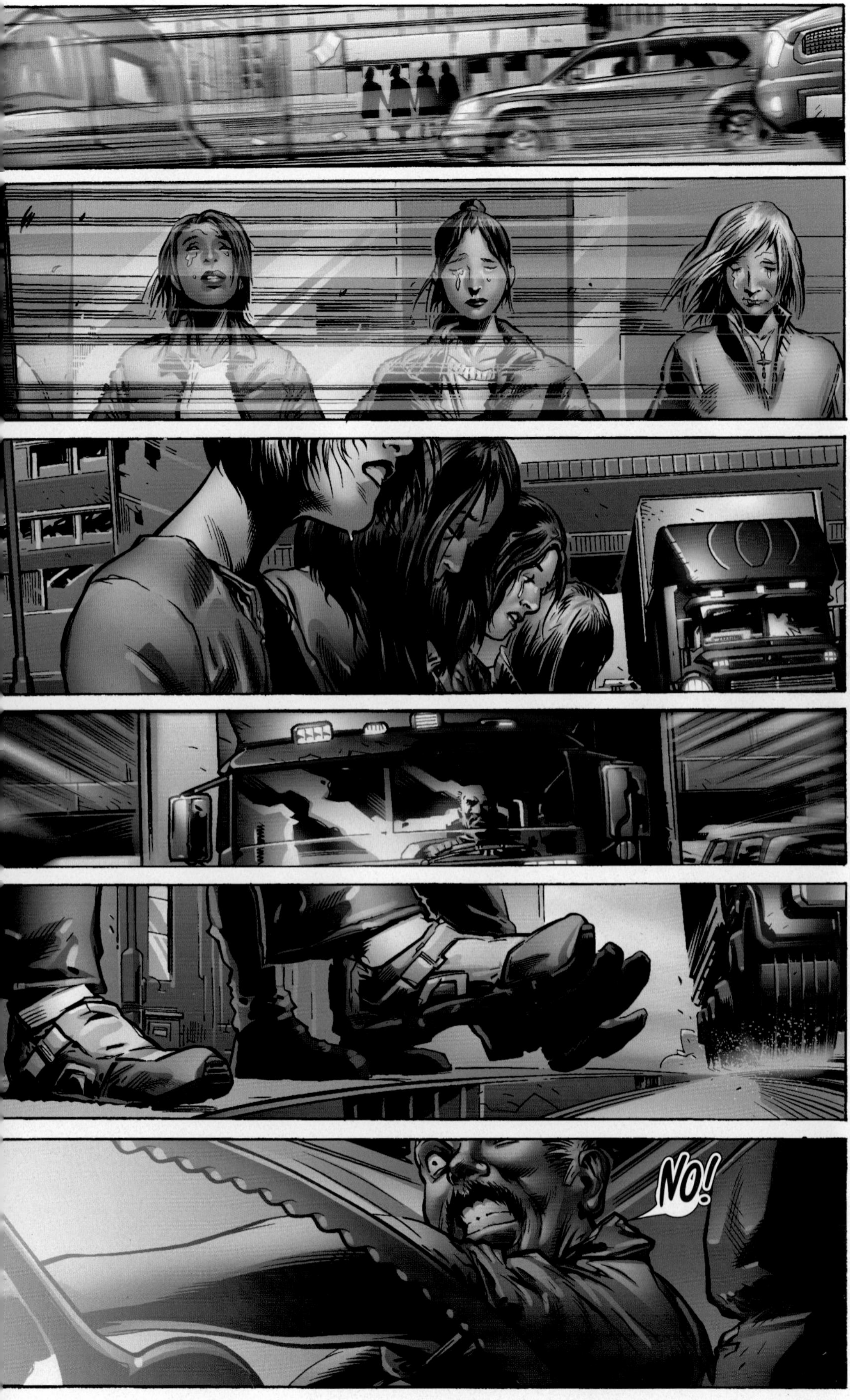
NO!

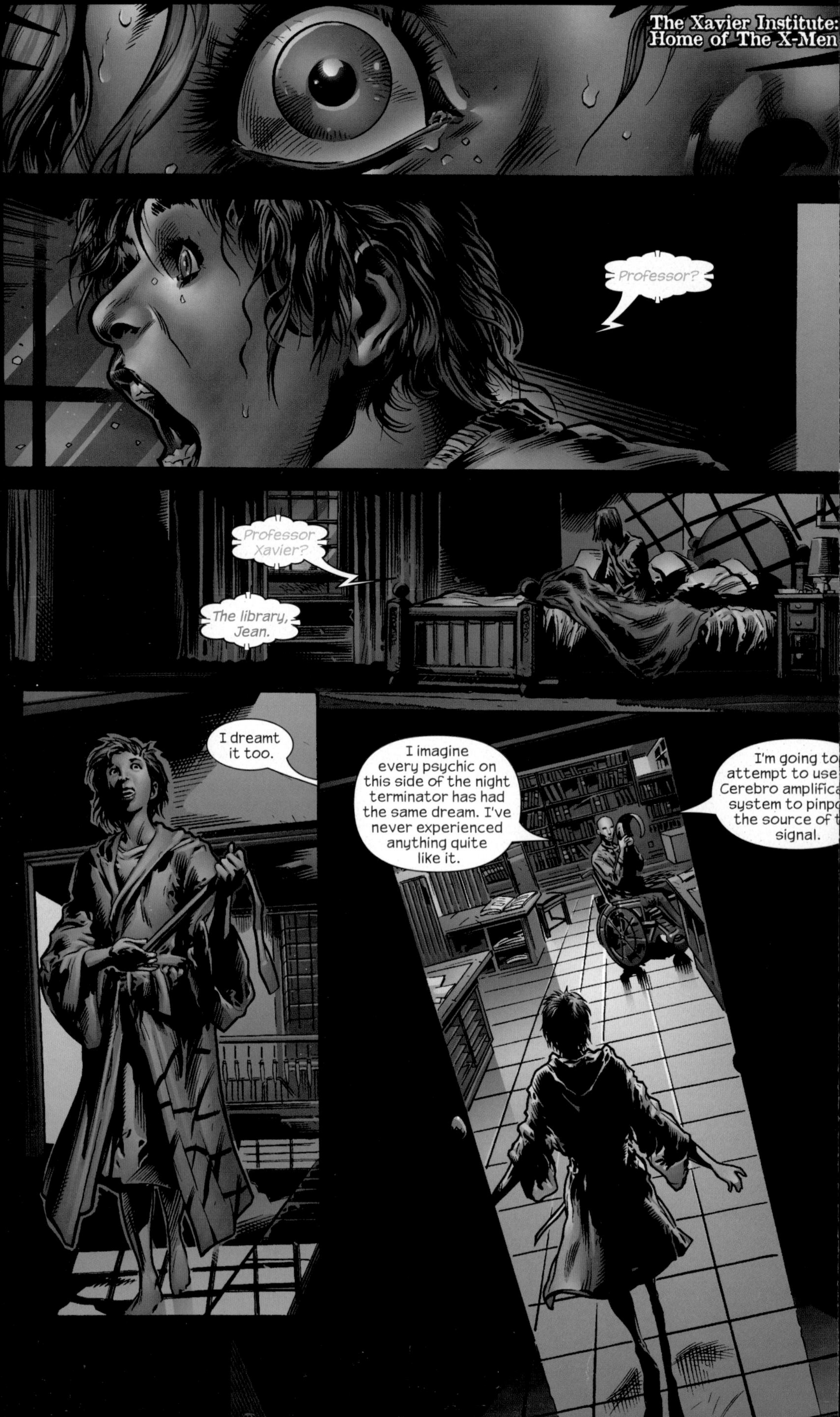
The Xavier Institute:
Home of The X-Men
Professor?
Professor Xavier?
The library, Jean.
I dreamt it too.
I imagine every psychic on this side of the night terminator has had the same dream. I've never experienced anything quite like it.
I'm going to attempt to use Cerebro amplifica system to pinpo the source of t signal.

It felt like... like someone was playing me a recording, almost.

Indeed. Surreal as the sequence was, it had the authentic tenor of direct experience. It's not an artificial construct.

Is it an attack?

I don't think so. I think it's a cry for help.

Perhaps... imagine a traumatized teenager, factor positive and emerging into full-blown homo sapiens novus.

Trying to communicate what they've experienced, but filtered through the fantasies they've evolved to cope.

Visual metaphors for loneliness and abuse.

Young, scared, confused, and the most powerful broadcast telepath we've ever encountered...

...there.

Jean, I'd like you to wake up Logan and Peter.

We've a rescue mission to mount.

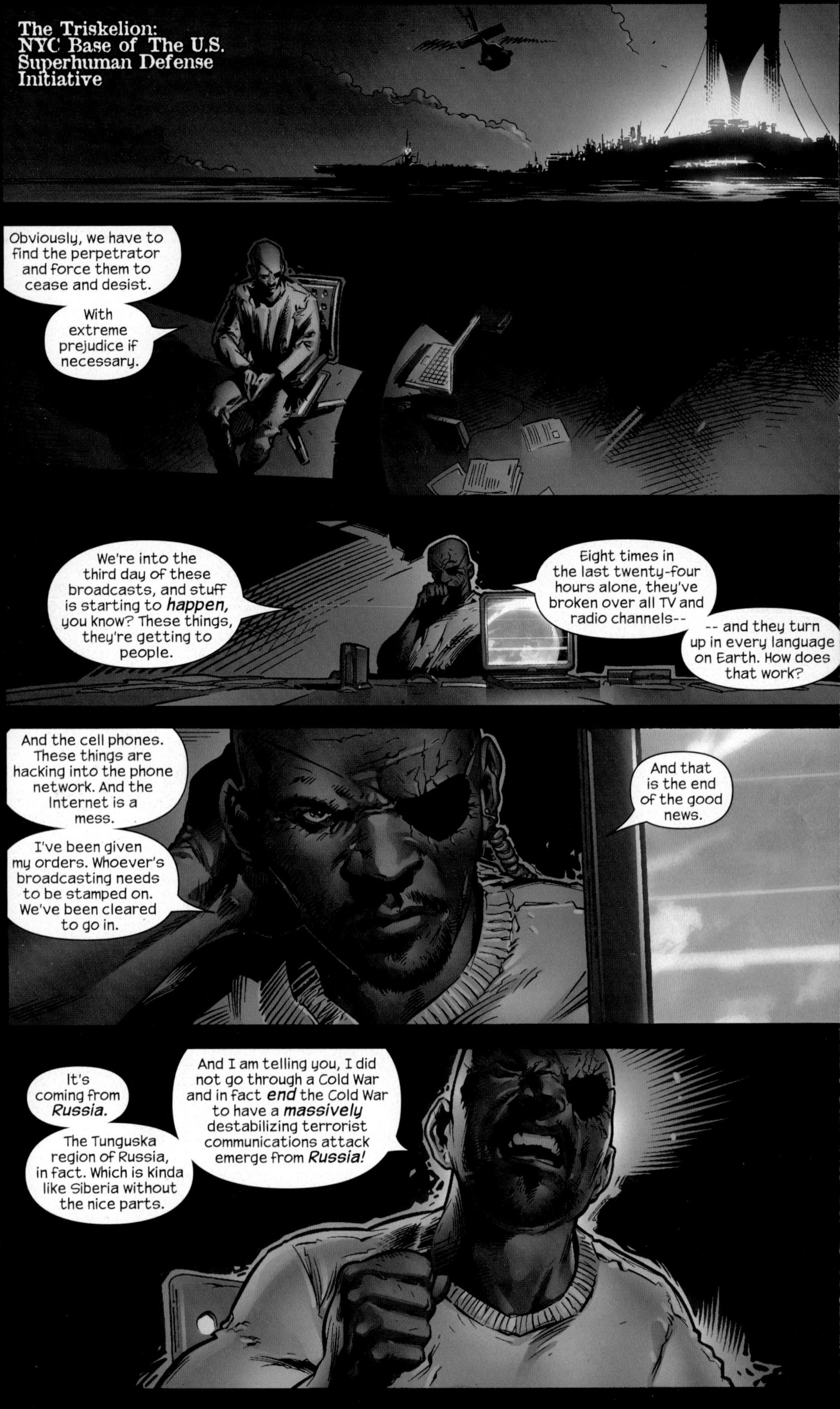
The Triskelion:
NYC Base of The U.S. Superhuman Defense Initiative
Obviously, we have to find the perpetrator and force them to cease and desist.
With extreme prejudice if necessary.
We're into the third day of these broadcasts, and stuff is starting to *happen,* you know? These things, they're getting to people.
Eight times in the last twenty-four hours alone, they've broken over all TV and radio channels--
-- and they turn up in every language on Earth. How does that work?
And the cell phones. These things are hacking into the phone network. And the Internet is a mess.
I've been given my orders. Whoever's broadcasting needs to be stamped on. We've been cleared to go in.
And that is the end of the good news.
It's coming from *Russia.*
The Tunguska region of Russia, in fact. Which is kinda like Siberia without the nice parts.
And I am telling you, I did not go through a Cold War and in fact *end* the Cold War to have a *massively* destabilizing terrorist communications attack emerge from *Russia!*

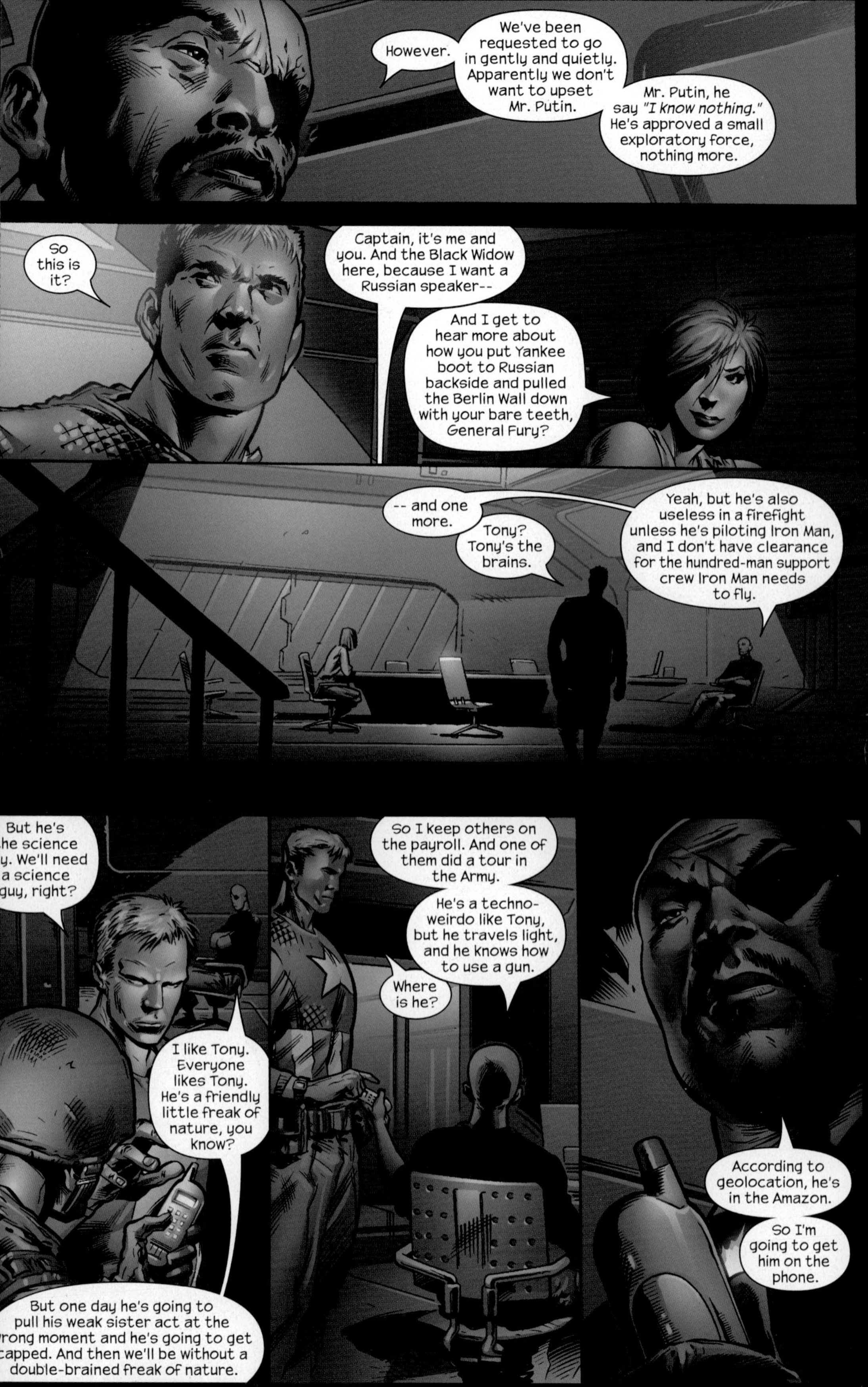
However.
We've been requested to go in gently and quietly. Apparently we don't want to upset Mr. Putin.
Mr. Putin, he say *"I know nothing."* He's approved a small exploratory force, nothing more.
So this is it?
Captain, it's me and you. And the Black Widow here, because I want a Russian speaker--
And I get to hear more about how you put Yankee boot to Russian backside and pulled the Berlin Wall down with your bare teeth, General Fury?
-- and one more.
Tony? Tony's the brains.
Yeah, but he's also useless in a firefight unless he's piloting Iron Man, and I don't have clearance for the hundred-man support crew Iron Man needs to fly.
But he's he science y. We'll need a science guy, right?
I like Tony. Everyone likes Tony. He's a friendly little freak of nature, you know?
But one day he's going to pull his weak sister act at the rong moment and he's going to get capped. And then we'll be without a double-brained freak of nature.
So I keep others on the payroll. And one of them did a tour in the Army.
He's a techno-weirdo like Tony, but he travels light, and he knows how to use a gun.
Where is he?
According to geolocation, he's in the Amazon.
So I'm going to get him on the phone.

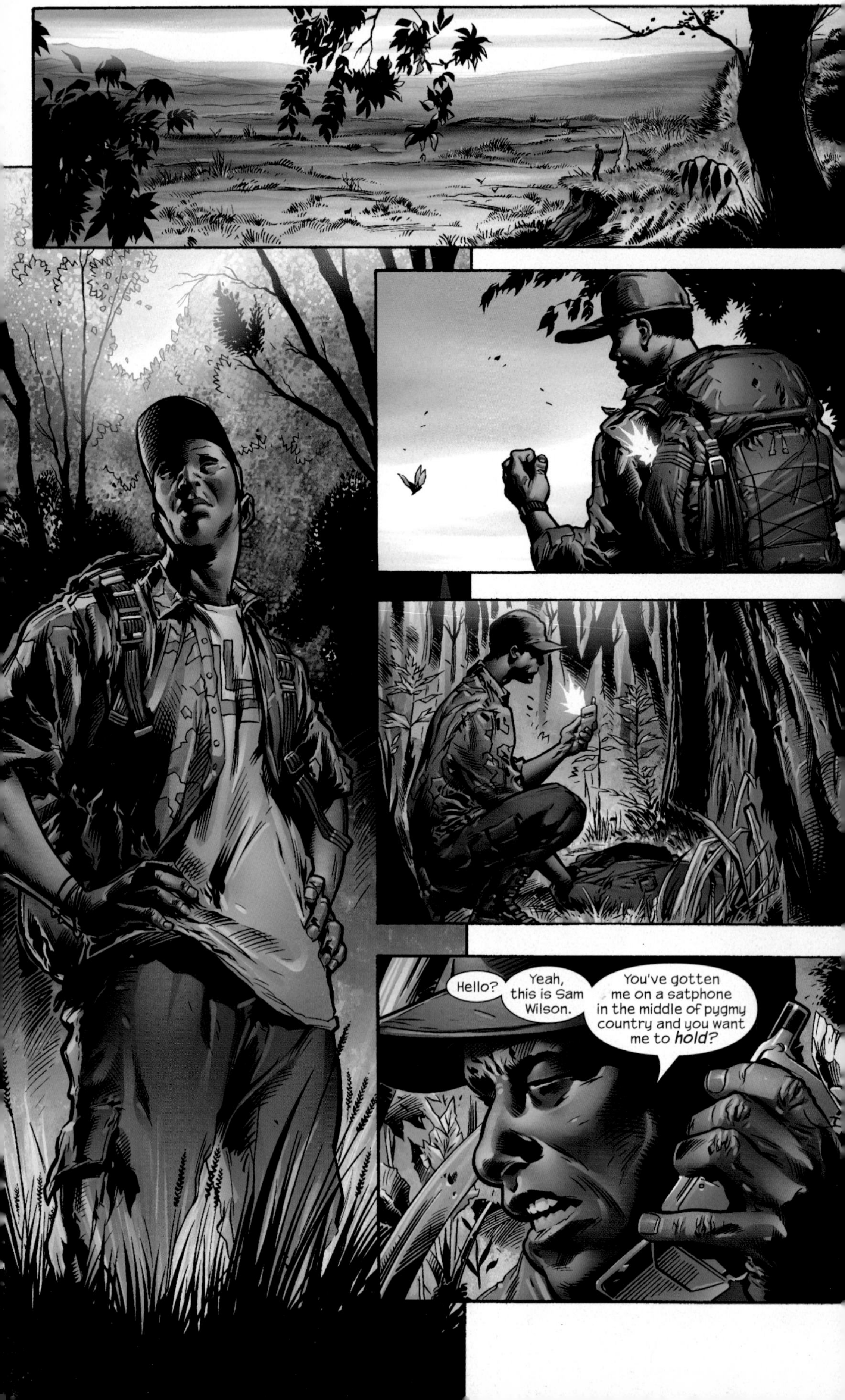
Hello?
Yeah, this is Sam Wilson.
You've gotten me on a satphone in the middle of pygmy country and you want me to *hold*?

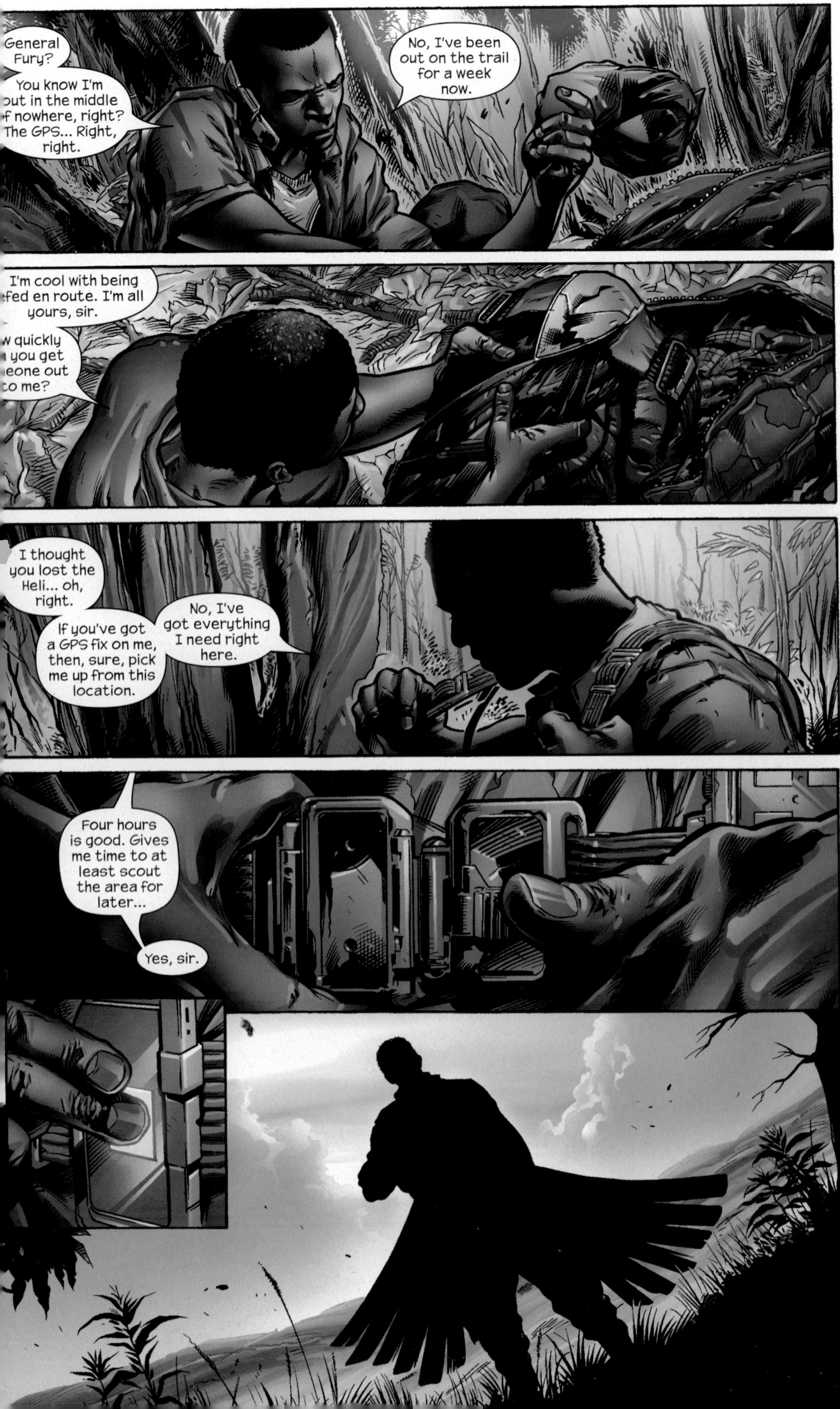

General Fury?
You know I'm
ut in the middle
f nowhere, right?
The GPS... Right, right.
No, I've been out on the trail for a week now.
I'm cool with being
fed en route. I'm all yours, sir.
w quickly
you get
eone out
to me?
I thought you lost the Heli... oh, right.
If you've got a GPS fix on me, then, sure, pick me up from this location.
No, I've got everything I need right here.
Four hours is good. Gives me time to at least scout the area for later...
Yes, sir.

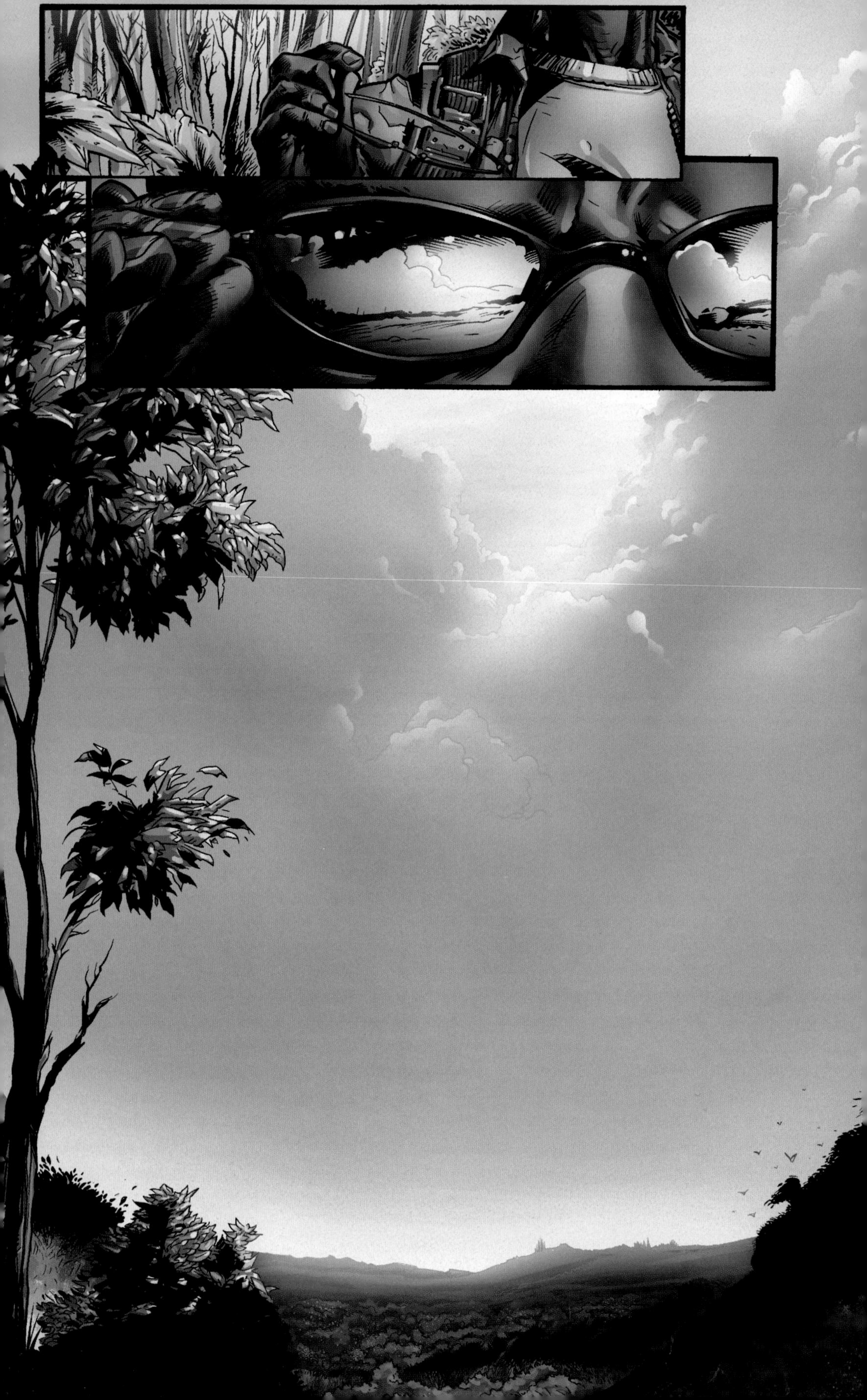

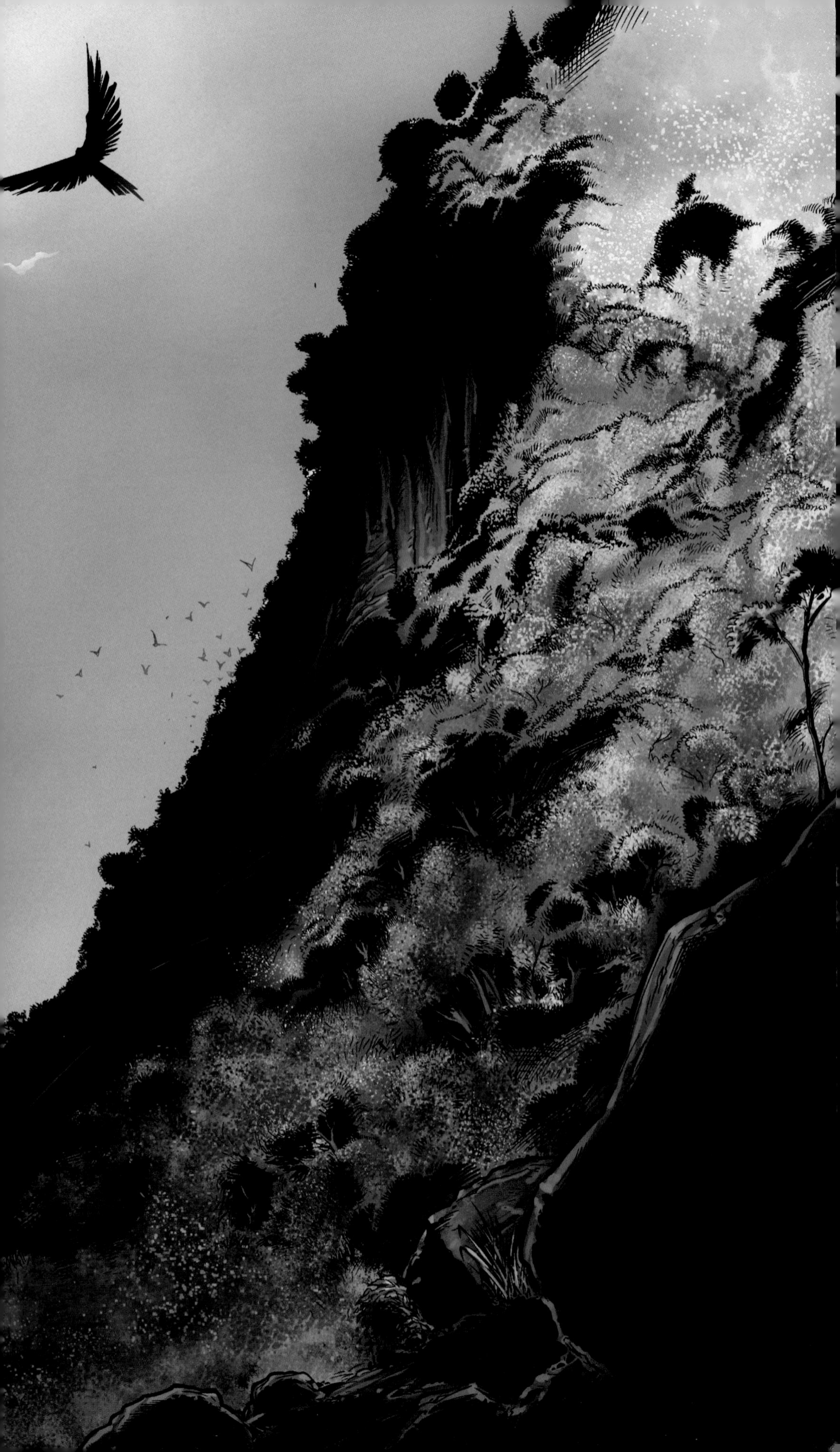

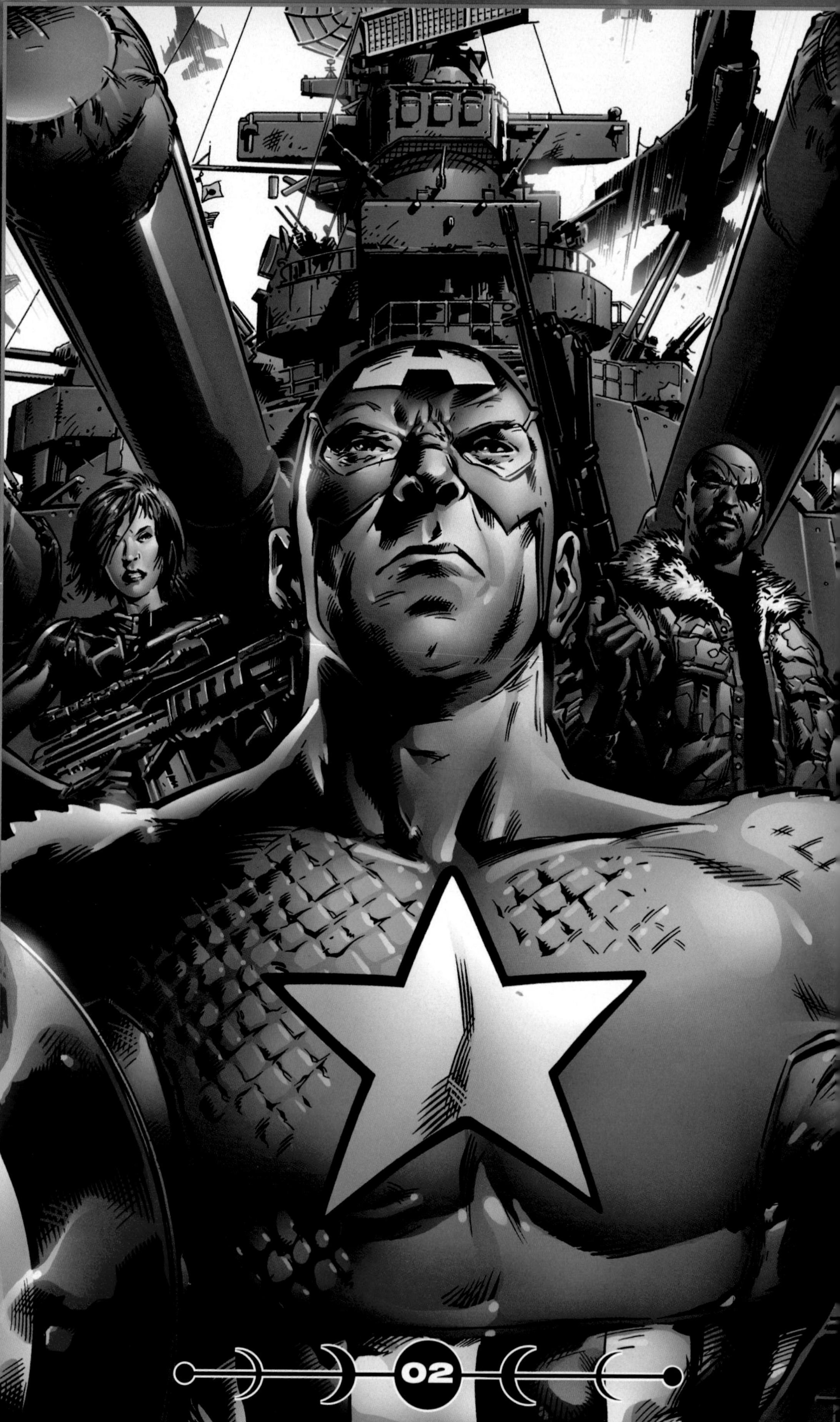

02

stan lee presents:

ULTIMATE NIGHTMARE

CHAPTER TWO

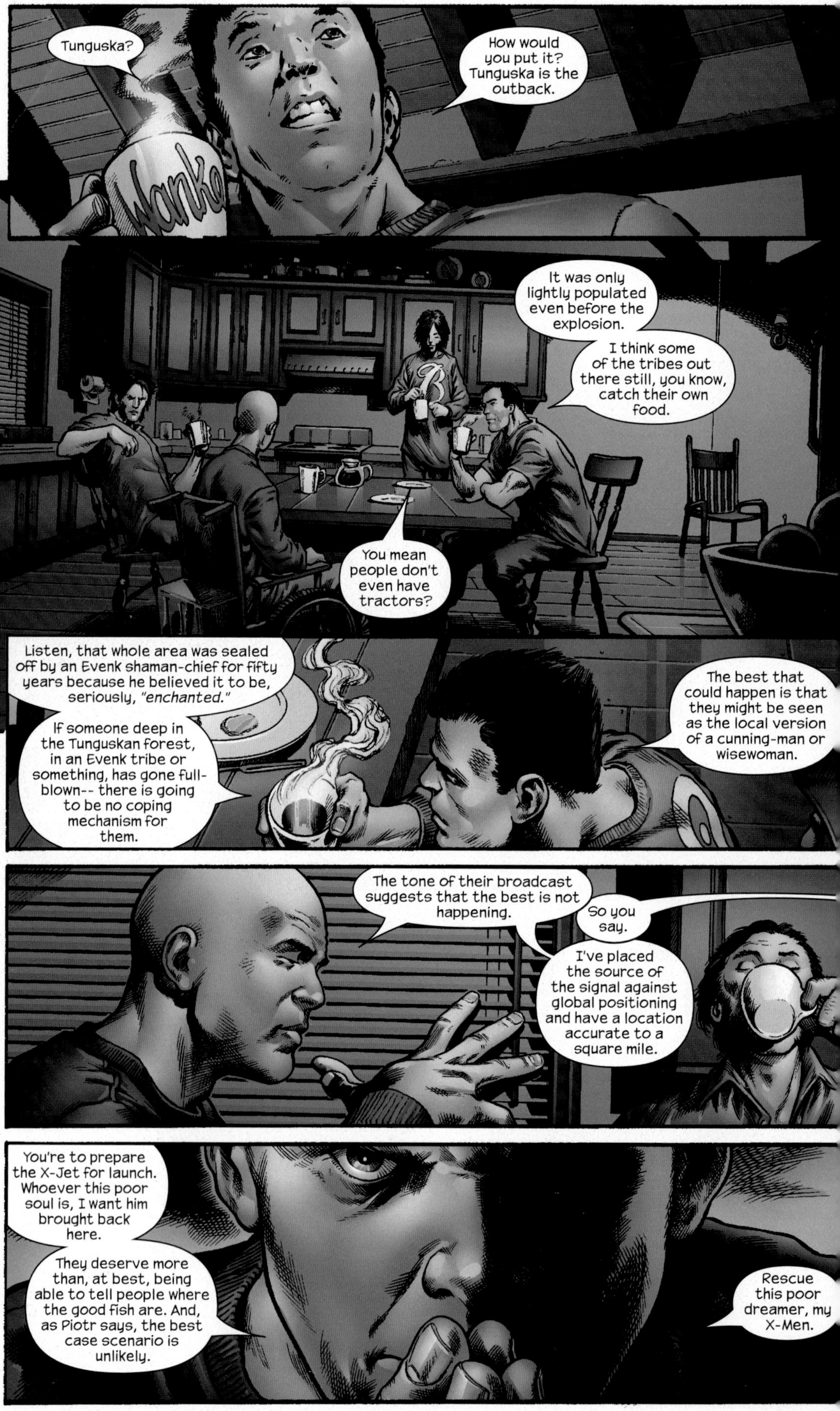

Tungusha?
How would you put it? Tunguska is the outback.
It was only lightly populated even before the explosion.
I think some of the tribes out there still, you know, catch their own food.
You mean people don't even have tractors?
Listen, that whole area was sealed off by an Evenk shaman-chief for fifty years because he believed it to be, seriously, "enchanted."
If someone deep in the Tunguskan forest, in an Evenk tribe or something, has gone full-blown-- there is going to be no coping mechanism for them.
The best that could happen is that they might be seen as the local version of a cunning-man or wisewoman.
The tone of their broadcast suggests that the best is not happening.
So you say.
I've placed the source of the signal against global positioning and have a location accurate to a square mile.
You're to prepare the X-Jet for launch. Whoever this poor soul is, I want him brought back here.
They deserve more than, at best, being able to tell people where the good fish are. And, as Piotr says, the best case scenario is unlikely.
Rescue this poor dreamer, my X-Men.

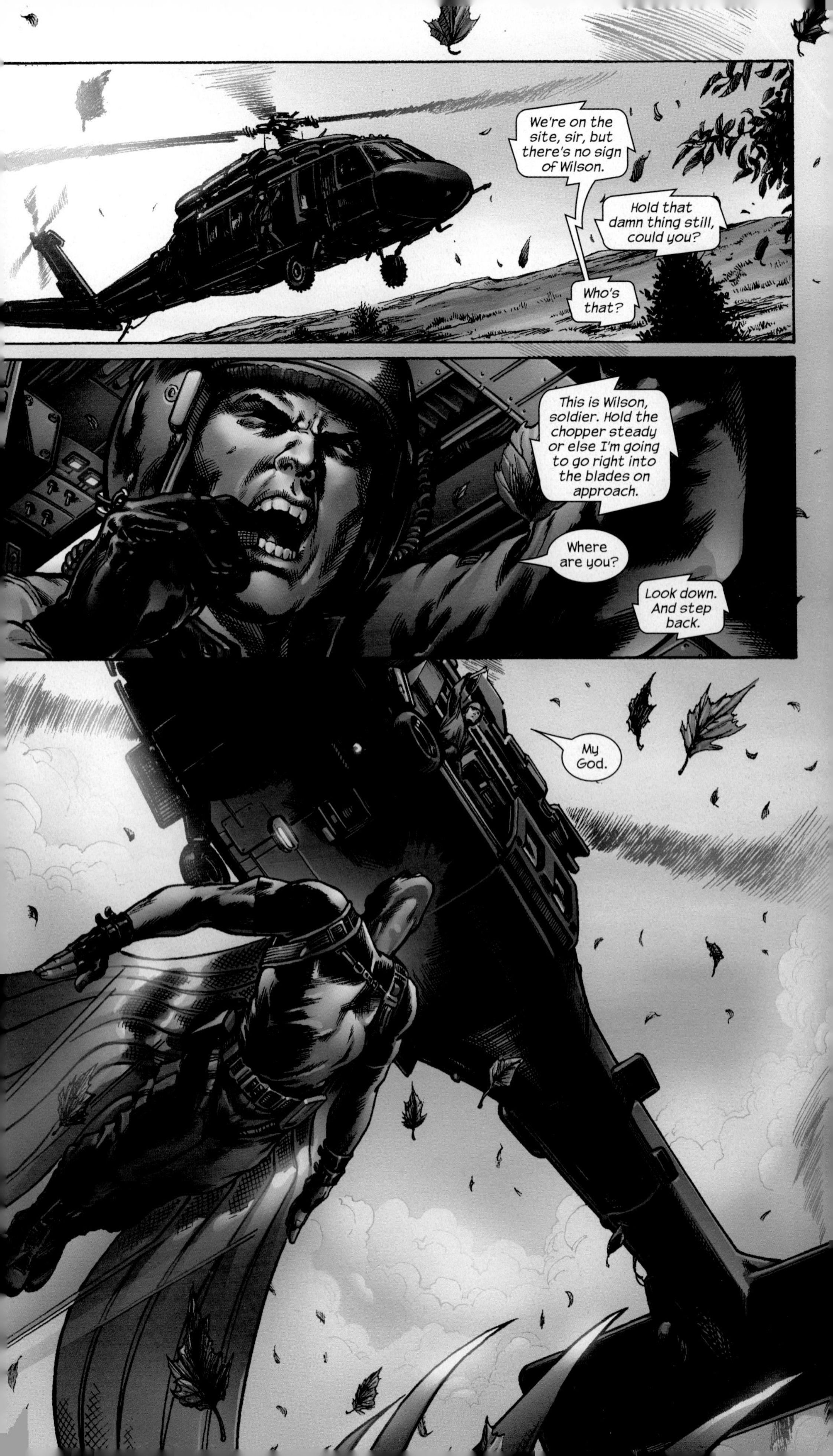

We're on the site, sir, but there's no sign of Wilson.
Hold that damn thing still, could you?
Who's that?
This is Wilson, soldier. Hold the chopper steady or else I'm going to go right into the blades on approach.
Where are you?
Look down. And step back.
My God.

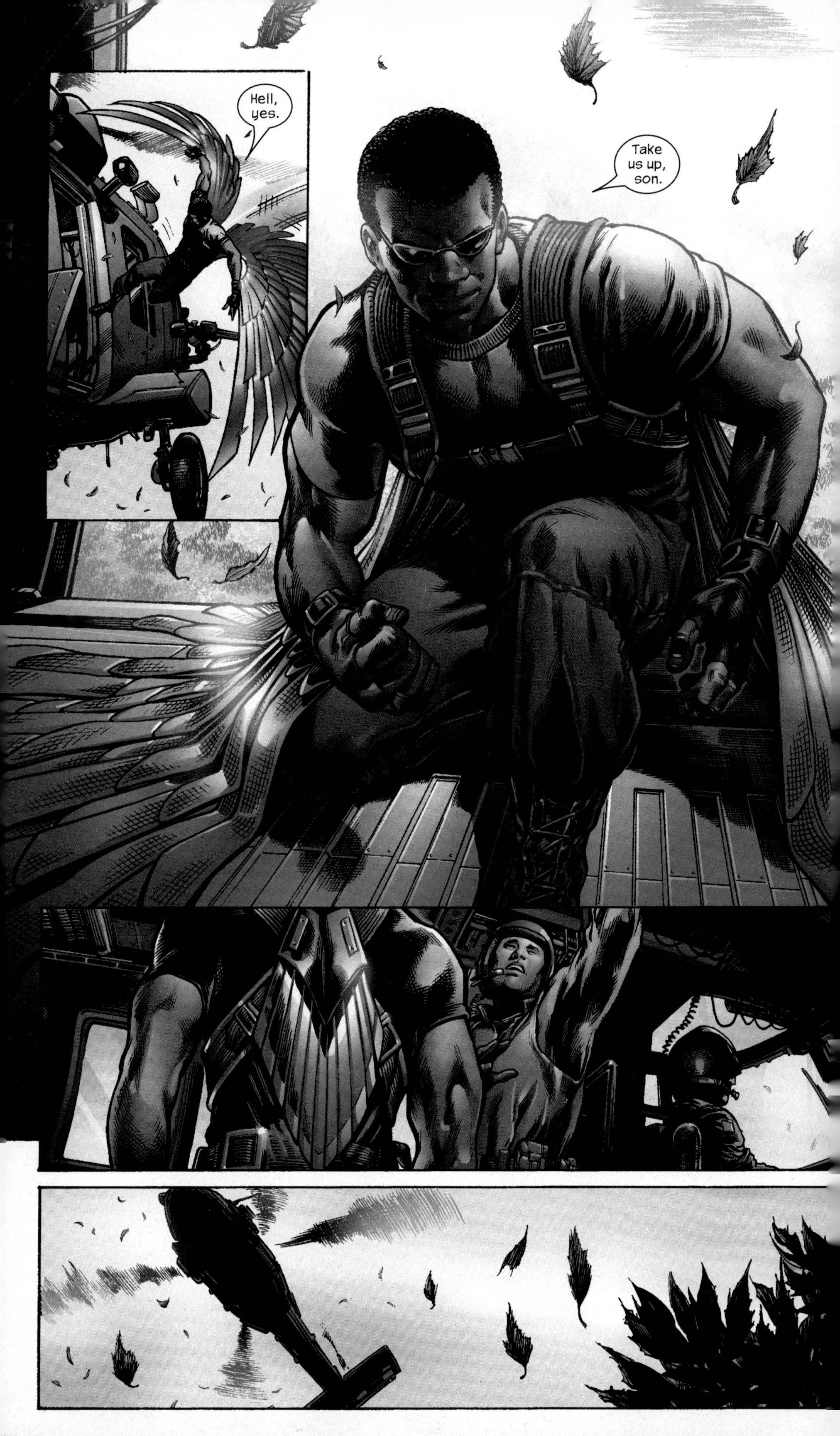
Hell, yes.
Take us up, son.

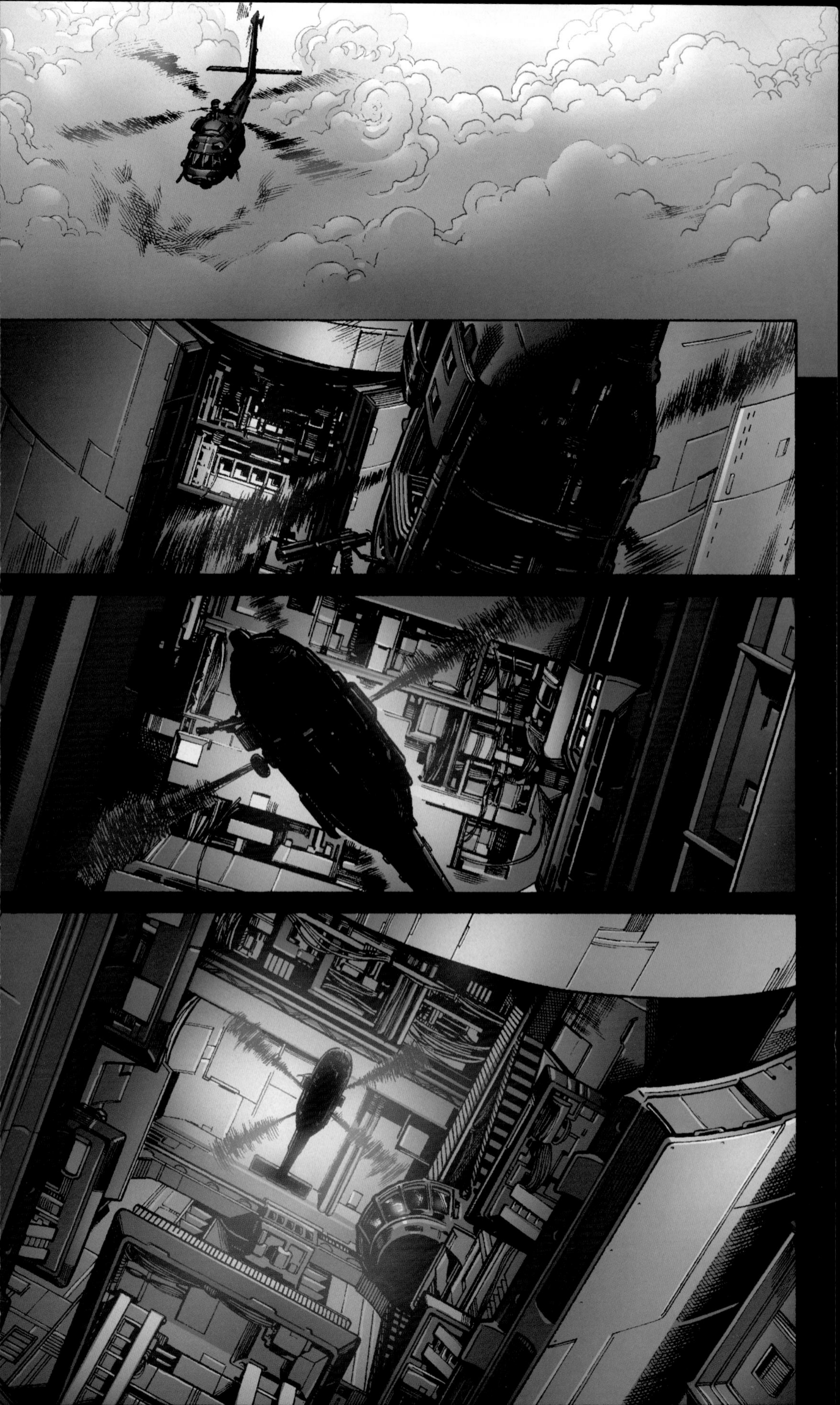

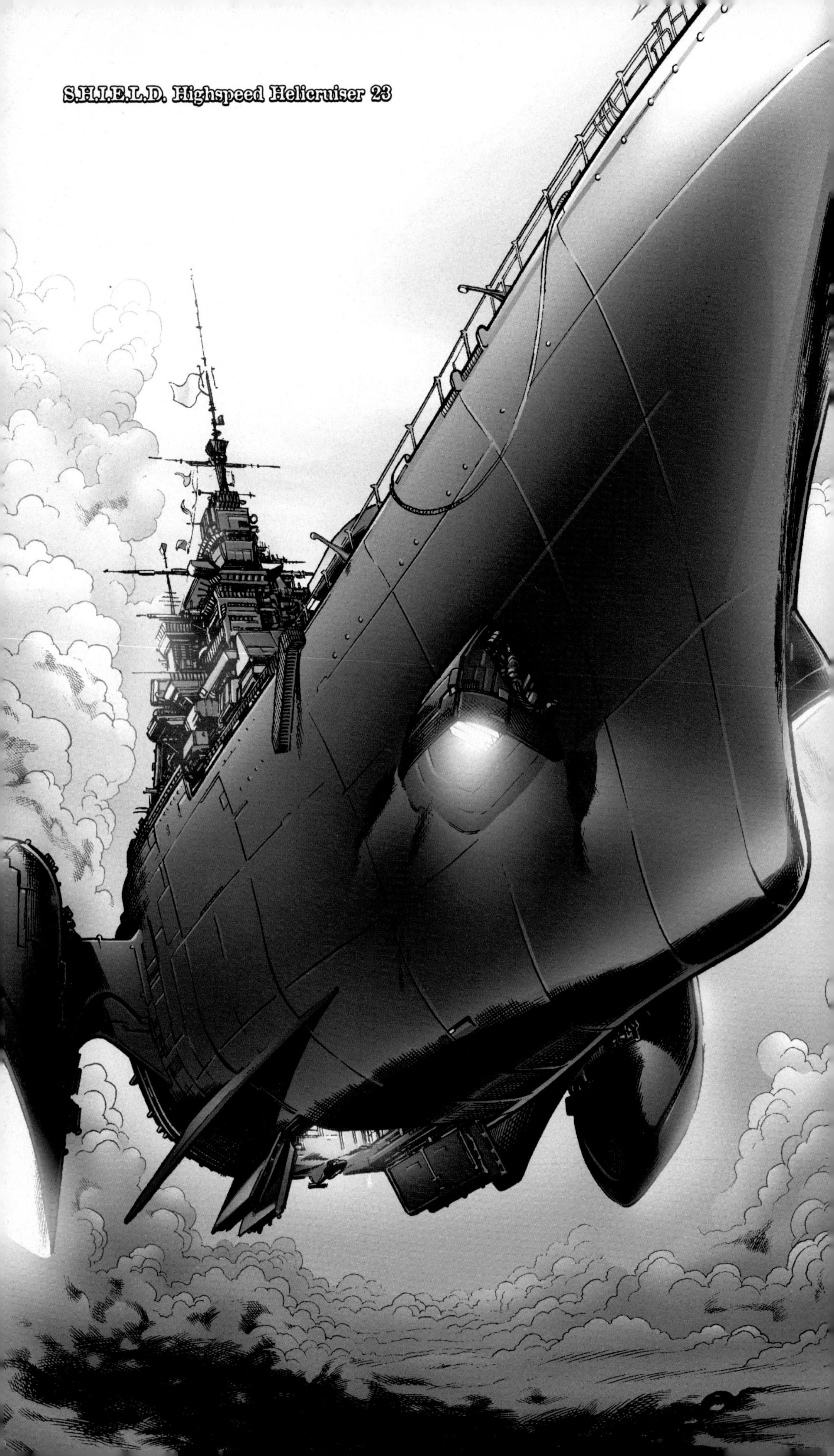
S.H.I.E.L.D. Highspeed Helicruiser 23

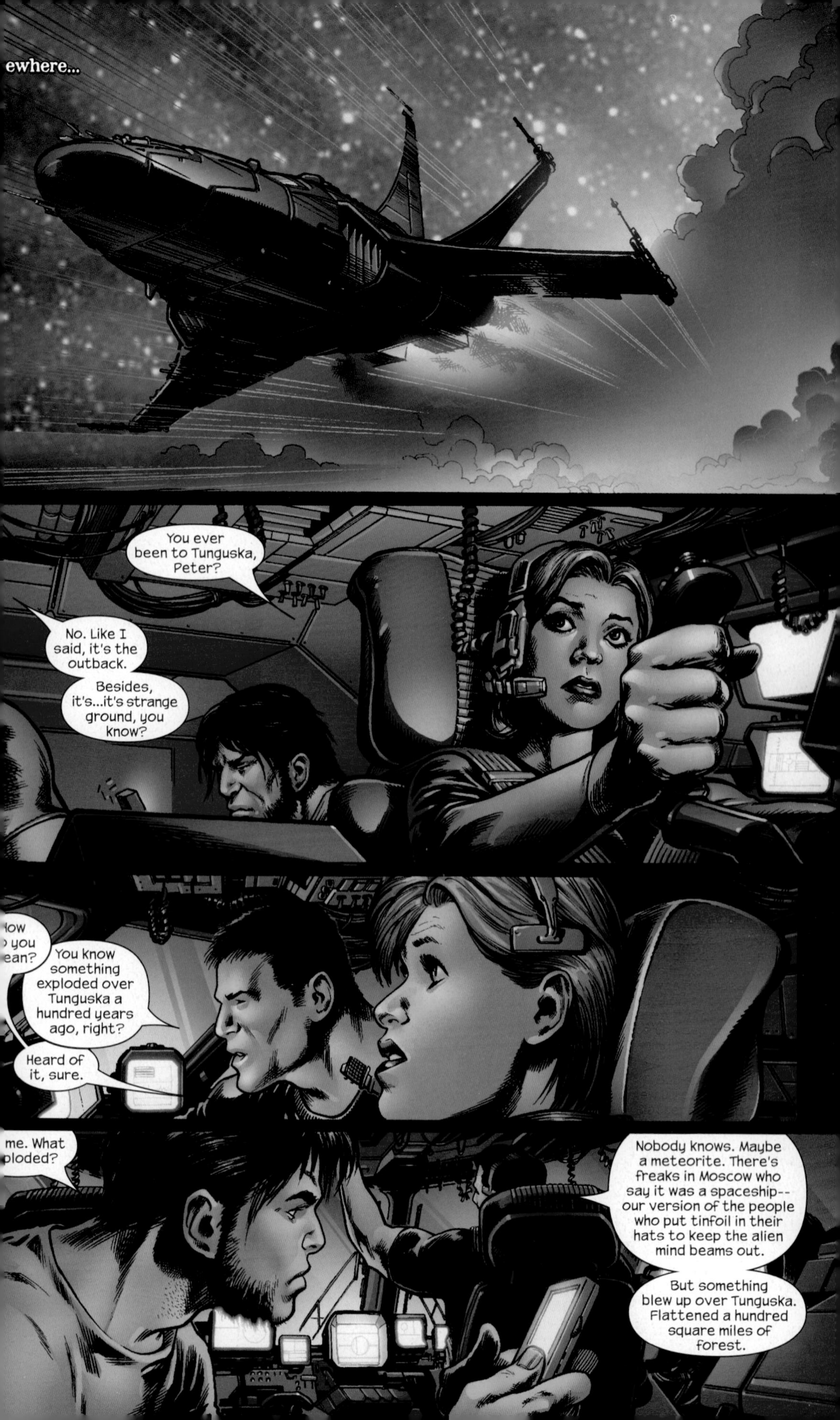
ewhere...
You ever been to Tunguska, Peter?
No. Like I said, it's the outback.
Besides, it's...it's strange ground, you know?
You know something exploded over Tunguska a hundred years ago, right?
Heard of it, sure.
me. What ploded?
Nobody knows. Maybe a meteorite. There's freaks in Moscow who say it was a spaceship-- our version of the people who put tinfoil in their hats to keep the alien mind beams out.
But something blew up over Tunguska. Flattened a hundred square miles of forest.

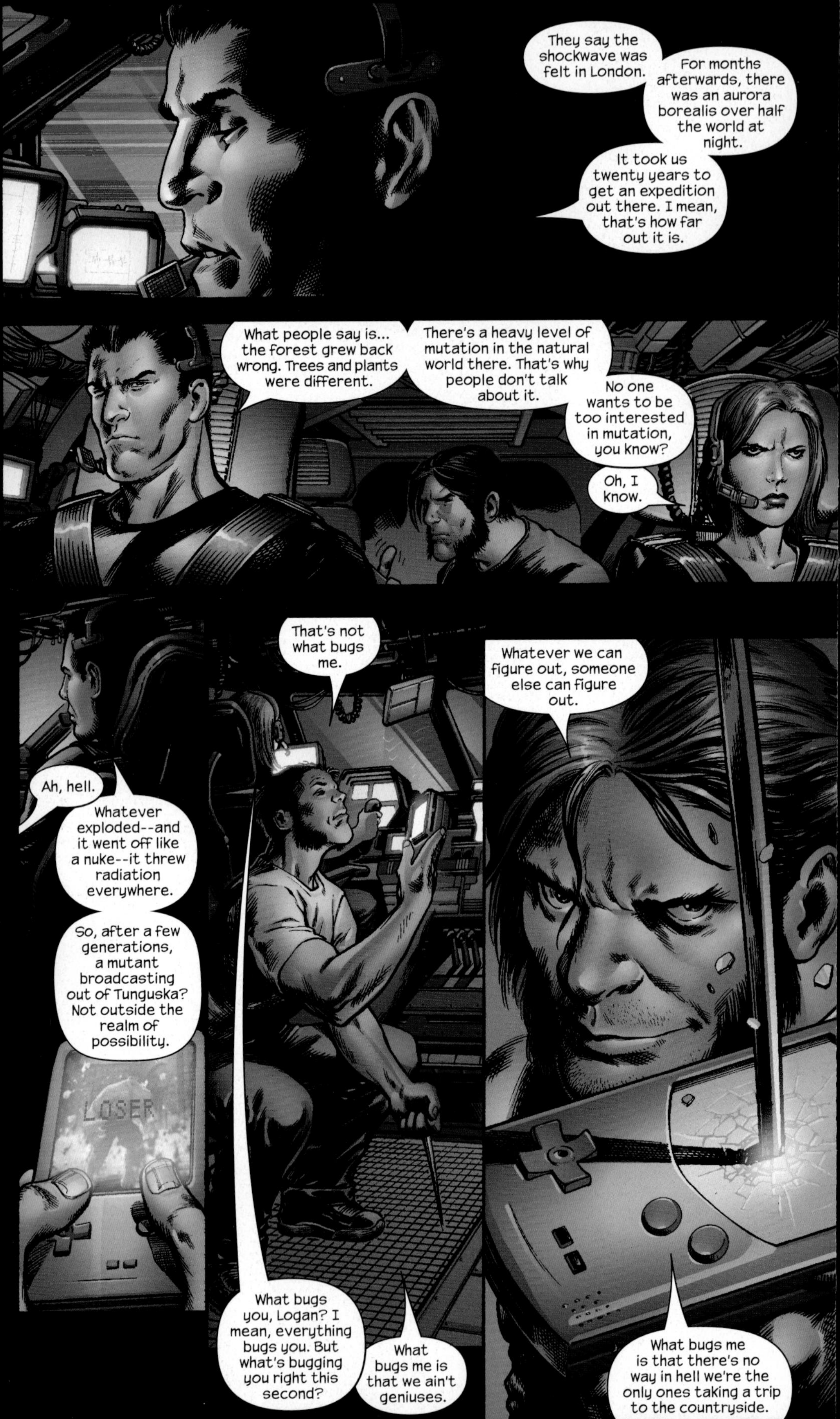

They say the shockwave was felt in London.
For months afterwards, there was an aurora borealis over half the world at night.
It took us twenty years to get an expedition out there. I mean, that's how far out it is.
What people say is... the forest grew back wrong. Trees and plants were different.
There's a heavy level of mutation in the natural world there. That's why people don't talk about it.
No one wants to be too interested in mutation, you know?
Oh, I know.
Ah, hell.
Whatever exploded--and it went off like a nuke--it threw radiation everywhere.
So, after a few generations, a mutant broadcasting out of Tunguska? Not outside the realm of possibility.
LOSER
That's not what bugs me.
What bugs you, Logan? I mean, everything bugs you. But what's bugging you right this second?
What bugs me is that we ain't geniuses.
Whatever we can figure out, someone else can figure out.
What bugs me is that there's no way in hell we're the only ones taking a trip to the countryside.

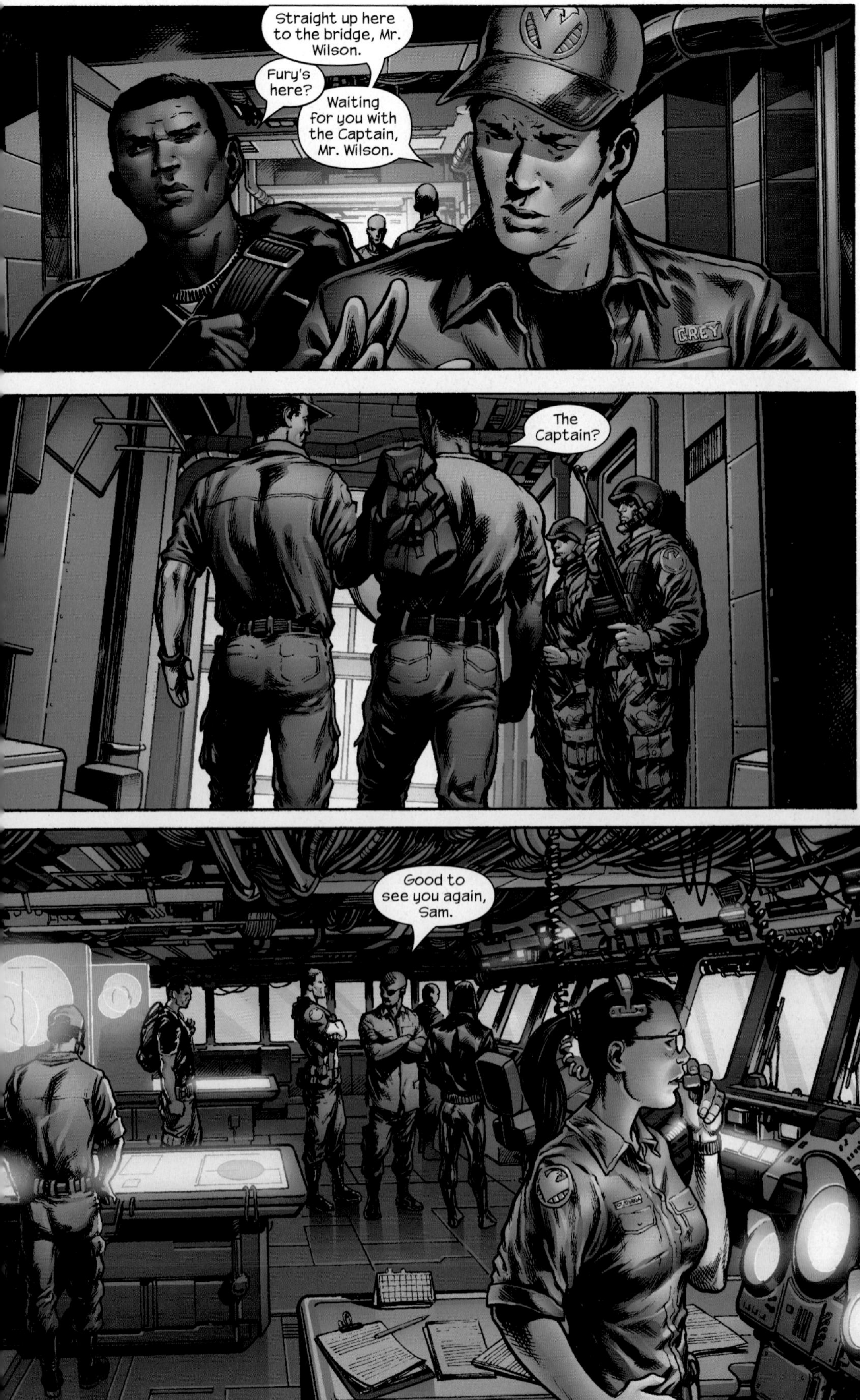
Straight up here to the bridge, Mr. Wilson.
Fury's here?
Waiting for you with the Captain, Mr. Wilson.
GREY
The Captain?
Good to see you again, Sam.

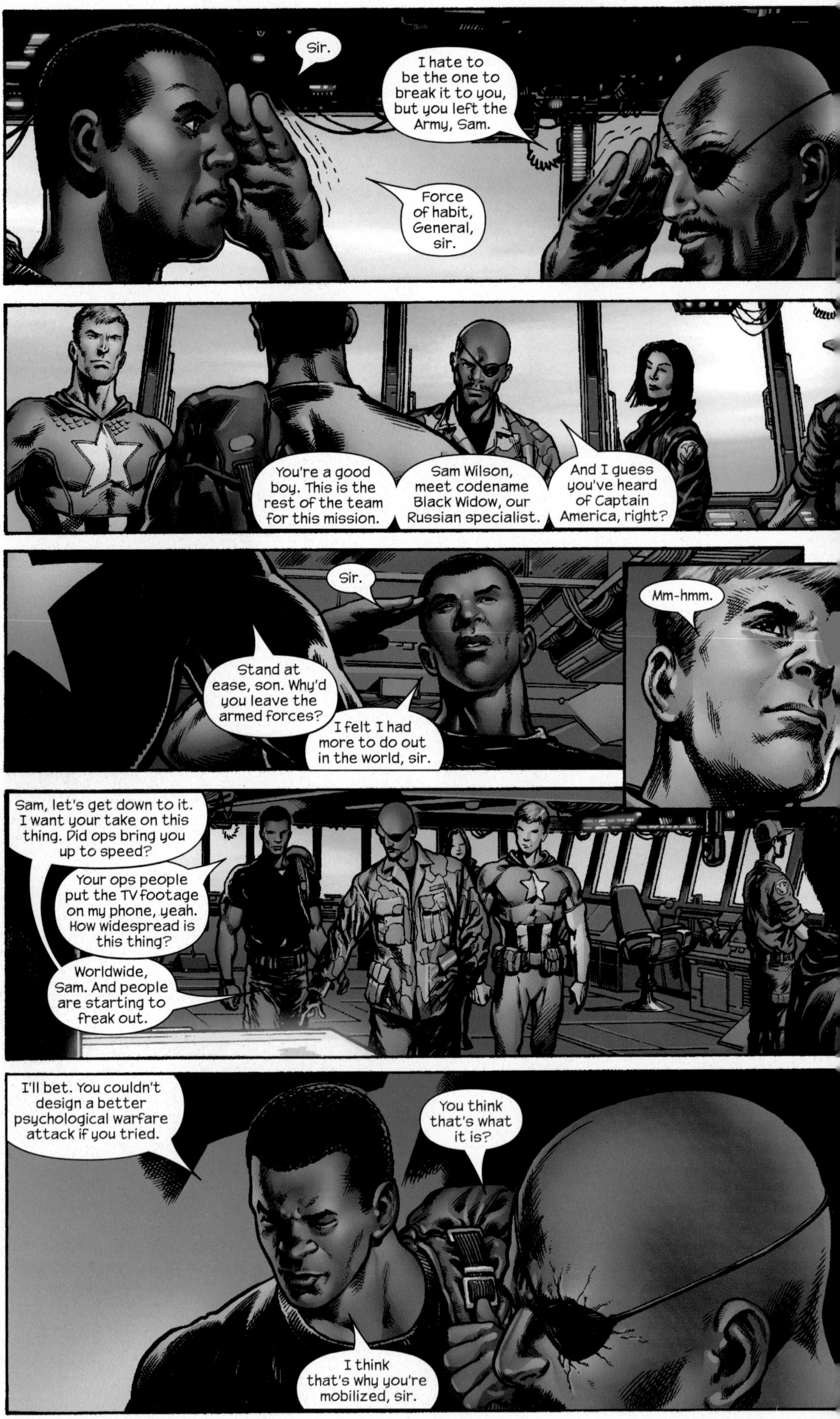
Sir.
I hate to be the one to break it to you, but you left the Army, Sam.
Force of habit, General, sir.
You're a good boy. This is the rest of the team for this mission.
Sam Wilson, meet codename Black Widow, our Russian specialist.
And I guess you've heard of Captain America, right?
Sir.
Stand at ease, son. Why'd you leave the armed forces?
I felt I had more to do out in the world, sir.
Mm-hmm.
Sam, let's get down to it. I want your take on this thing. Did ops bring you up to speed?
Your ops people put the TV footage on my phone, yeah. How widespread is this thing?
Worldwide, Sam. And people are starting to freak out.
I'll bet. You couldn't design a better psychological warfare attack if you tried.
You think that's what it is?
I think that's why you're mobilized, sir.

But no, I don't think it is.

I think the effect is purely accidental.

"Black Widow"... do I have to call you that?

Nick?

You're not cleared for real names, Sam.

Excuse me, General, but if I'm on a S.H.I.E.L.D. Helicruiser for a black ops mission into the middle of Russia, I think I'm cleared for whatever I damn well please.

Sir.

Natasha.

Natasha. Do you think the Russian secret services have the funding for a stunt like this?

No.

No. At the height of the Cold War, they were limited to short-range radio and microwave transmission.

On the best day of our lives, General, could we take control of every communications device on Earth?

We're working on it.

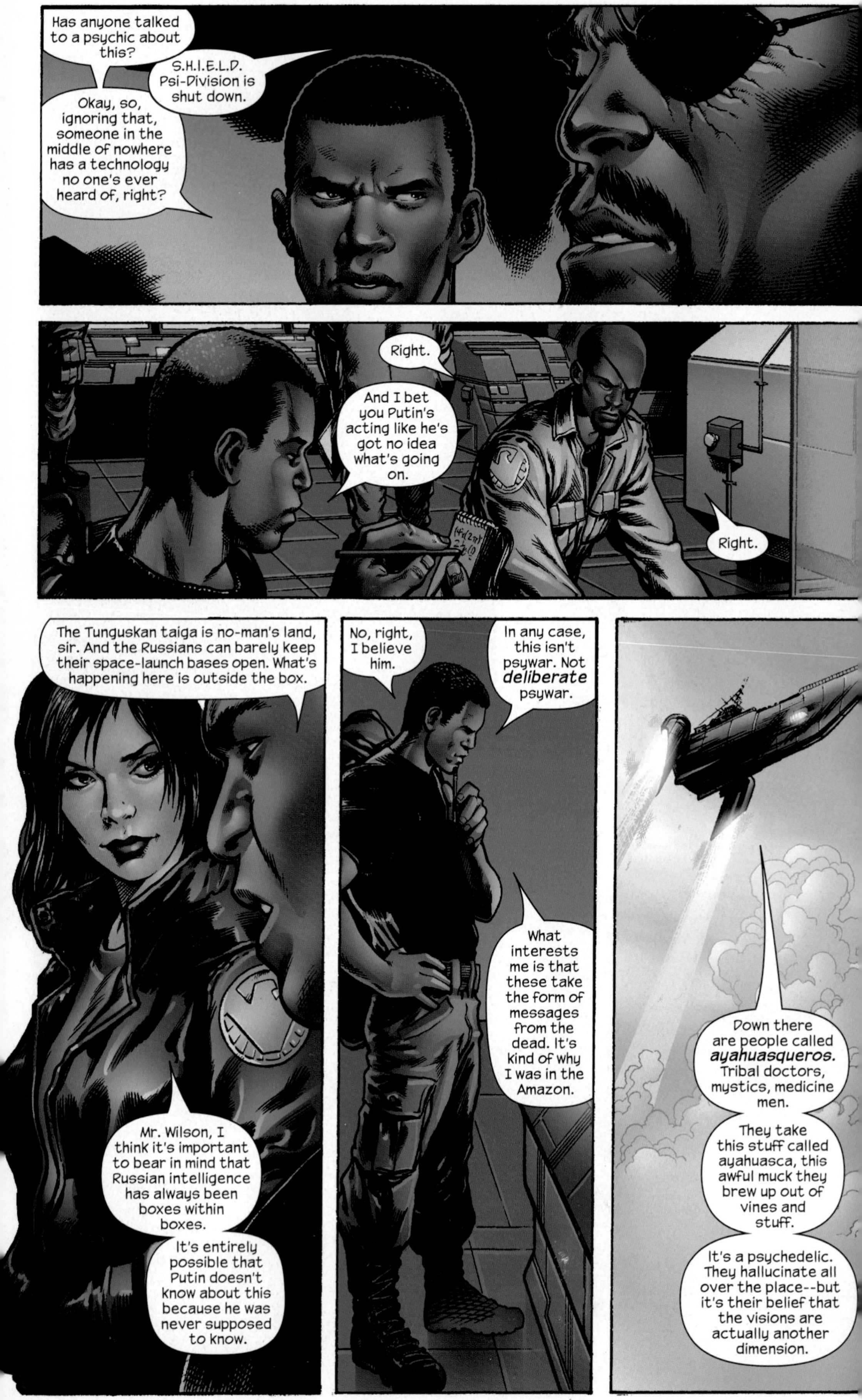

Has anyone talked to a psychic about this?
S.H.I.E.L.D. Psi-Division is shut down.
Okay, so, ignoring that, someone in the middle of nowhere has a technology no one's ever heard of, right?
Right.
And I bet you Putin's acting like he's got no idea what's going on.
Right.
The Tunguskan taiga is no-man's land, sir. And the Russians can barely keep their space-launch bases open. What's happening here is outside the box.
Mr. Wilson, I think it's important to bear in mind that Russian intelligence has always been boxes within boxes.
It's entirely possible that Putin doesn't know about this because he was never supposed to know.
No, right, I believe him.
In any case, this isn't psywar. Not *deliberate* psywar.
What interests me is that these take the form of messages from the dead. It's kind of why I was in the Amazon.
Down there are people called ***ayahuasqueros.*** Tribal doctors, mystics, medicine men.
They take this stuff called ayahuasca, this awful muck they brew up out of vines and stuff.
It's a psychedelic. They hallucinate all over the place--but it's their belief that the visions are actually another dimension.

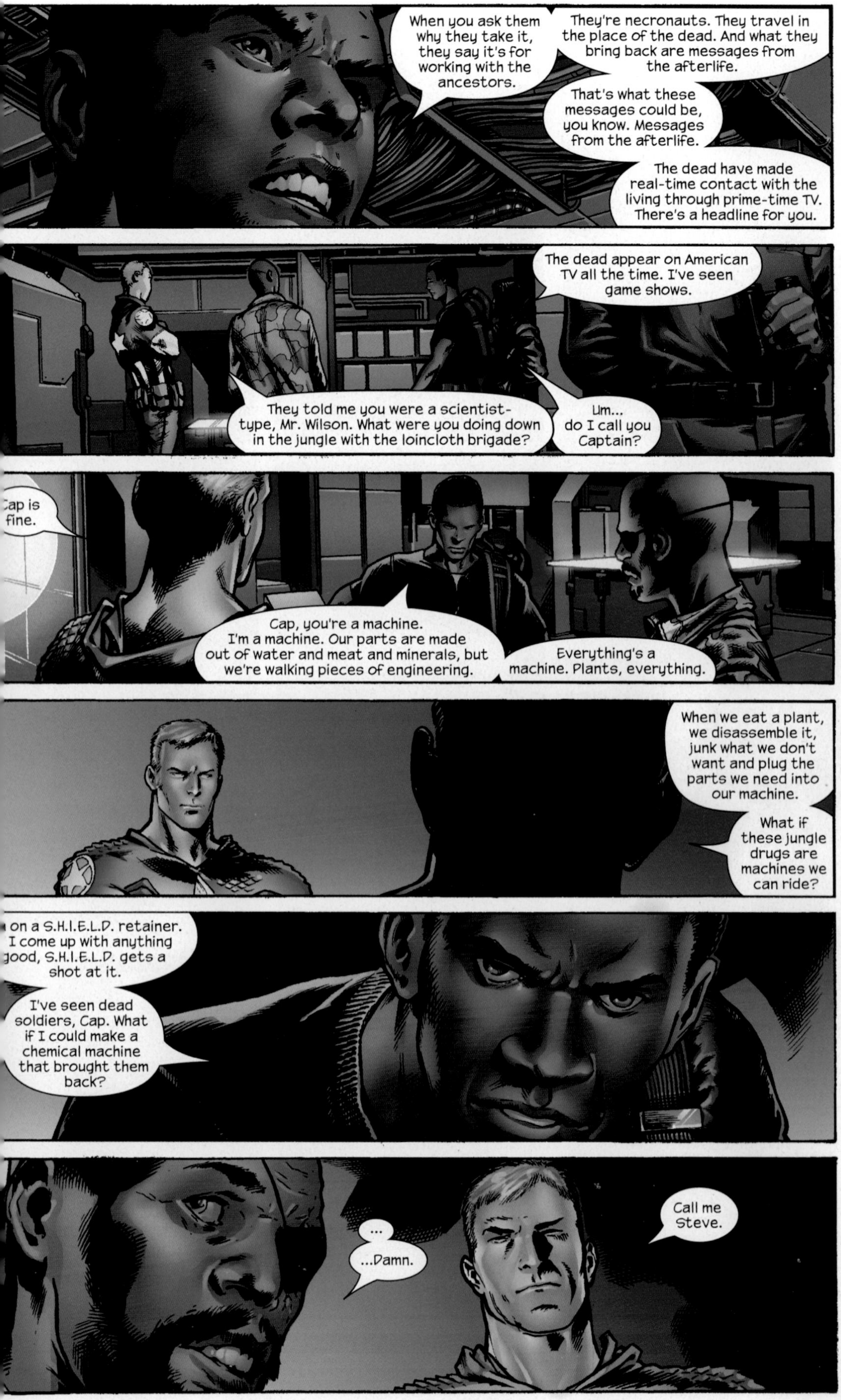
When you ask them why they take it, they say it's for working with the ancestors.
They're necronauts. They travel in the place of the dead. And what they bring back are messages from the afterlife.
That's what these messages could be, you know. Messages from the afterlife.
The dead have made real-time contact with the living through prime-time TV. There's a headline for you.
The dead appear on American TV all the time. I've seen game shows.
They told me you were a scientist-type, Mr. Wilson. What were you doing down in the jungle with the loincloth brigade?
Um... do I call you Captain?
Cap is fine.
Cap, you're a machine. I'm a machine. Our parts are made out of water and meat and minerals, but we're walking pieces of engineering.
Everything's a machine. Plants, everything.
When we eat a plant, we disassemble it, junk what we don't want and plug the parts we need into our machine.
What if these jungle drugs are machines we can ride?
on a S.H.I.E.L.D. retainer. I come up with anything good, S.H.I.E.L.D. gets a shot at it.
I've seen dead soldiers, Cap. What if I could make a chemical machine that brought them back?
...
...Damn.
Call me Steve.

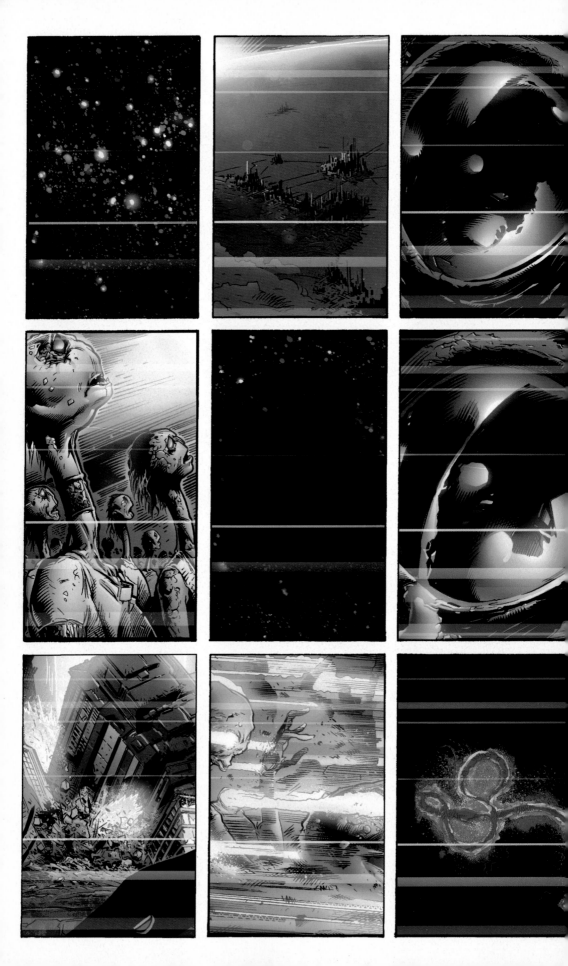

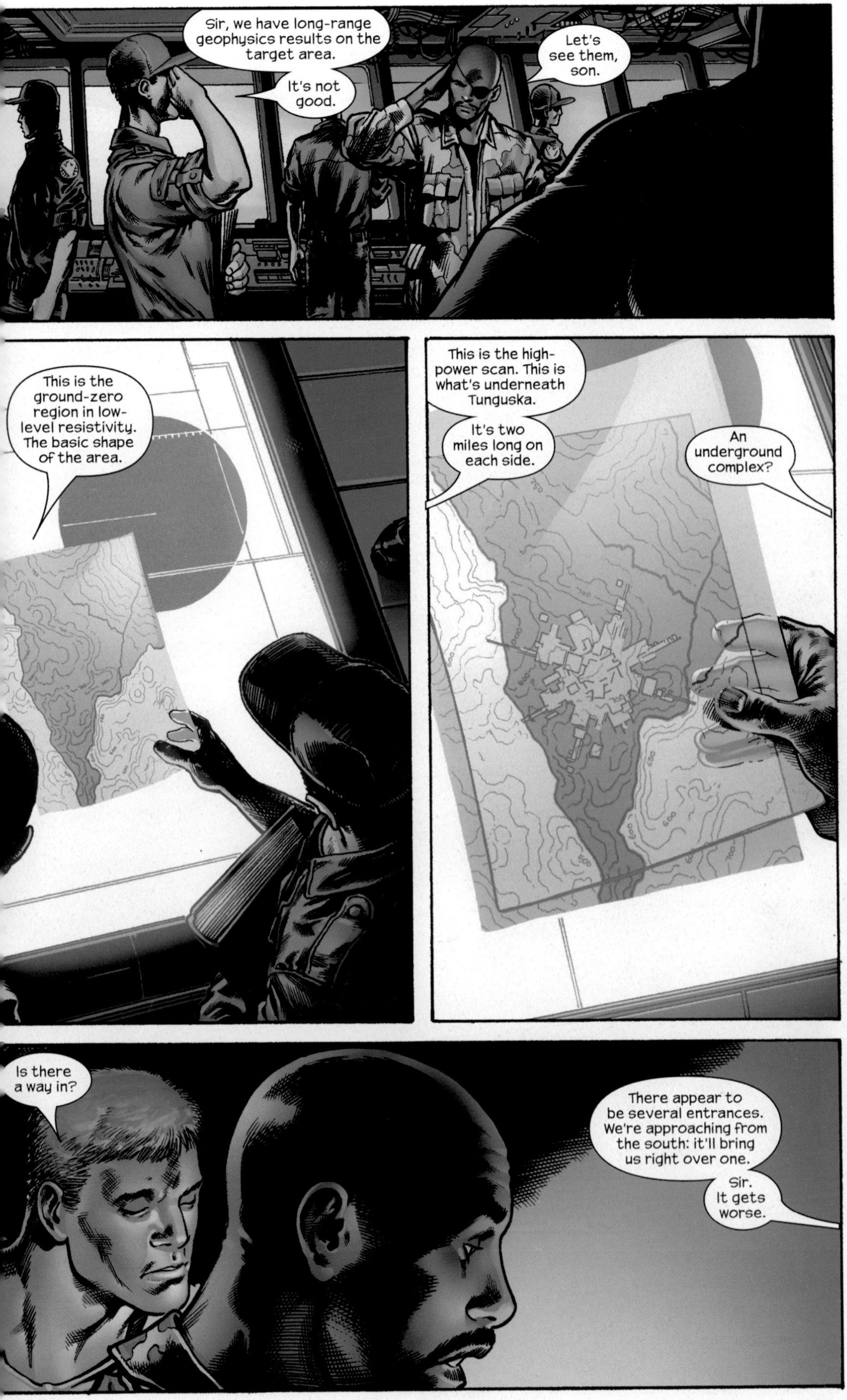
Sir, we have long-range geophysics results on the target area.
It's not good.
Let's see them, son.
This is the ground-zero region in low-level resistivity. The basic shape of the area.
This is the high-power scan. This is what's underneath Tunguska.
It's two miles long on each side.
An underground complex?
Is there a way in?
There appear to be several entrances. We're approaching from the south: it'll bring us right over one.
Sir. It gets worse.

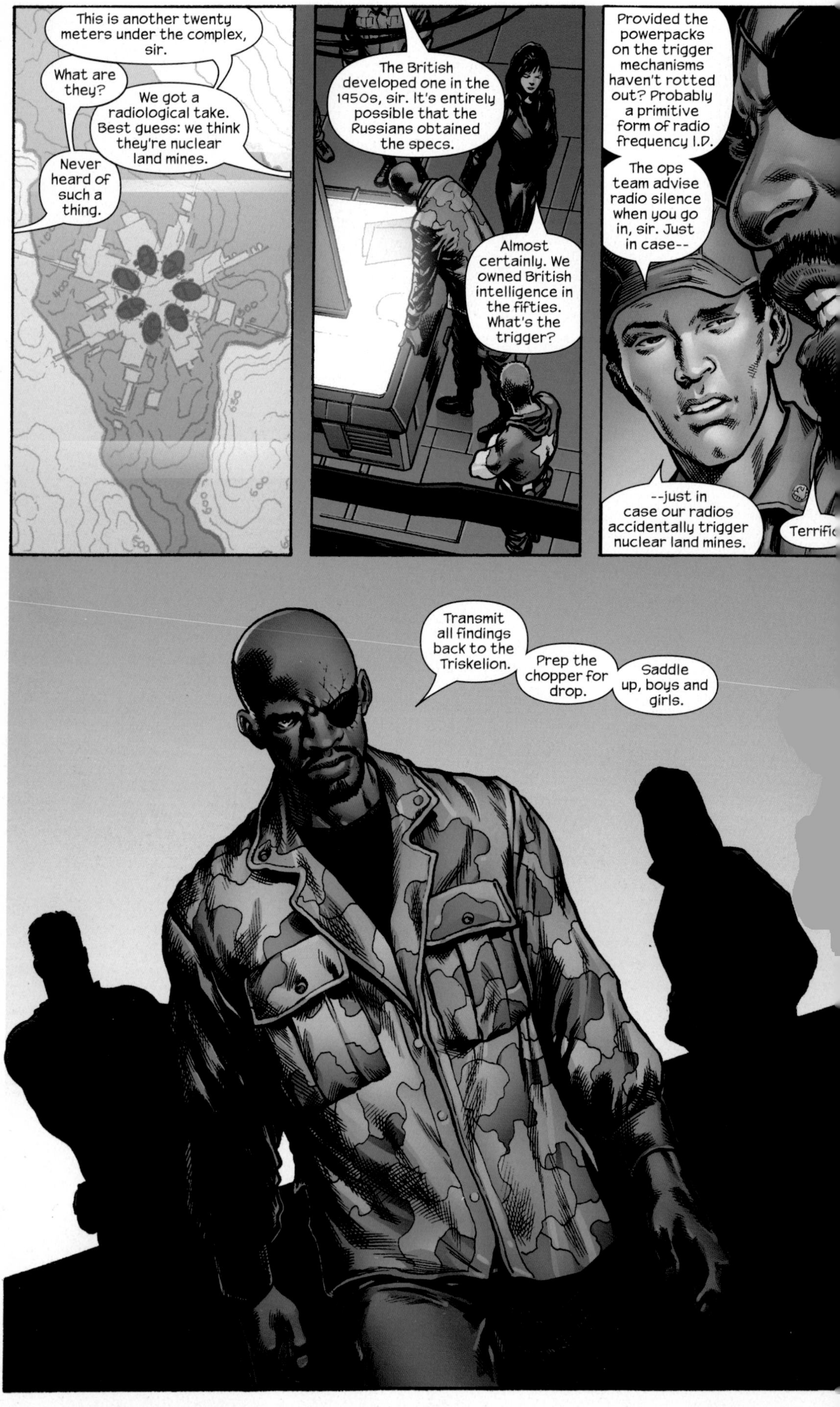
This is another twenty meters under the complex, sir.
What are they?
We got a radiological take. Best guess: we think they're nuclear land mines.
Never heard of such a thing.
The British developed one in the 1950s, sir. It's entirely possible that the Russians obtained the specs.
Almost certainly. We owned British intelligence in the fifties. What's the trigger?
Provided the powerpacks on the trigger mechanisms haven't rotted out? Probably a primitive form of radio frequency I.D.
The ops team advise radio silence when you go in, sir. Just in case--
--just in case our radios accidentally trigger nuclear land mines.
Terrific
Transmit all findings back to the Triskelion.
Prep the chopper for drop.
Saddle up, boys and girls.

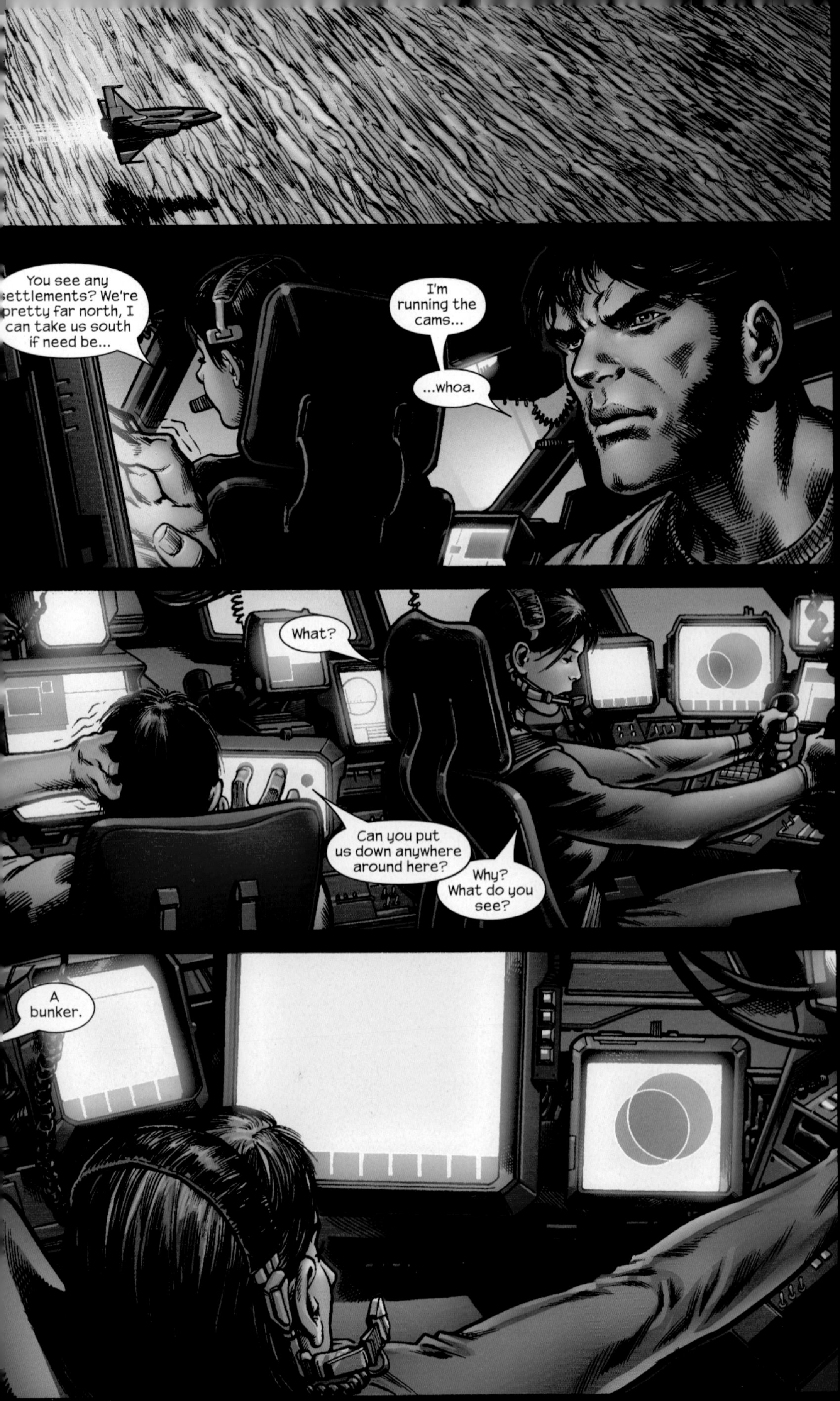

You see any settlements? We're pretty far north, I can take us south if need be...
I'm running the cams...
...whoa.
What?
Can you put us down anywhere around here?
Why? What do you see?
A bunker.

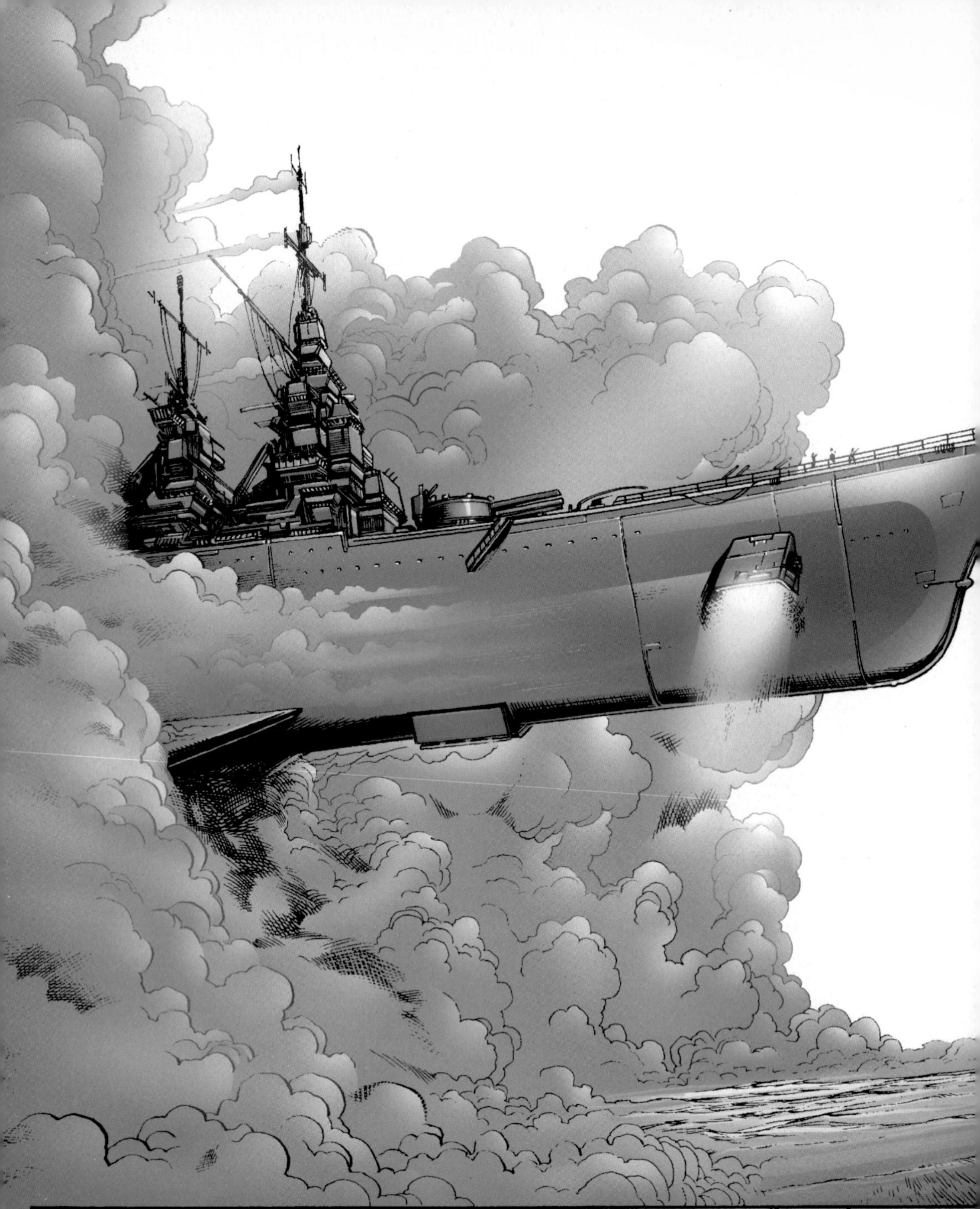
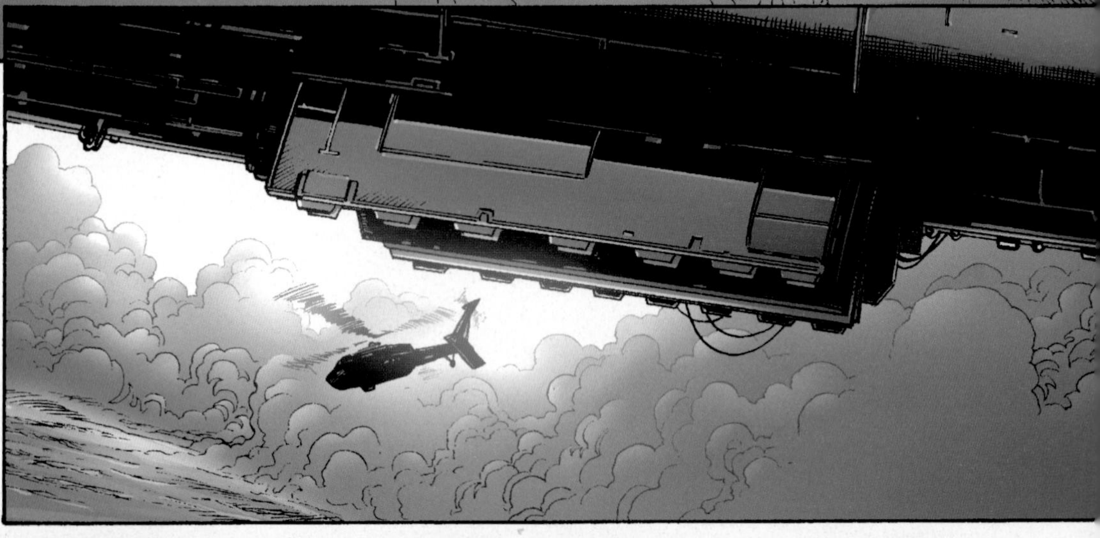

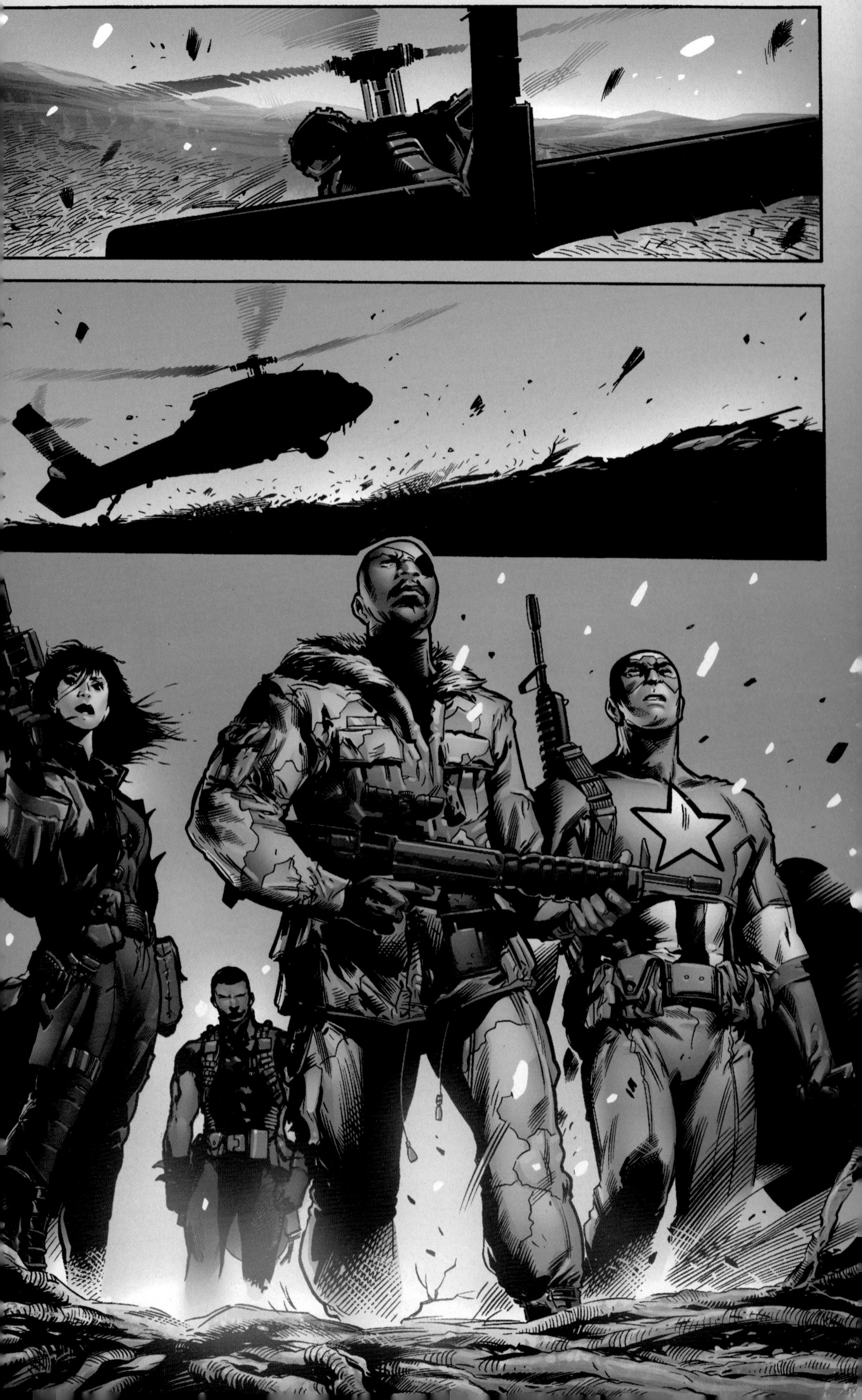

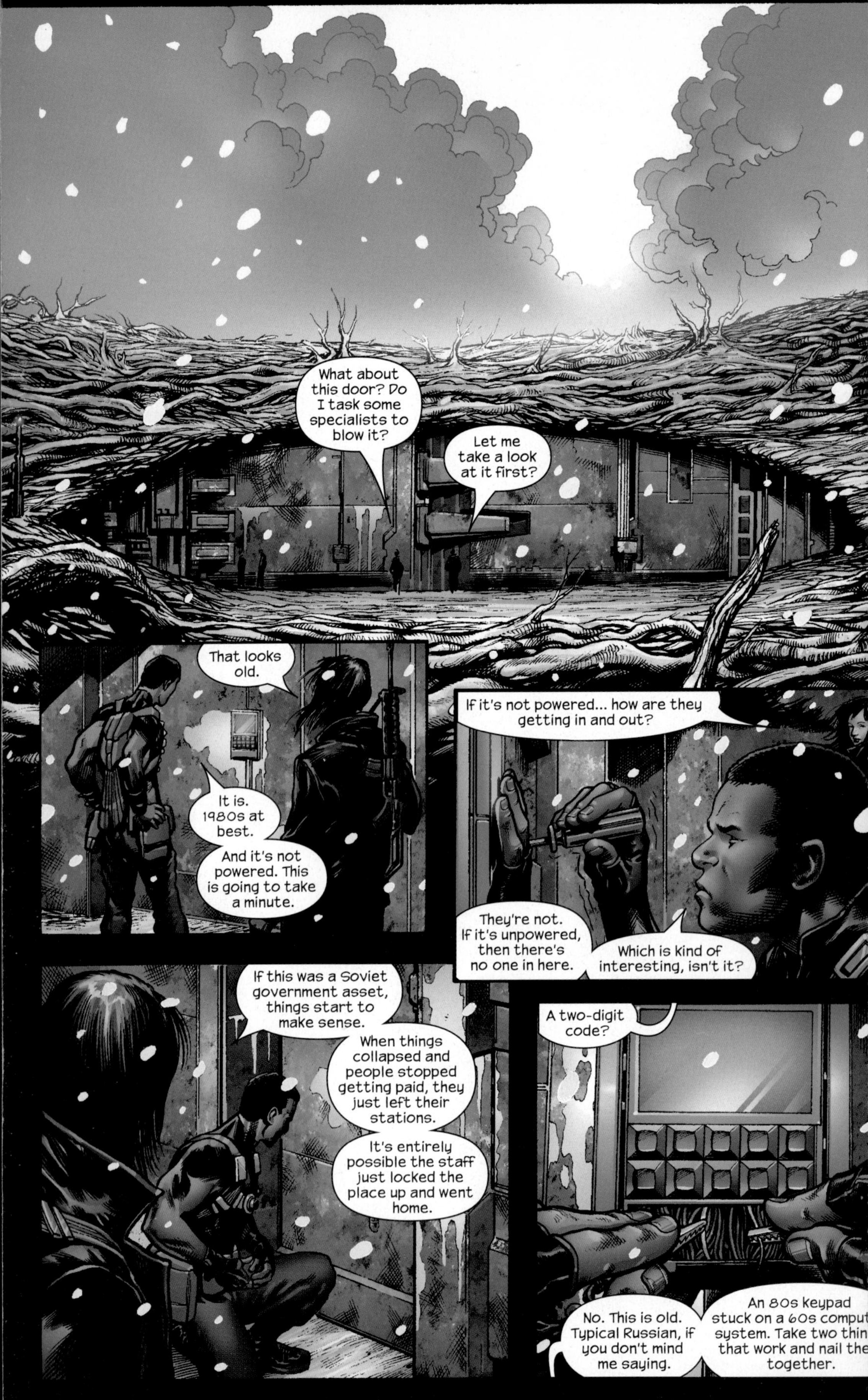
What about this door? Do I task some specialists to blow it?
Let me take a look at it first?
That looks old.
It is. 1980s at best.
And it's not powered. This is going to take a minute.
If it's not powered... how are they getting in and out?
They're not. If it's unpowered, then there's no one in here.
Which is kind of interesting, isn't it?
If this was a Soviet government asset, things start to make sense.
When things collapsed and people stopped getting paid, they just left their stations.
It's entirely possible the staff just locked the place up and went home.
A two-digit code?
No. This is old. Typical Russian, if you don't mind me saying.
An 80s keypad stuck on a 60s comput system. Take two thin that work and nail the together.

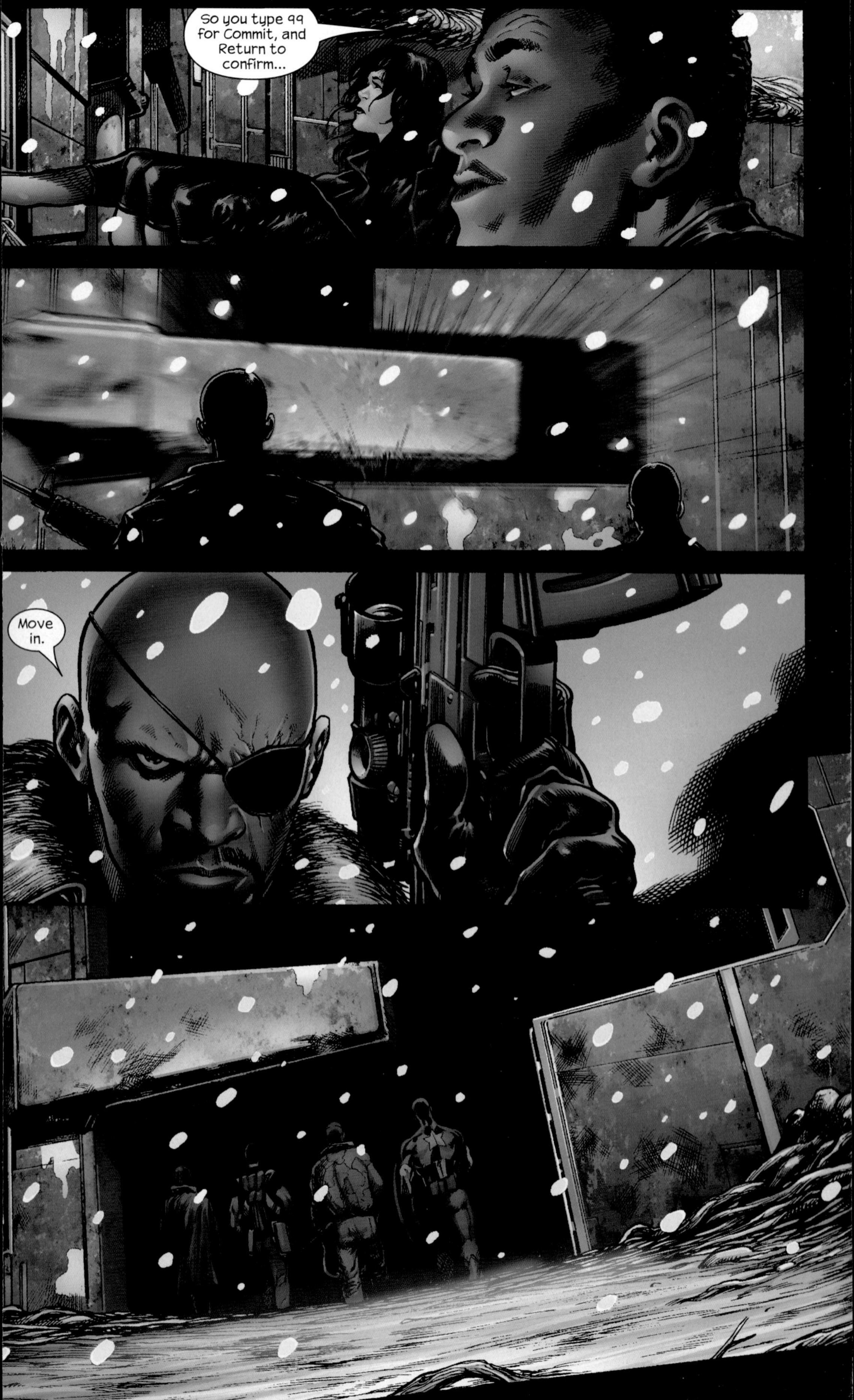
So you type 99 for Commit, and Return to confirm...
Move in.

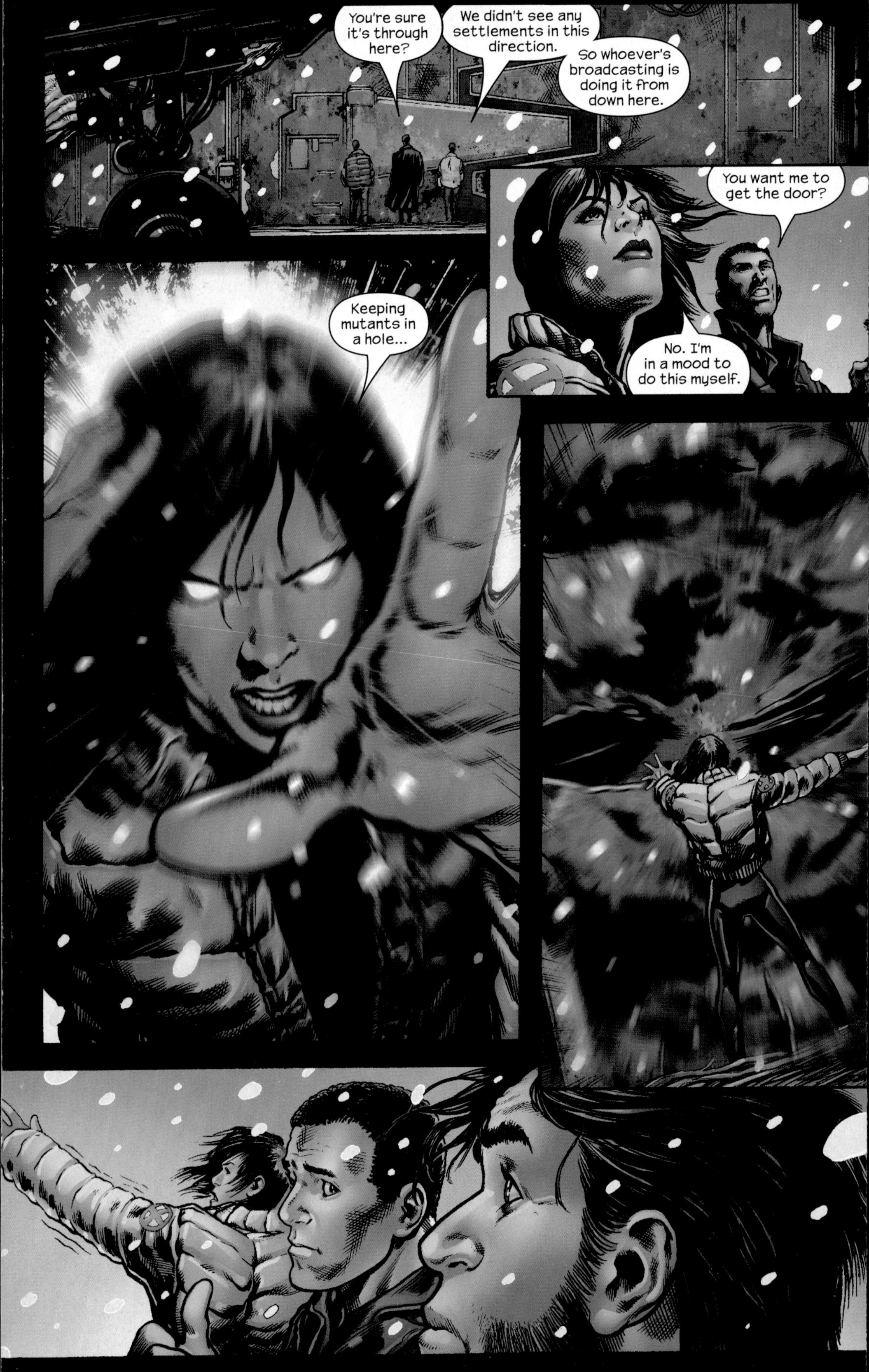
You're sure it's through here?
We didn't see any settlements in this direction.
So whoever's broadcasting is doing it from down here.
You want me to get the door?
No. I'm in a mood to do this myself.
Keeping mutants in a hole...

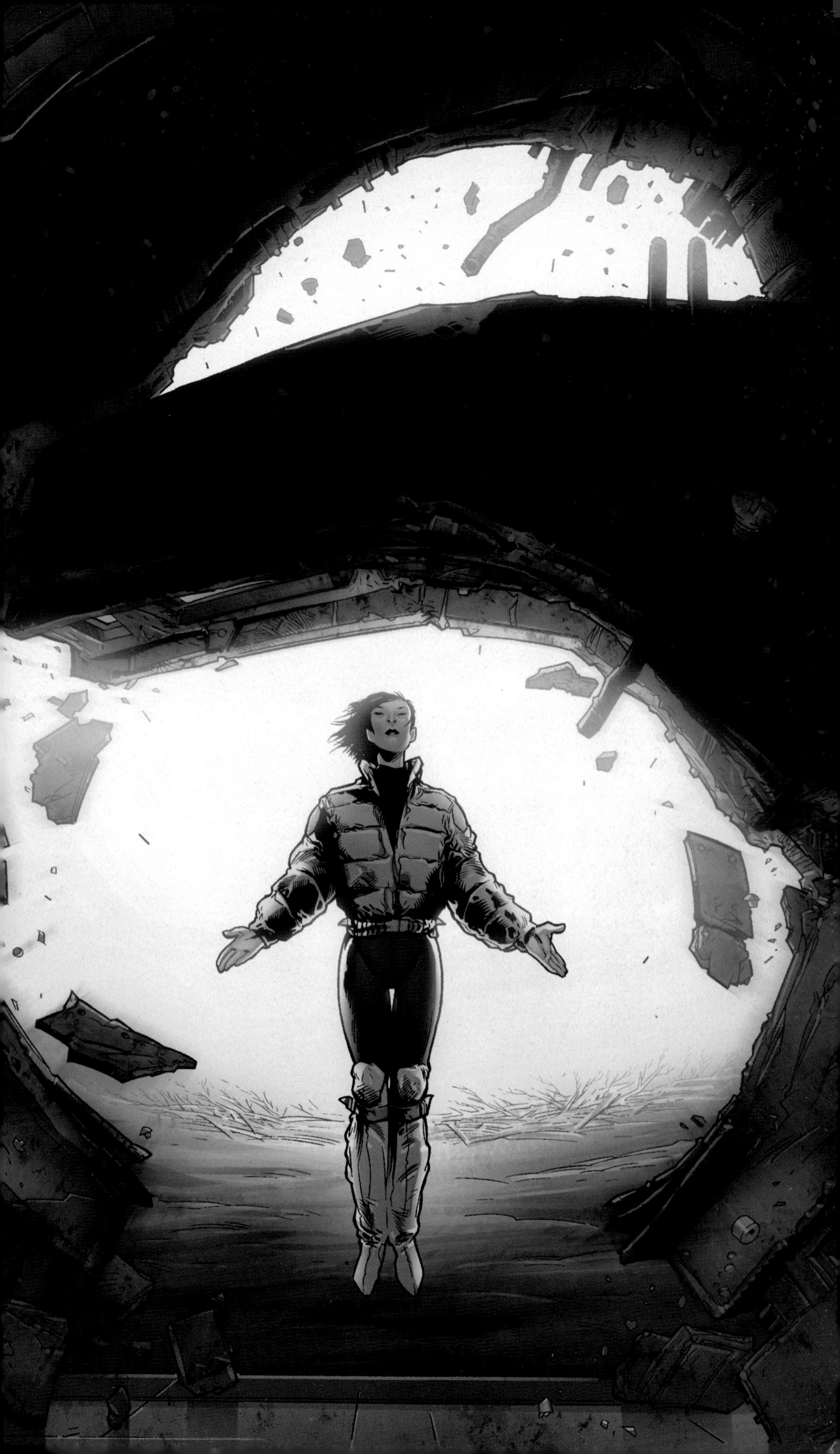

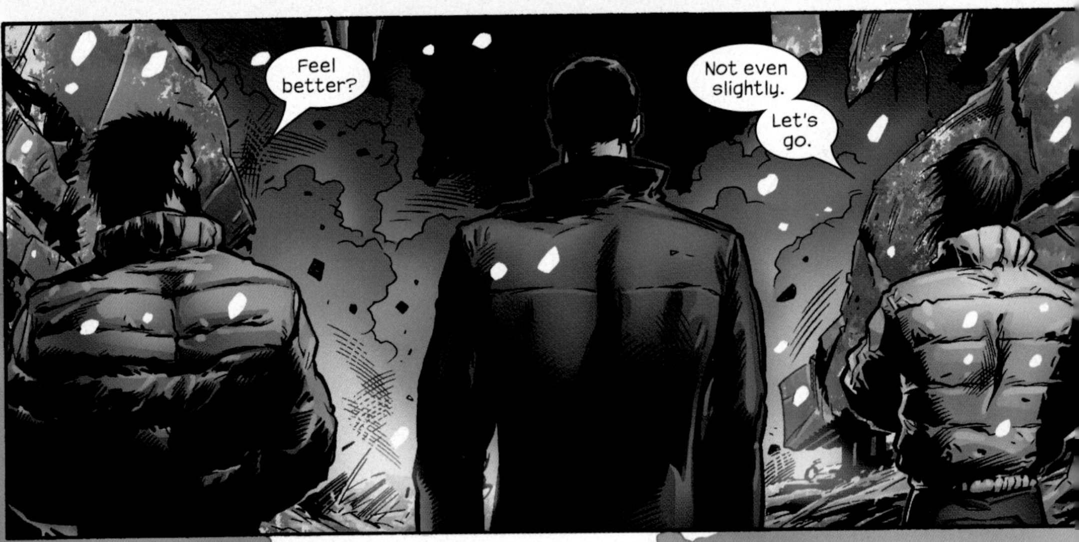
Feel better?
Not even slightly.
Let's go.

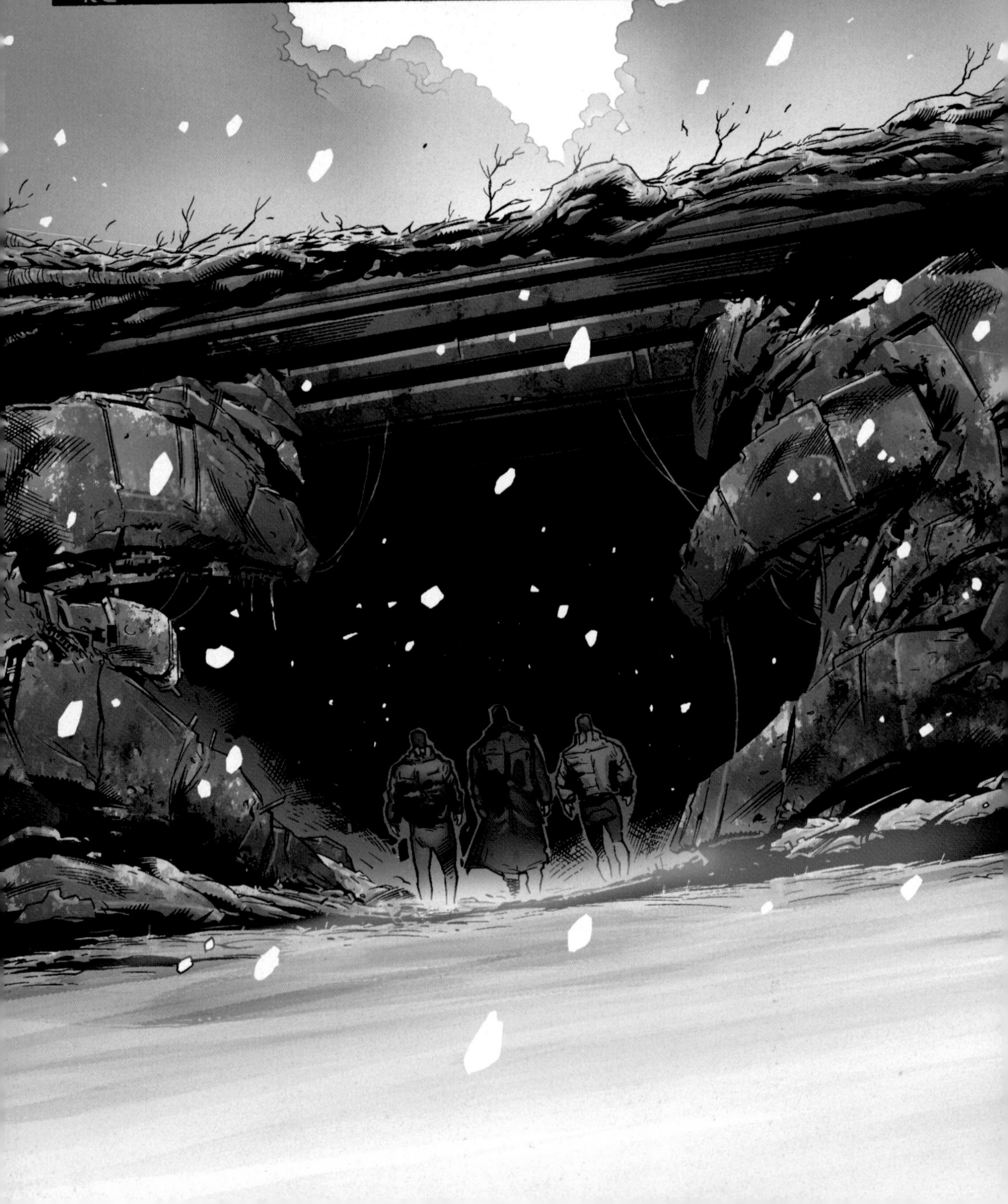

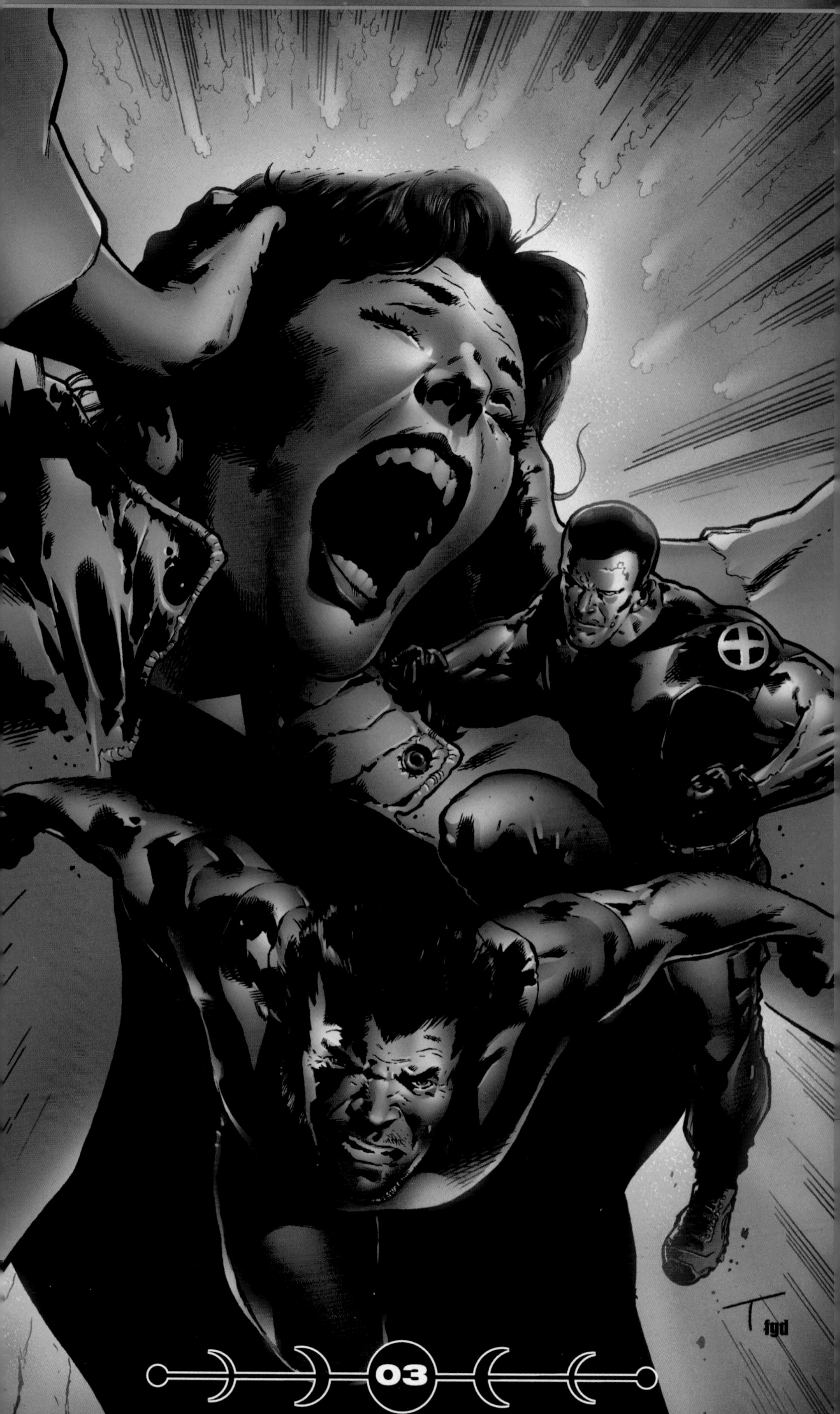

03

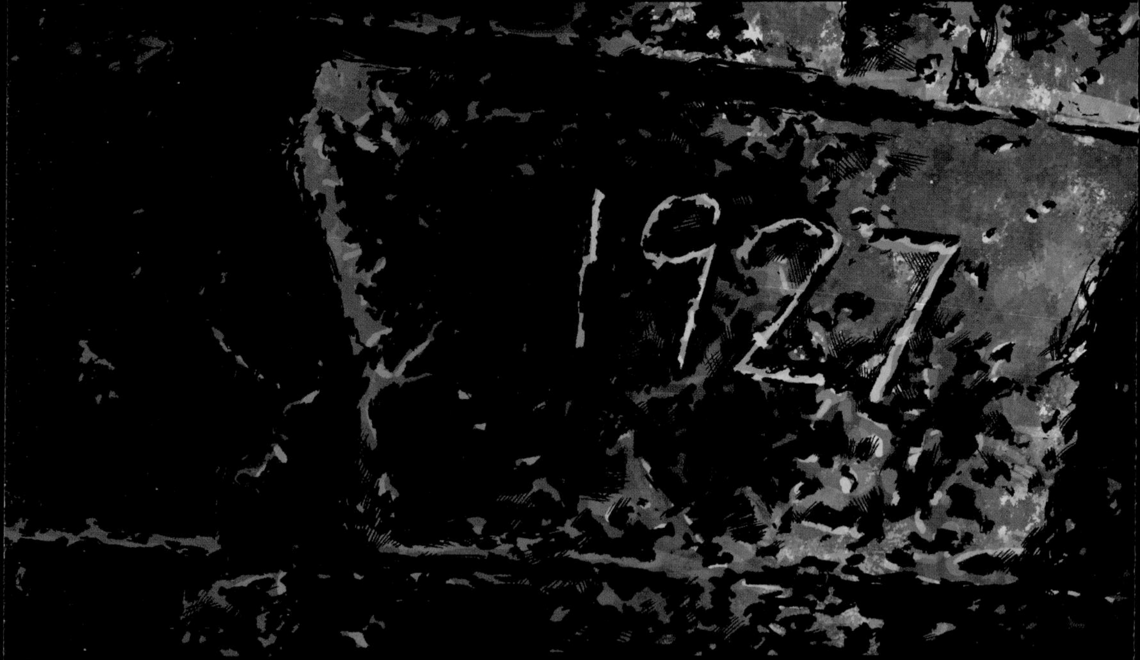
1927

Stan Lee presents

ULTIMATE NIGHTMARE

CHAPTER THREE

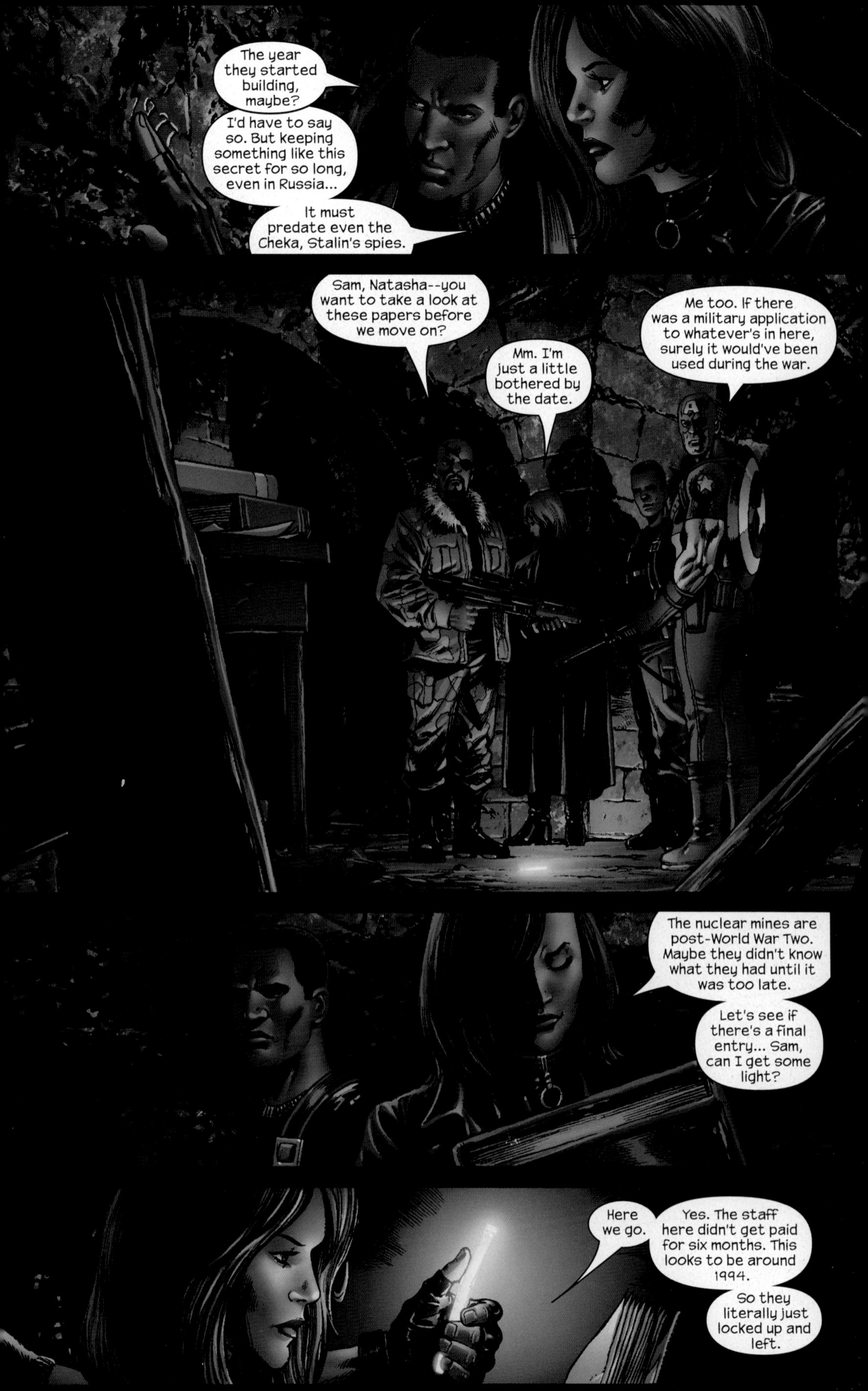
The year they started building, maybe?
I'd have to say so. But keeping something like this secret for so long, even in Russia...
It must predate even the Cheka, Stalin's spies.
Sam, Natasha--you want to take a look at these papers before we move on?
Mm. I'm just a little bothered by the date.
Me too. If there was a military application to whatever's in here, surely it would've been used during the war.
The nuclear mines are post-World War Two. Maybe they didn't know what they had until it was too late.
Let's see if there's a final entry... Sam, can I get some light?
Here we go.
Yes. The staff here didn't get paid for six months. This looks to be around 1994.
So they literally just locked up and left.

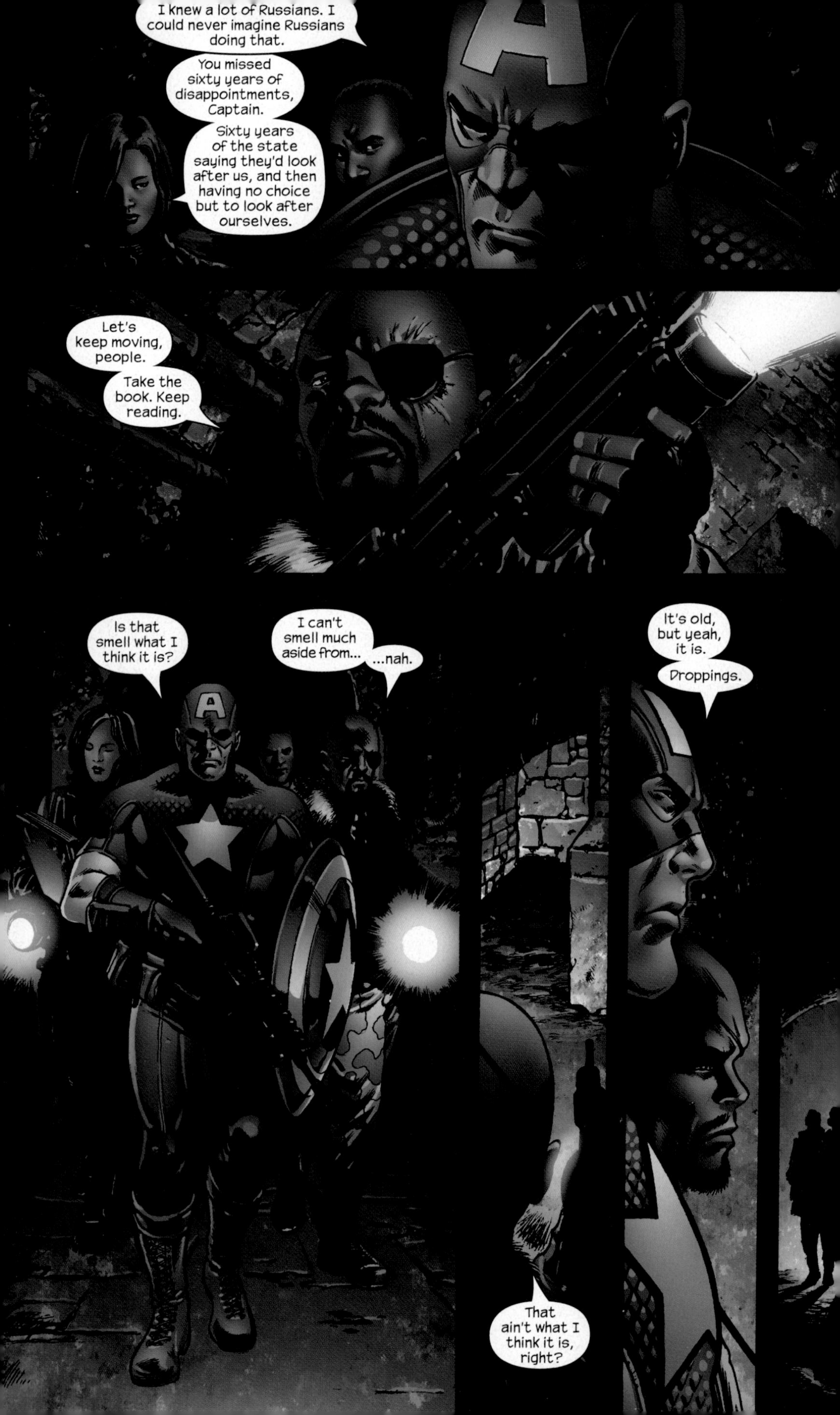
I knew a lot of Russians. I could never imagine Russians doing that.
You missed sixty years of disappointments, Captain.
Sixty years of the state saying they'd look after us, and then having no choice but to look after ourselves.
Let's keep moving, people.
Take the book. Keep reading.
Is that smell what I think it is?
I can't smell much aside from...
...nah.
It's old, but yeah, it is.
Droppings.
That ain't what I think it is, right?

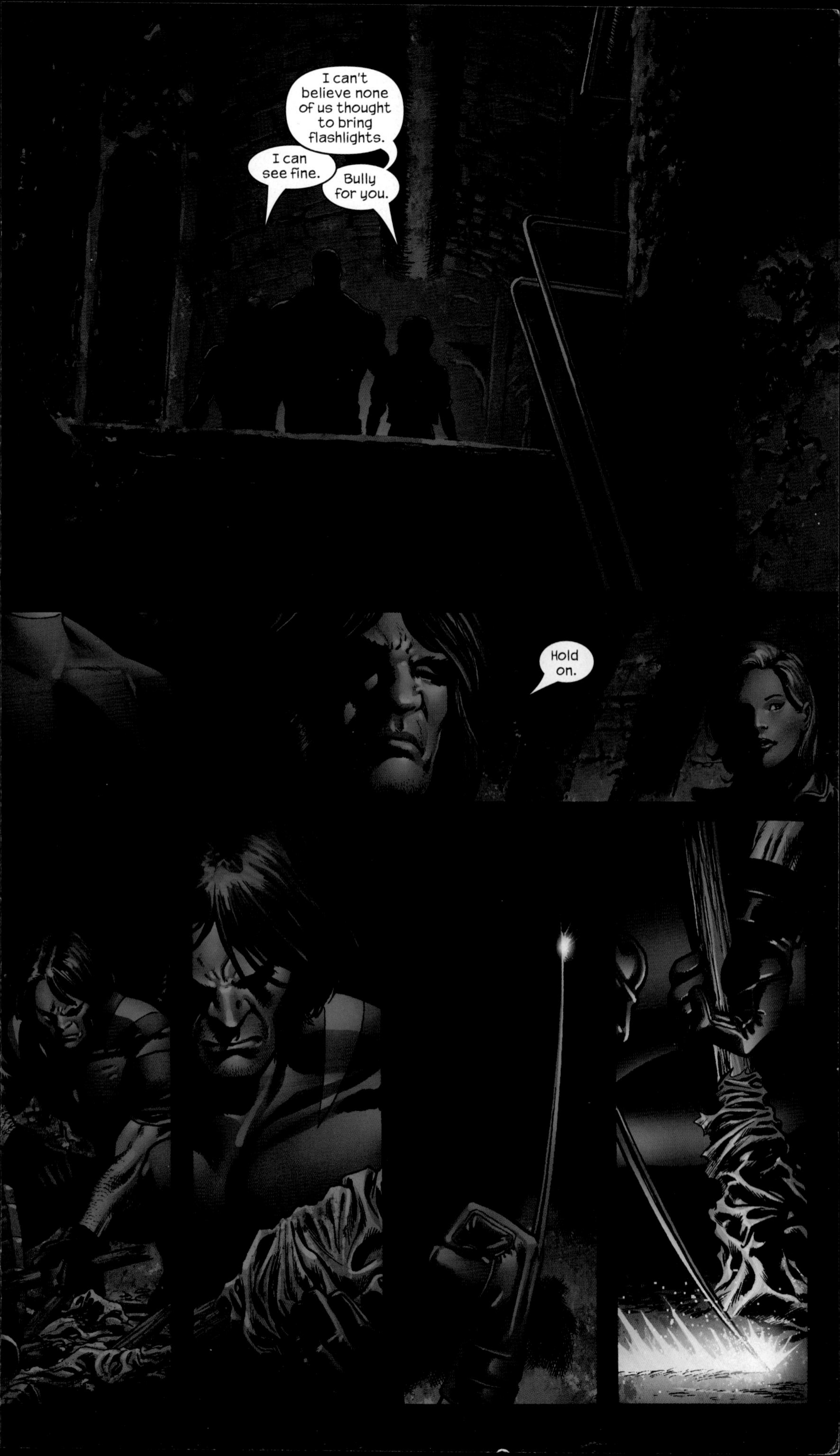
I can't believe none of us thought to bring flashlights.
I can see fine.
Bully for you.
Hold on.

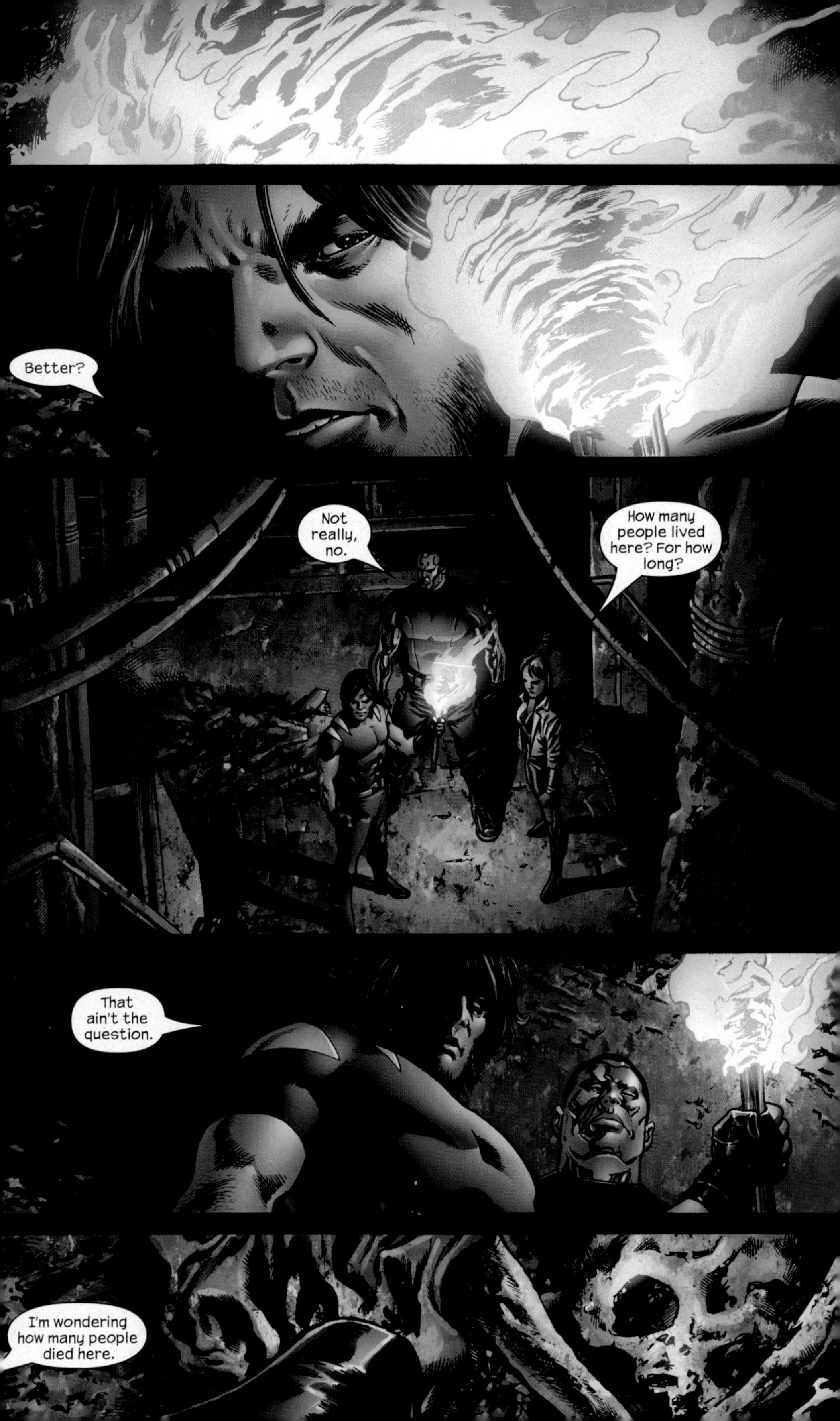
Better?
Not really, no.
How many people lived here? For how long?
That ain't the question.
I'm wondering how many people died here.

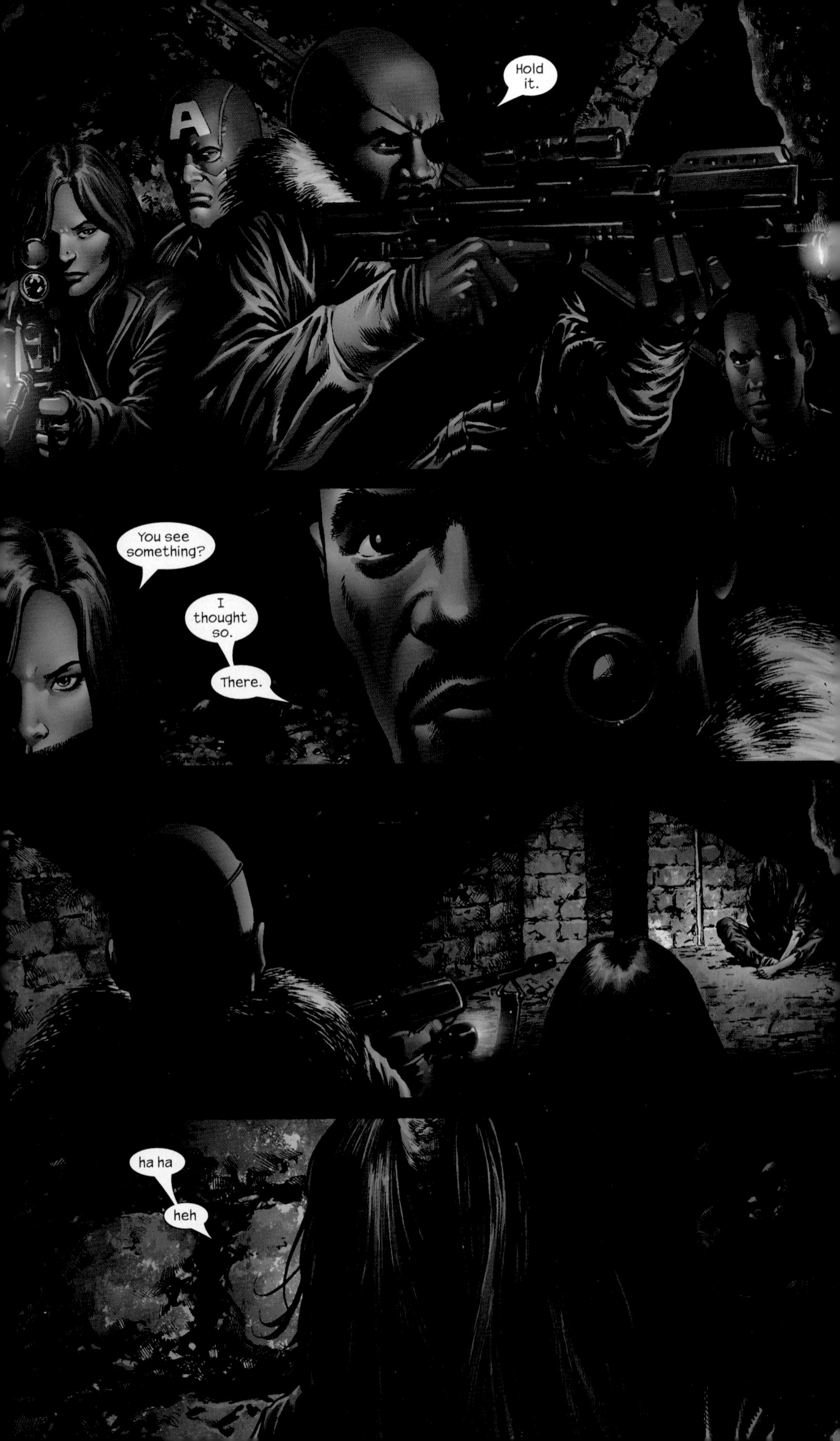
Hold it.
You see something?
I thought so.
There.
ha ha
heh

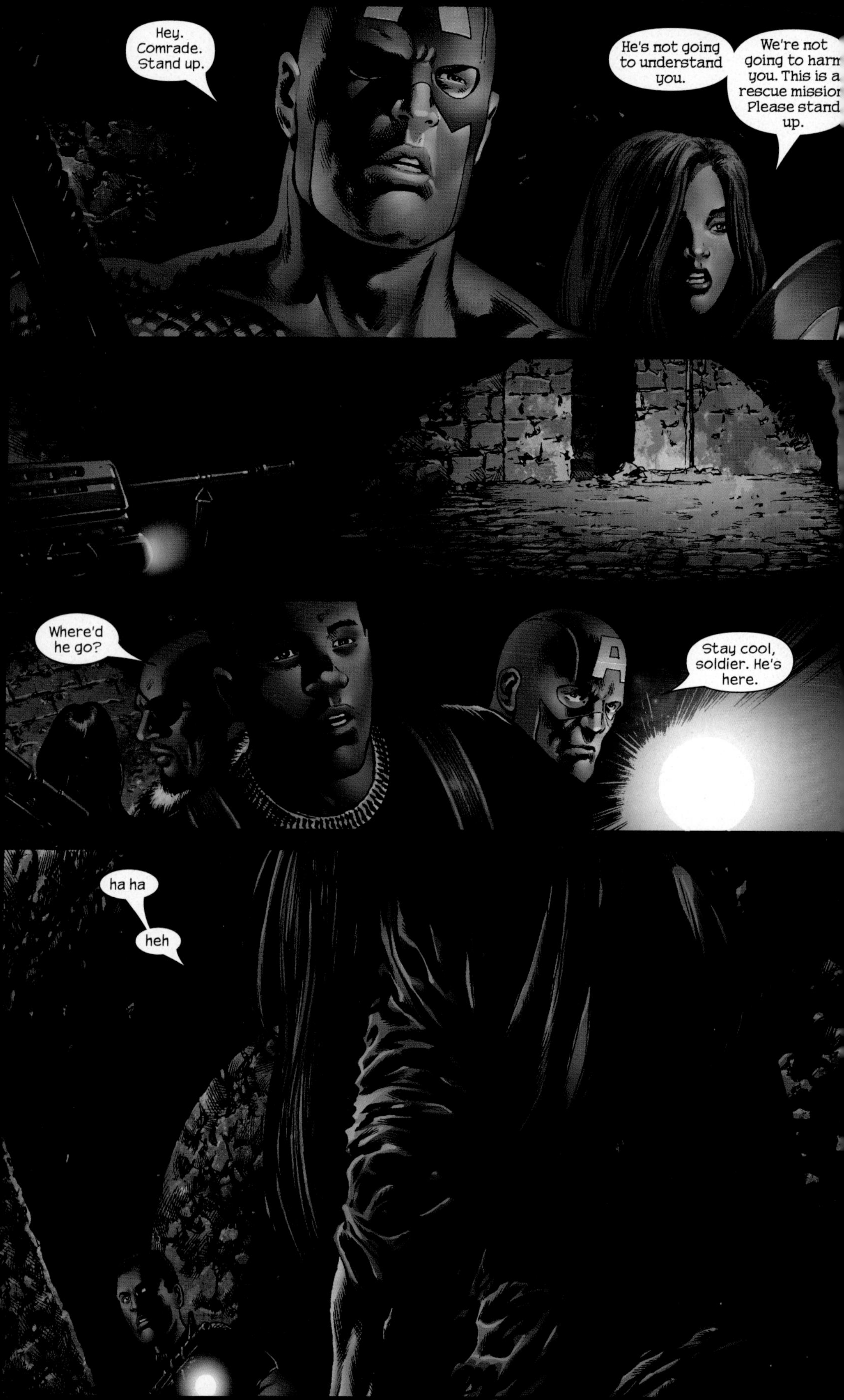

Hey. Comrade. Stand up.
He's not going to understand you.
We're not going to harm you. This is a rescue mission. Please stand up.
Where'd he go?
Stay cool, soldier. He's here.
ha ha
heh

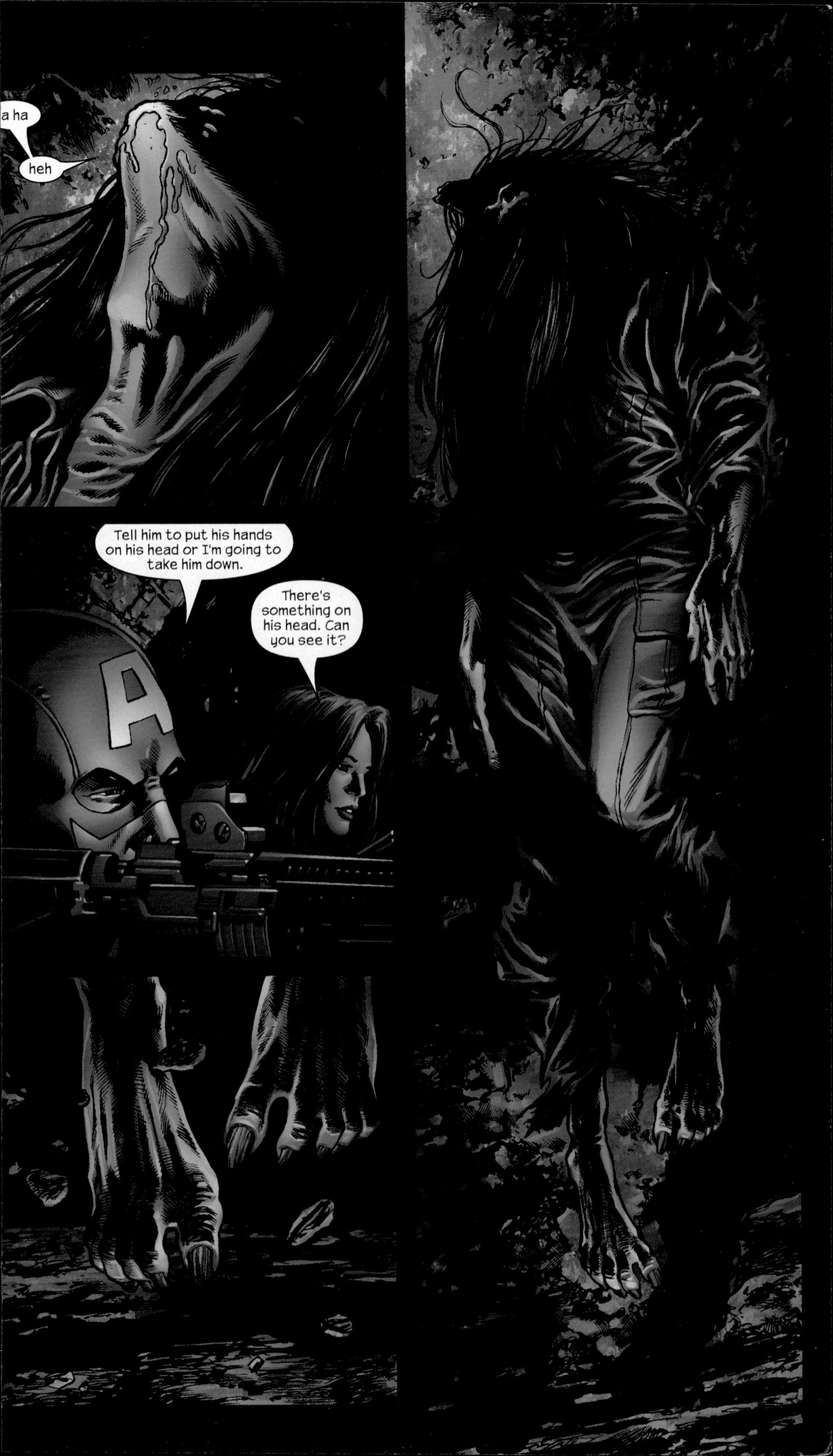
a ha
heh
Tell him to put his hands on his head or I'm going to take him down.
There's something on his head. Can you see it?

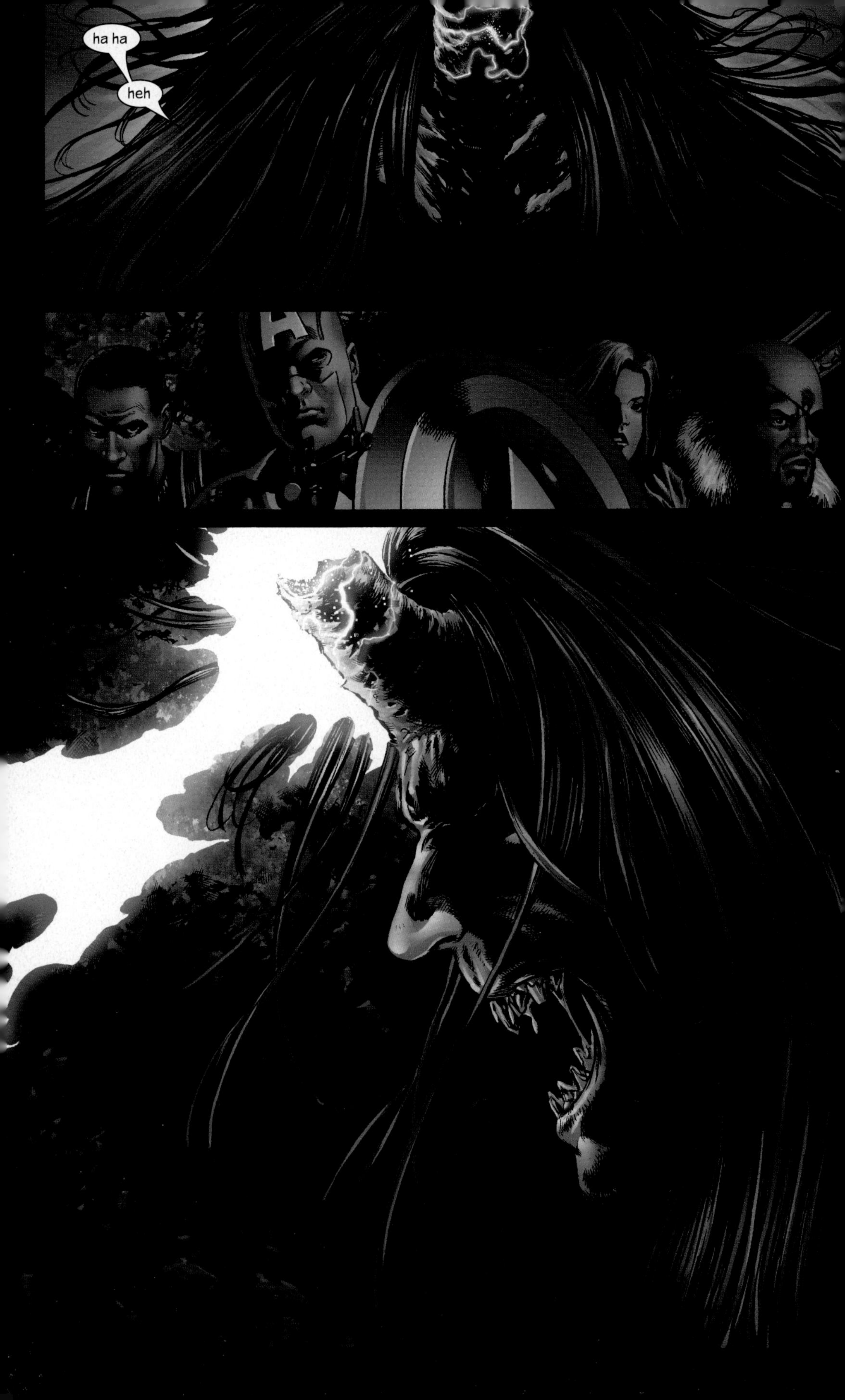
ha ha
heh

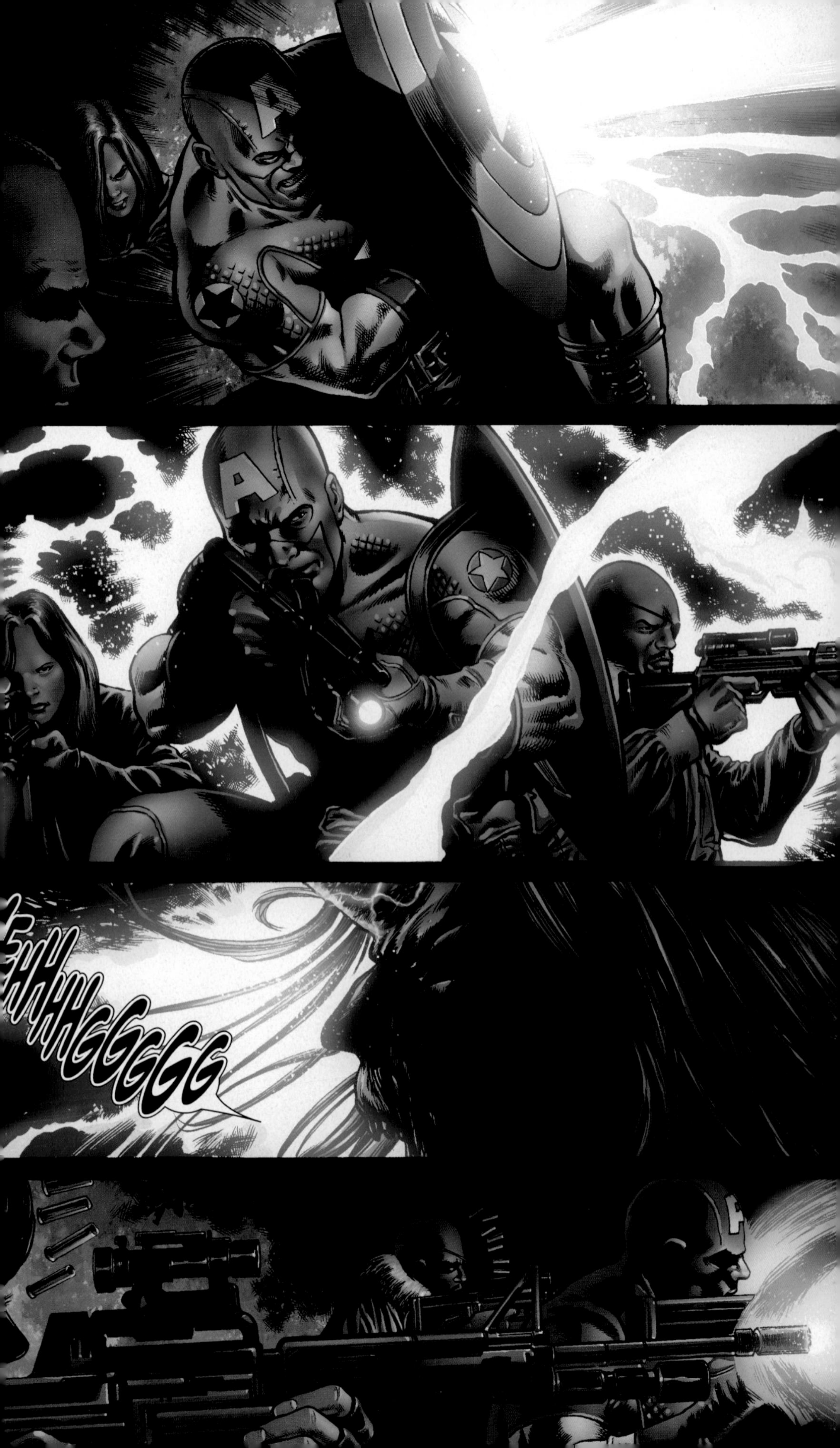
HHHHGGGGGG

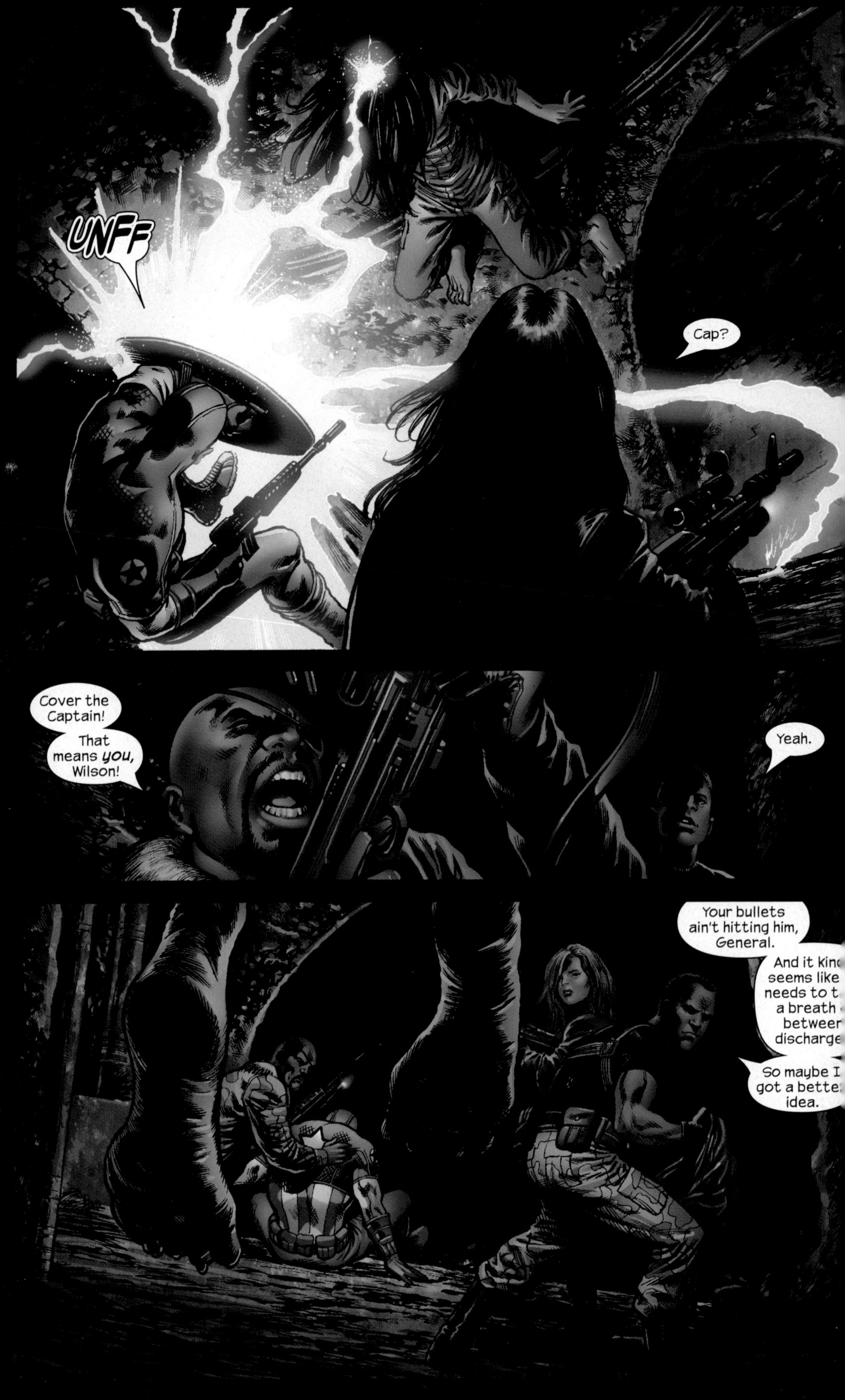
UNFF
Cap?
Cover the Captain!
That means you, Wilson!
Yeah.
Your bullets ain't hitting him, General.
So maybe I got a bette idea.

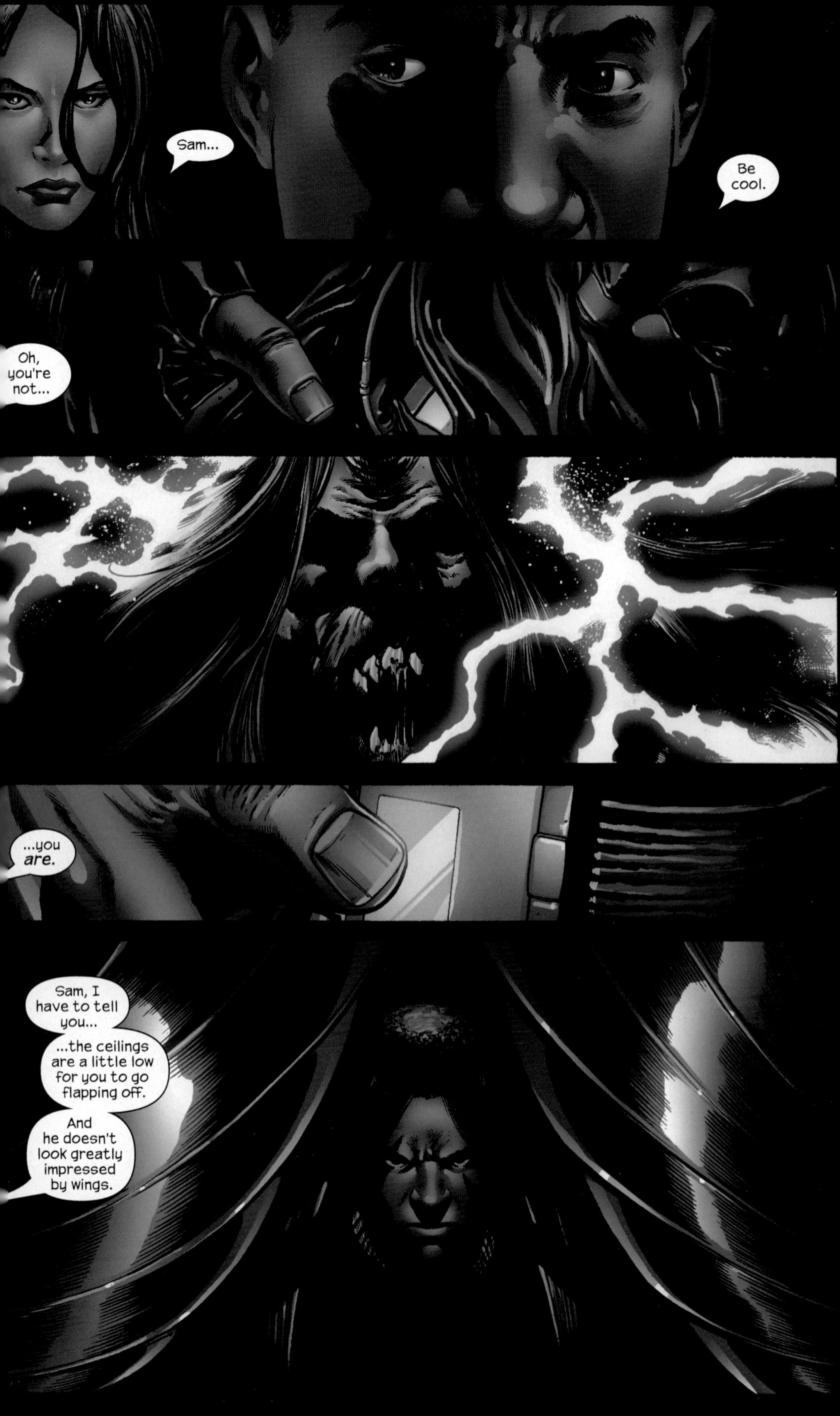
Sam...
Be cool.
Oh, you're not...
...you *are.*
Sam, I have to tell you...
...the ceilings are a little low for you to go flapping off.
And he doesn't look greatly impressed by wings.

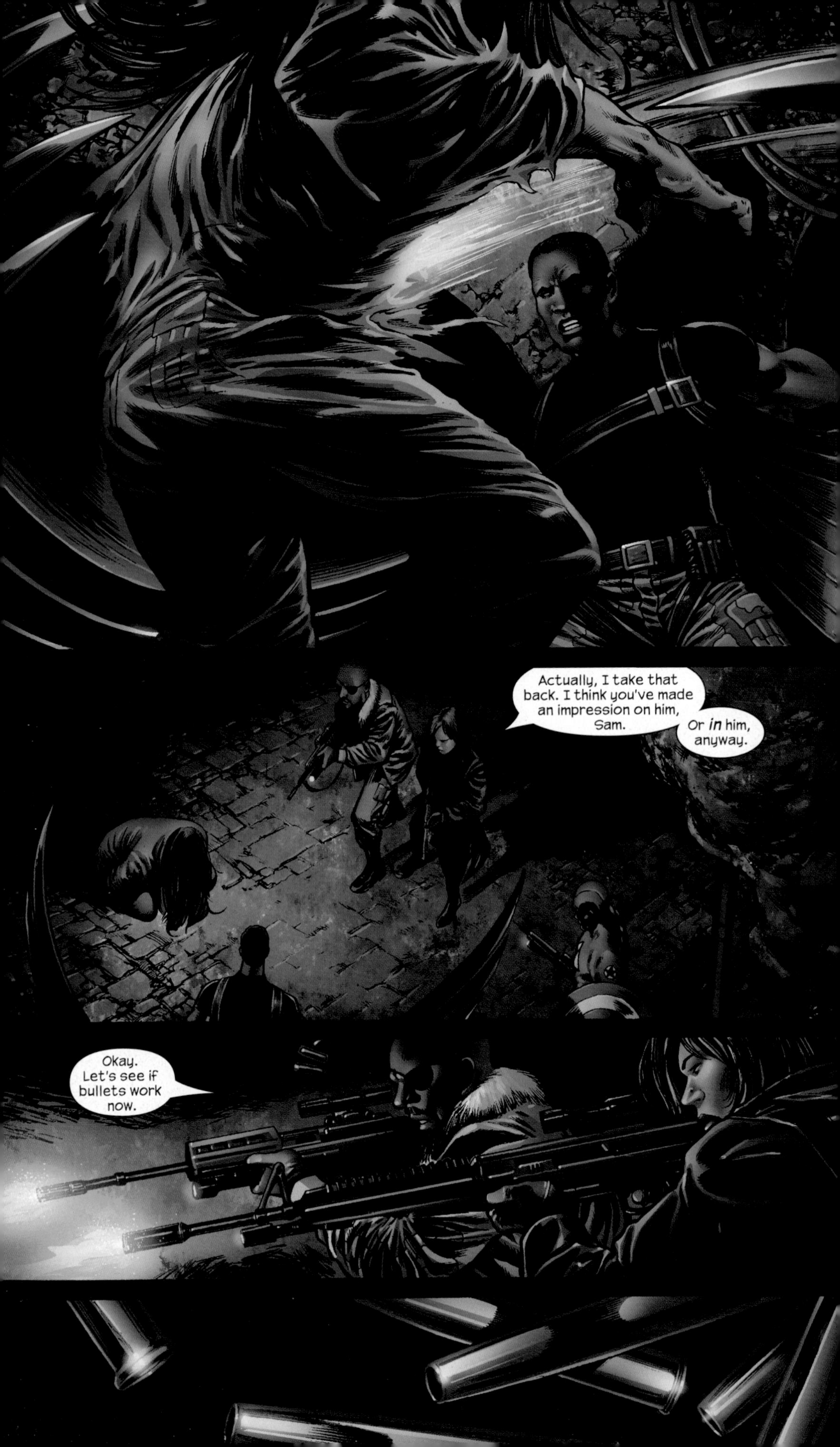
Actually, I take that back. I think you've made an impression on him, Sam.
Or *in* him, anyway.
Okay. Let's see if bullets work now.

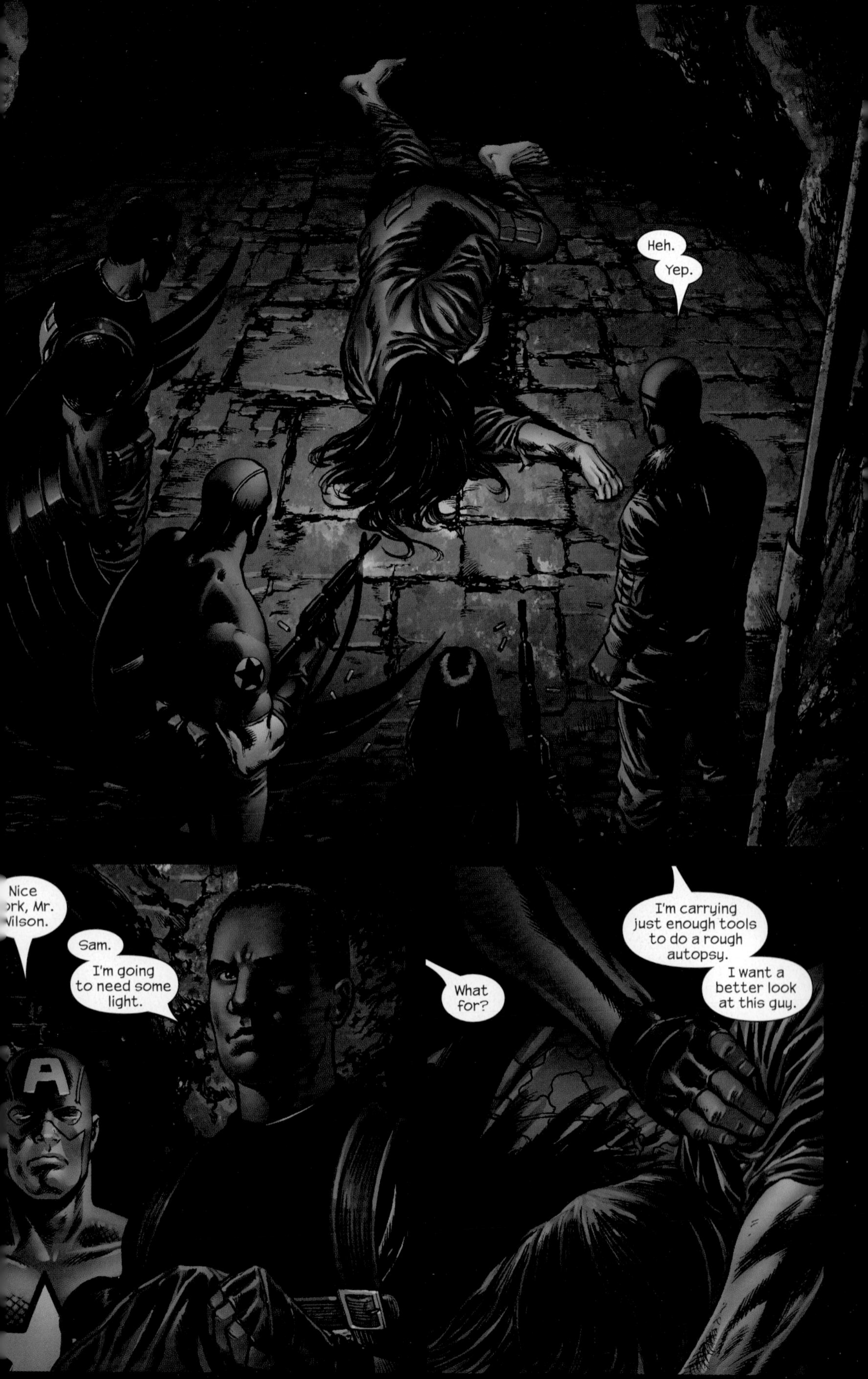
Heh.
Yep.
Nice rk, Mr. ilson.
Sam.
I'm going to need some light.
What for?
I'm carrying just enough tools to do a rough autopsy.
I want a better look at this guy.

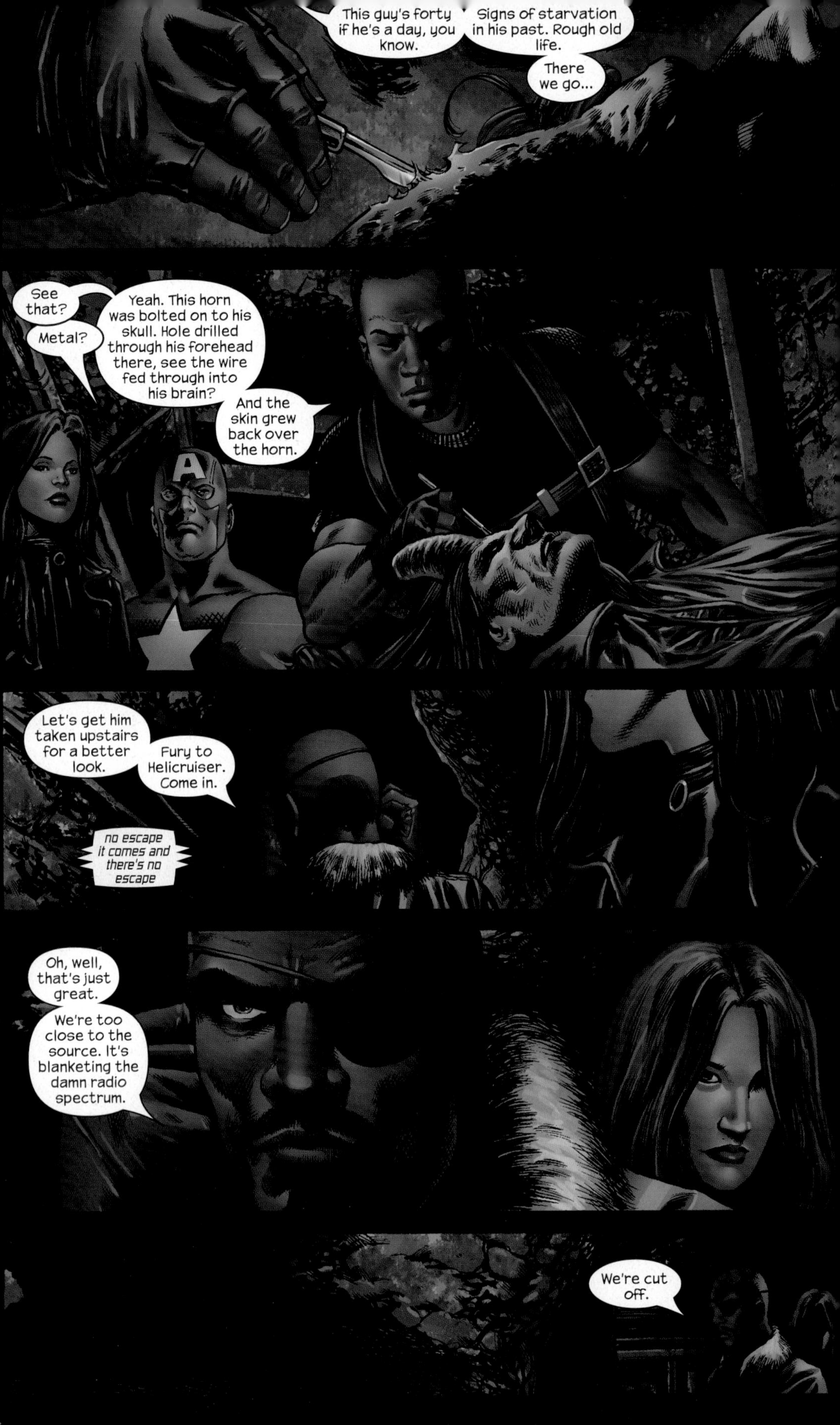
This guy's forty if he's a day, you know.
Signs of starvation in his past. Rough old life.
There we go...
See that?
Metal?
Yeah. This horn was bolted on to his skull. Hole drilled through his forehead there, see the wire fed through into his brain?
And the skin grew back over the horn.
Let's get him taken upstairs for a better look.
Fury to Helicruiser. Come in.
no escape it comes and there's no escape
Oh, well, that's just great.
We're too close to the source. It's blanketing the damn radio spectrum.
We're cut off.

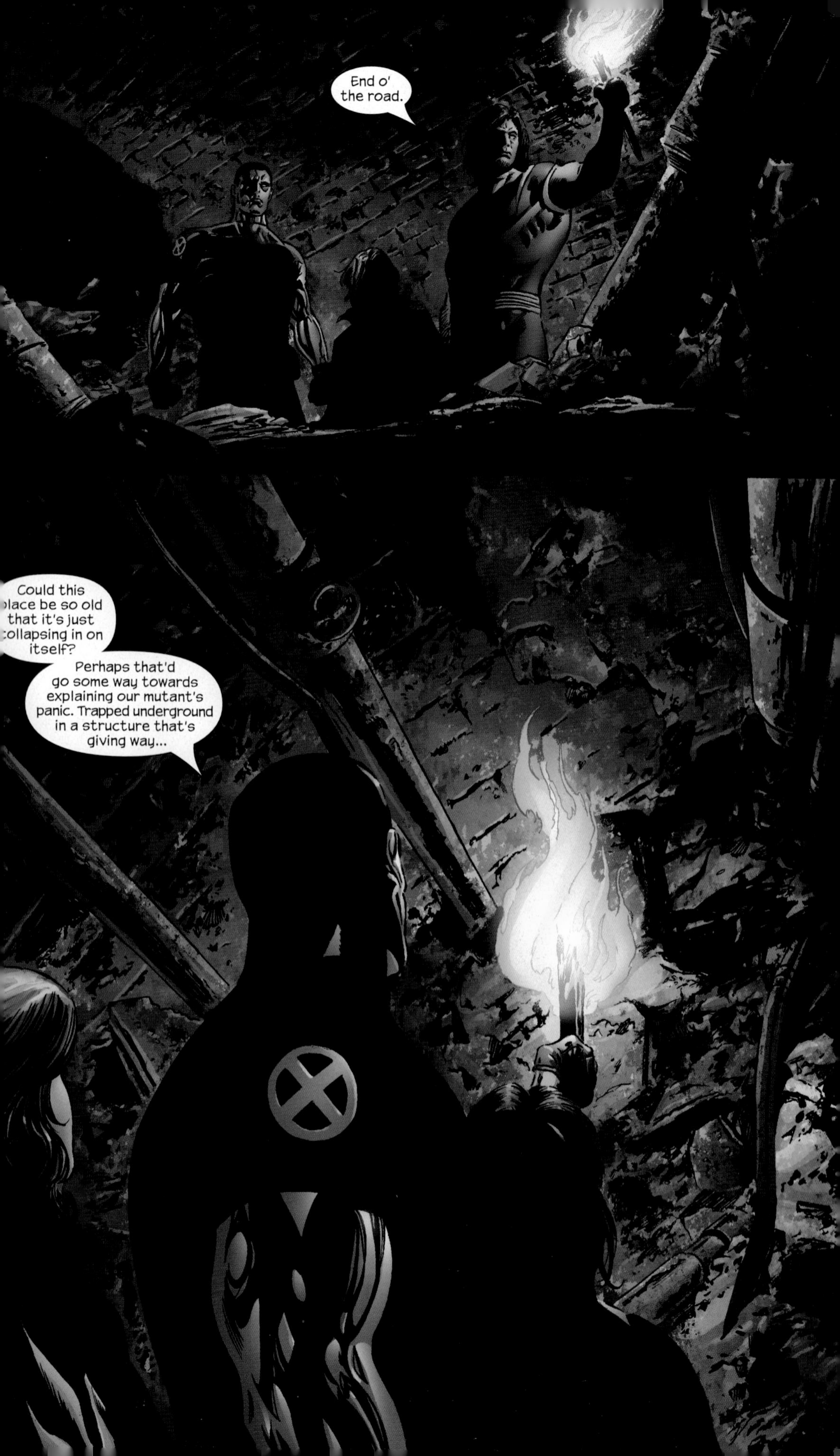
End o' the road.
Could this lace be so old that it's just ollapsing in on itself?
Perhaps that'd go some way towards explaining our mutant's panic. Trapped underground in a structure that's giving way...

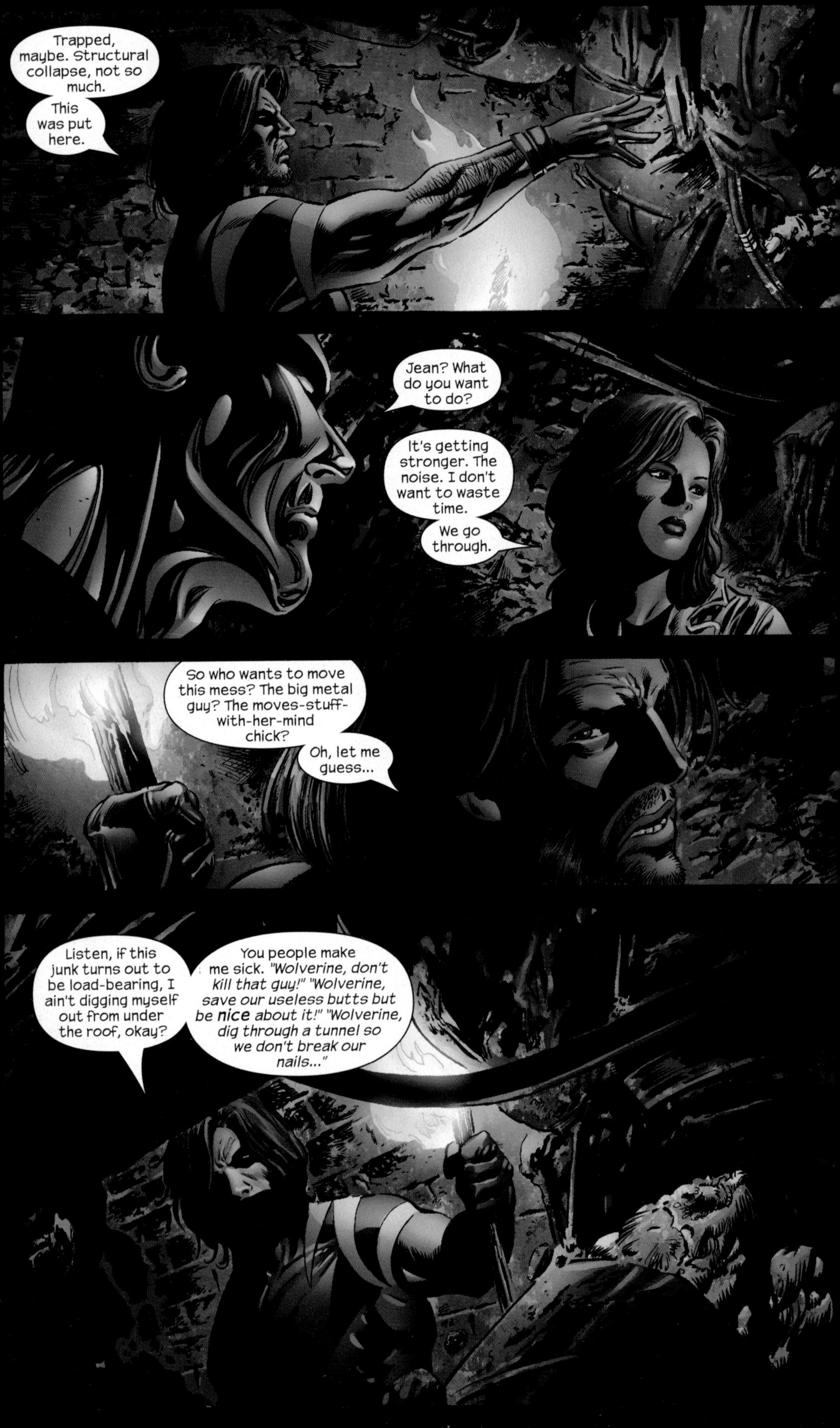
Trapped, maybe. Structural collapse, not so much.
This was put here.
Jean? What do you want to do?
It's getting stronger. The noise. I don't want to waste time.
We go through.
So who wants to move this mess? The big metal guy? The moves-stuff-with-her-mind chick?
Oh, let me guess...
Listen, if this junk turns out to be load-bearing, I ain't digging myself out from under the roof, okay?
You people make me sick. *"Wolverine, don't kill that guy!" "Wolverine, save our useless butts but be* ***nice*** *about it!" "Wolverine, dig through a tunnel so we don't break our nails..."*

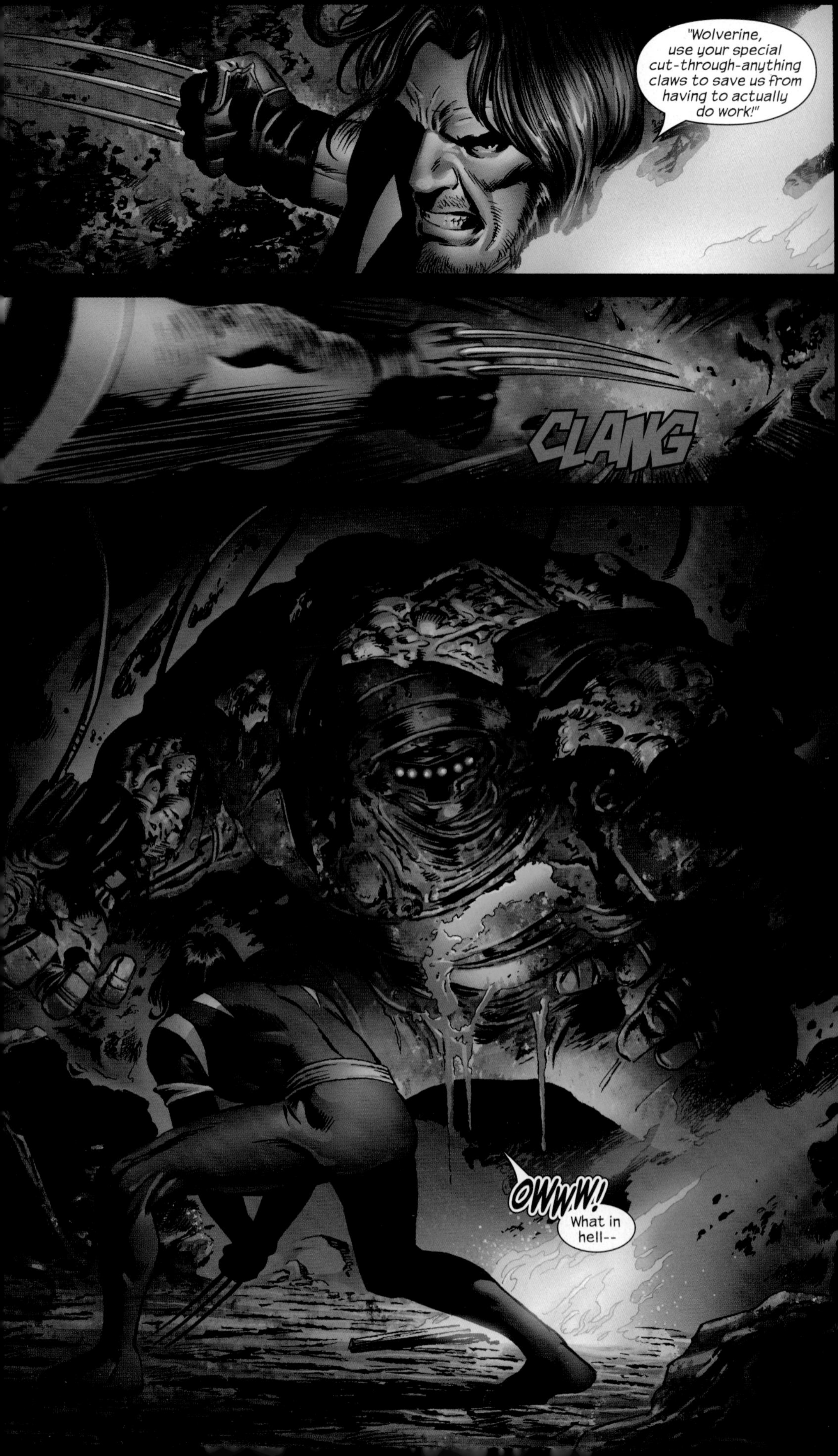
"Wolverine, use your special cut-through-anything claws to save us from having to actually do work!"
CLANG
OWWW!
What in hell--

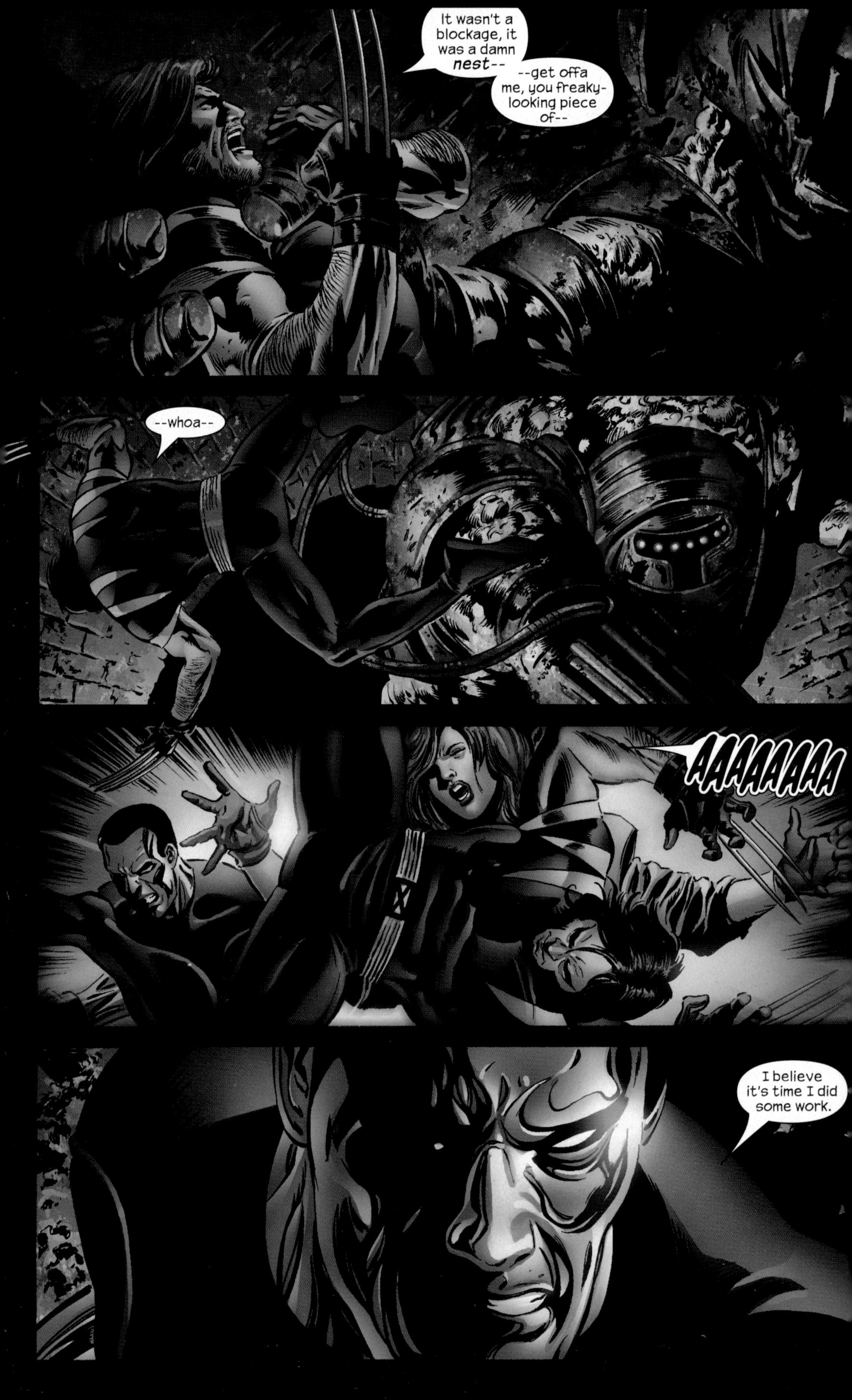
It wasn't a blockage, it was a damn *nest*--
--get offa me, you freaky-looking piece of--
--whoa--
AAAAAAAA
I believe it's time I did some work.

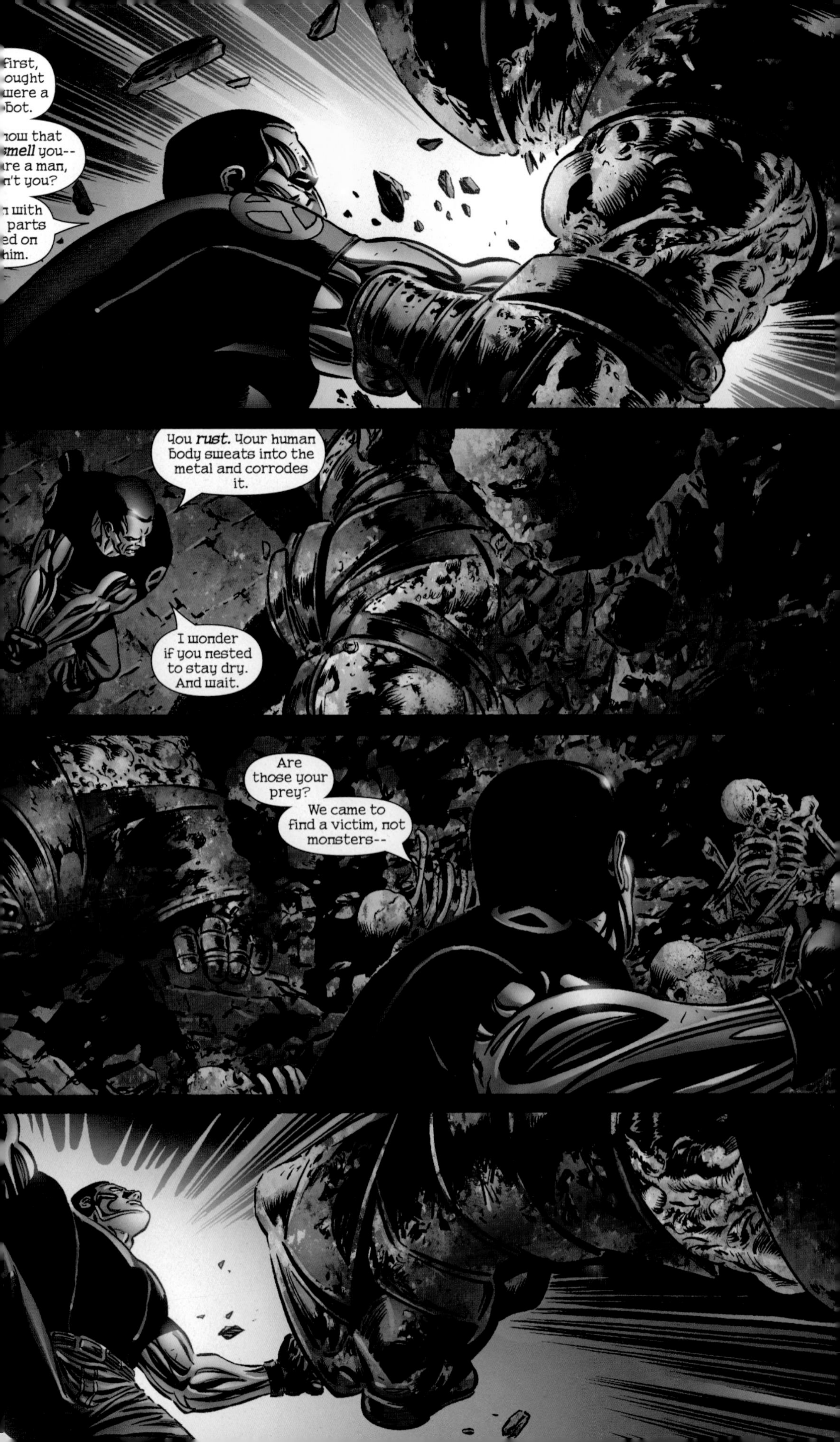
First, ought were a Bot.
now that smell you-- re a man, n't you?
n with parts ed on him.
You *rust.* Your human body sweats into the metal and corrodes it.
I wonder if you nested to stay dry. And wait.
Are those your prey?
We came to find a victim, not monsters--

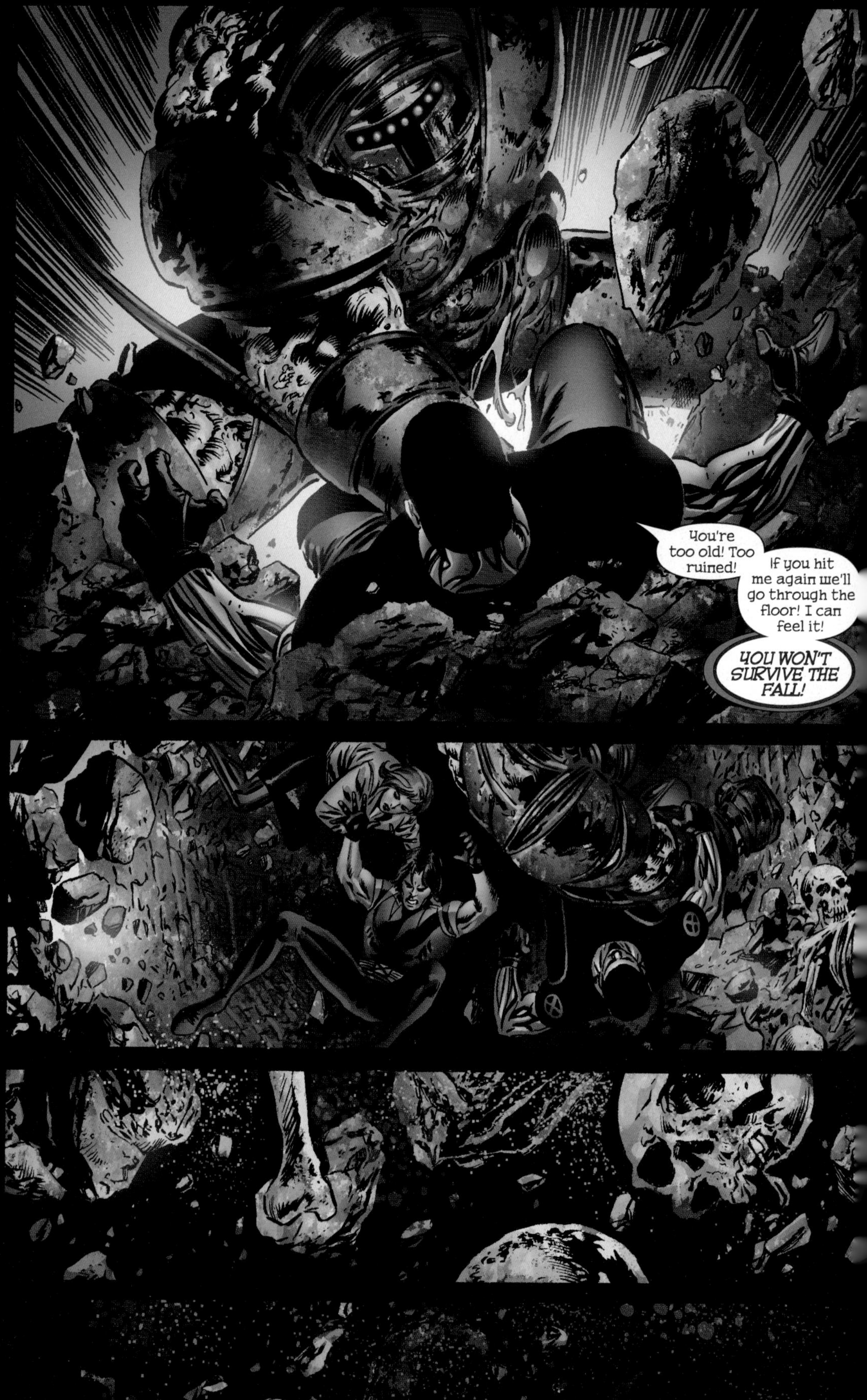
You're too old! Too ruined!
If you hit me again we'll go through the floor! I can feel it!
YOU WON'T SURVIVE THE FALL!

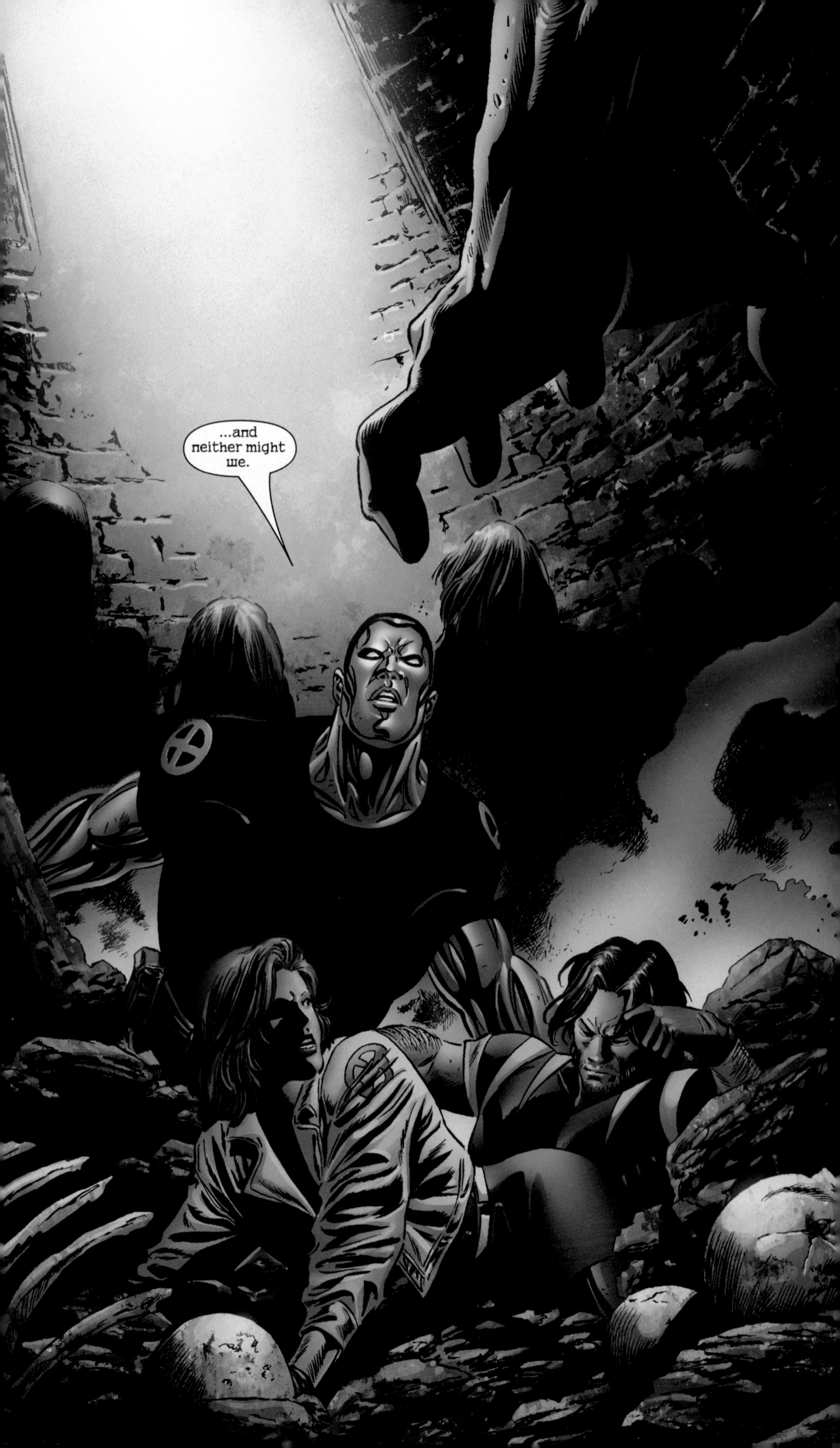
...and neither might we.

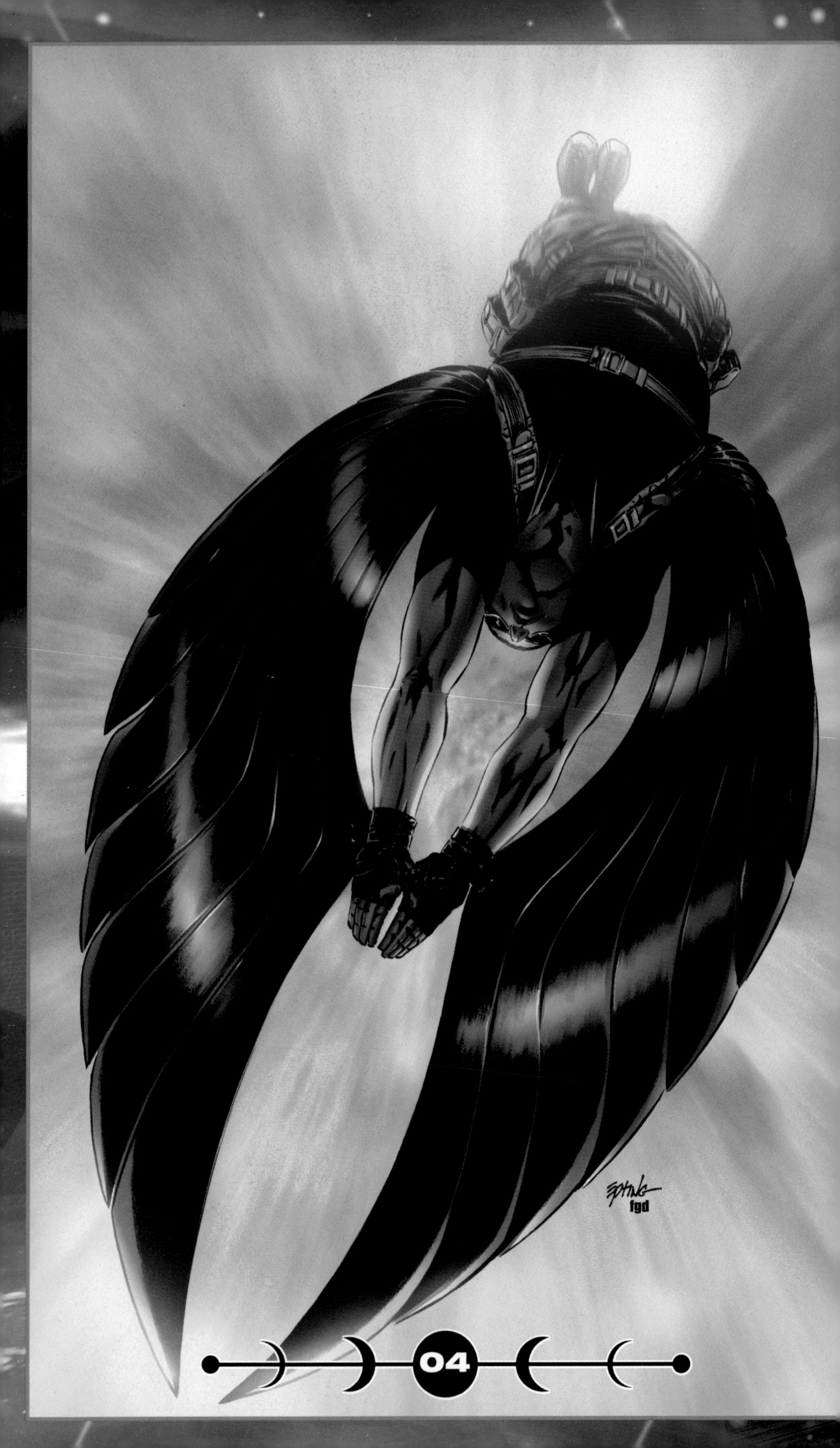
04

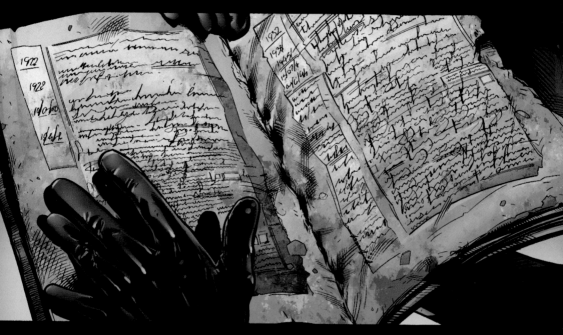

s t a n   l e e   p r e s e n t s :

ULTIMATE NIGHTMARE

C H A P T E R   F O U R

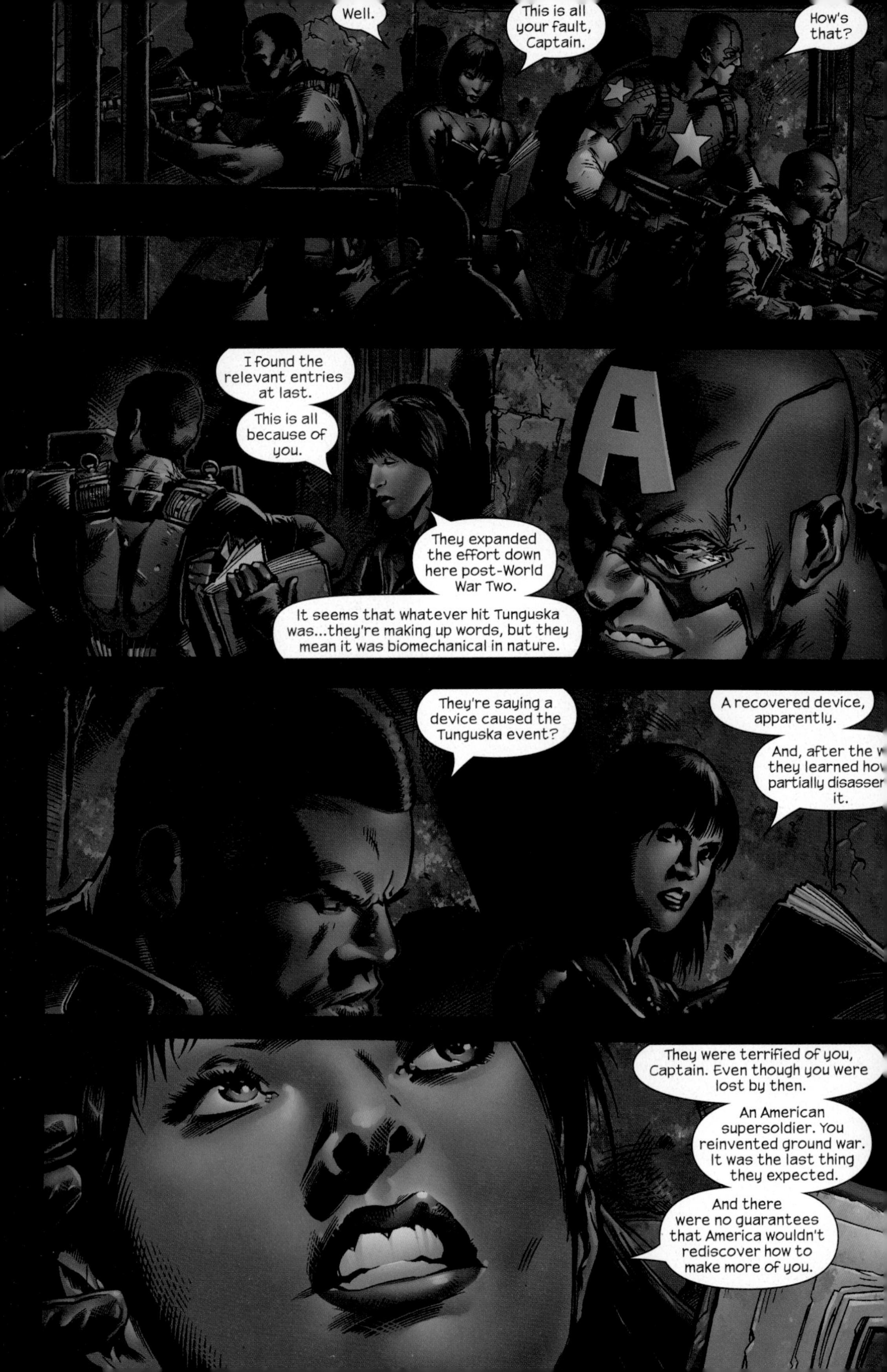
Well.
This is all your fault, Captain.
How's that?
I found the relevant entries at last.
This is all because of you.
They expanded the effort down here post-World War Two.
It seems that whatever hit Tunguska was...they're making up words, but they mean it was biomechanical in nature.
They're saying a device caused the Tunguska event?
A recovered device, apparently.
They were terrified of you, Captain. Even though you were lost by then.
An American supersoldier. You reinvented ground war. It was the last thing they expected.
And there were no guarantees that America wouldn't rediscover how to make more of you.

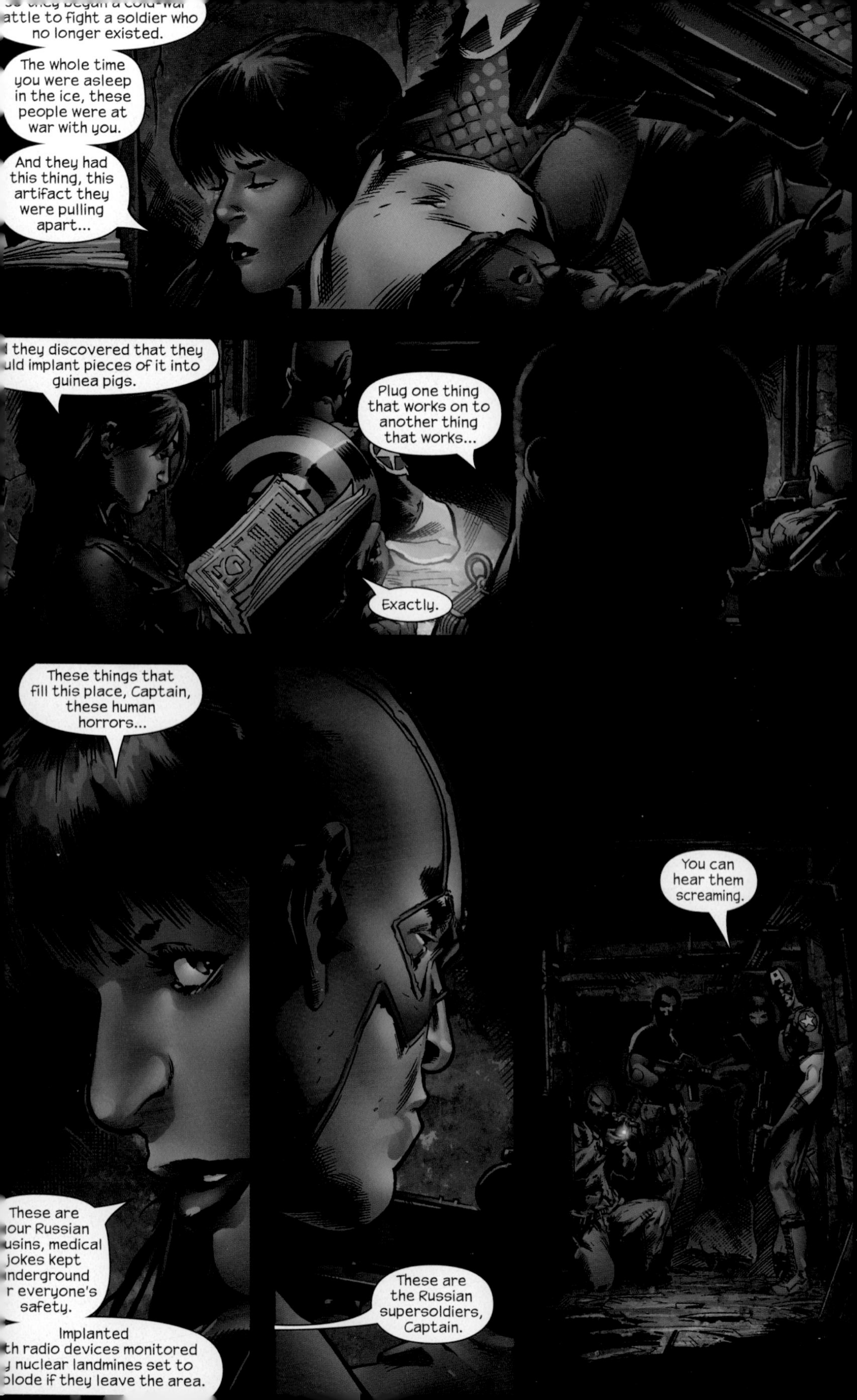

attle to fight a soldier who no longer existed.
The whole time you were asleep in the ice, these people were at war with you.
And they had this thing, this artifact they were pulling apart...
they discovered that they uld implant pieces of it into guinea pigs.
Plug one thing that works on to another thing that works...
Exactly.
These things that fill this place, Captain, these human horrors...
You can hear them screaming.
These are our Russian usins, medical jokes kept nderground r everyone's safety.
Implanted th radio devices monitored nuclear landmines set to plode if they leave the area.
These are the Russian supersoldiers, Captain.

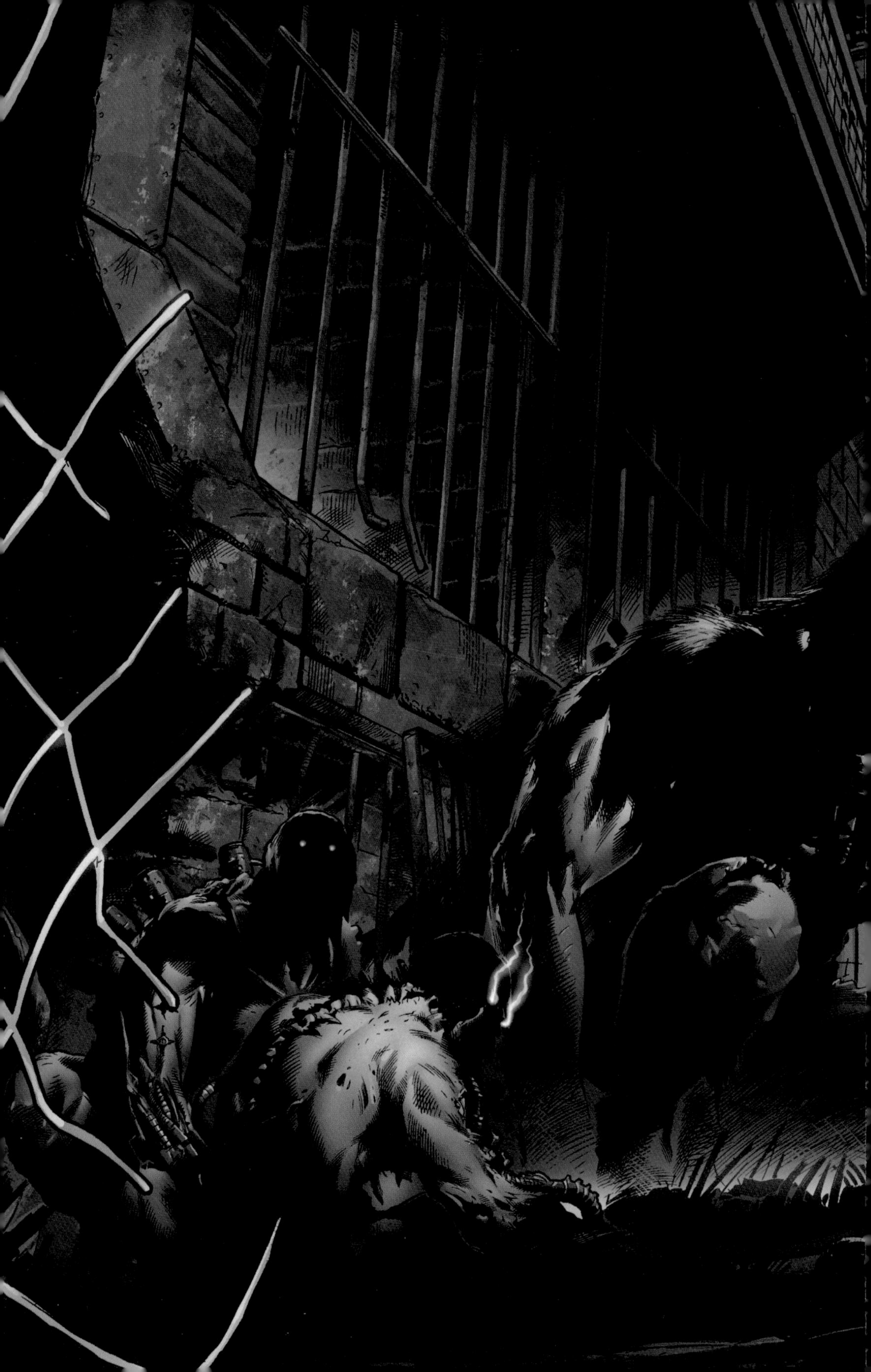

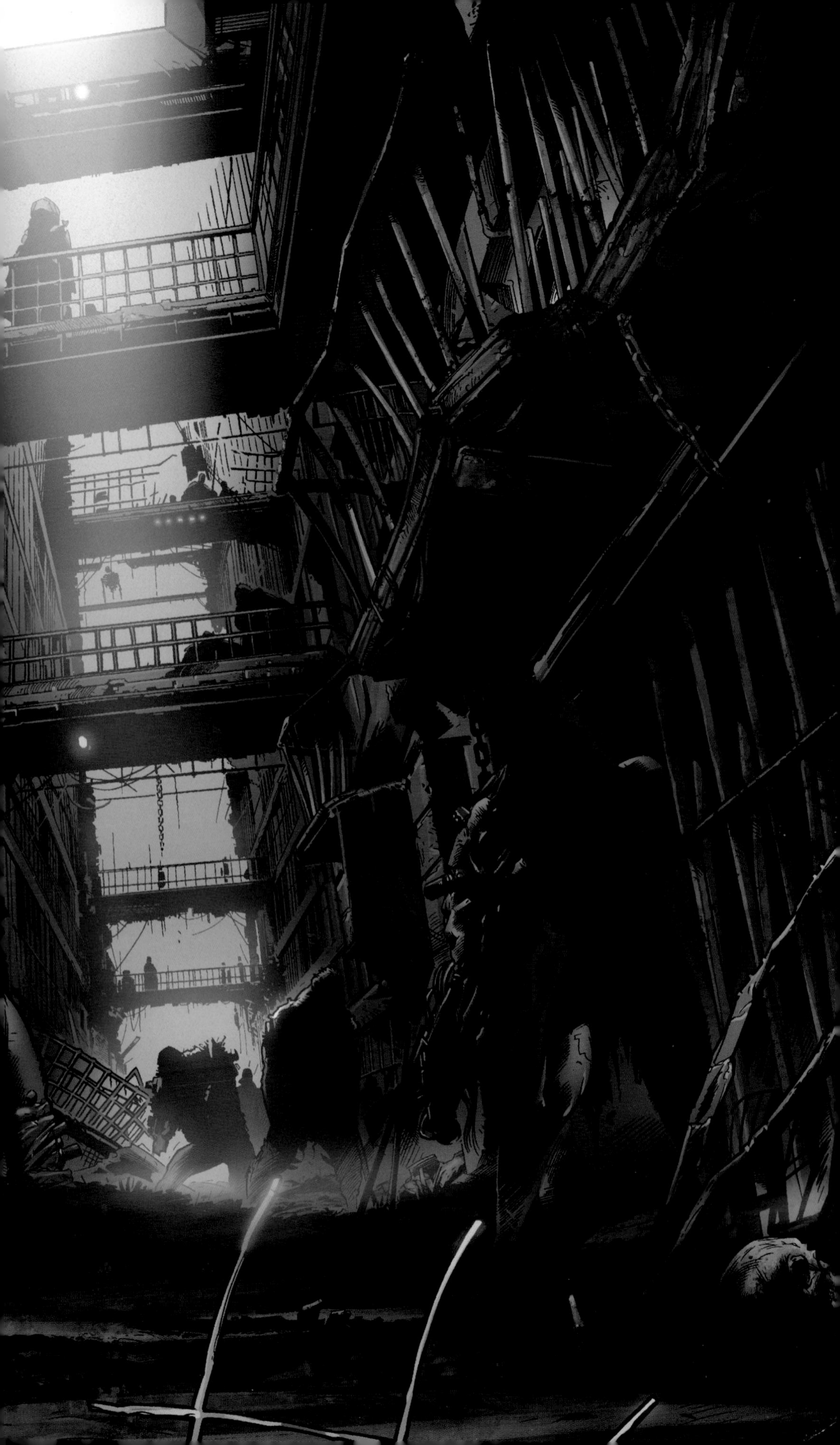

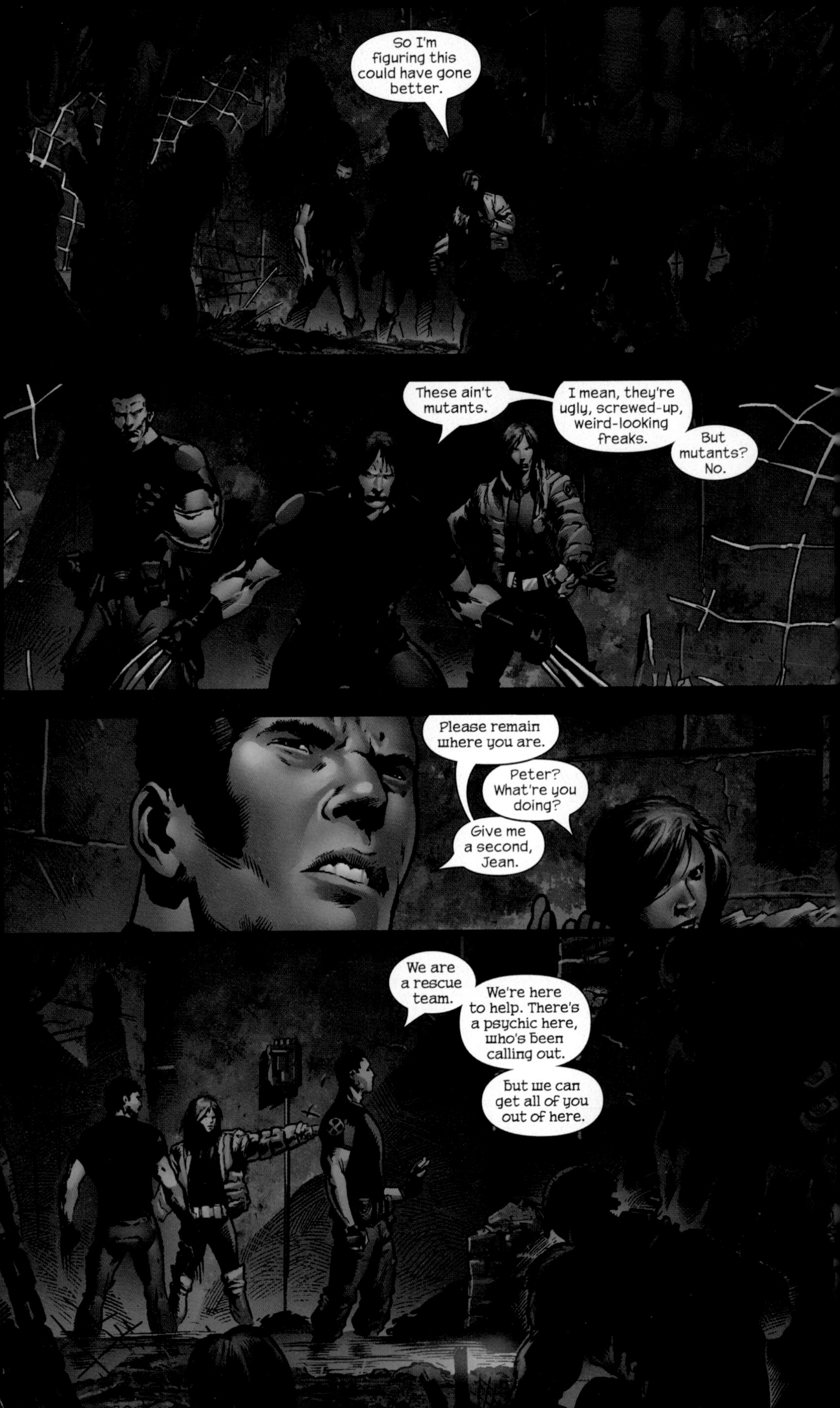
So I'm figuring this could have gone better.
These ain't mutants.
I mean, they're ugly, screwed-up, weird-looking freaks.
But mutants? No.
Please remain where you are.
Peter? What're you doing?
Give me a second, Jean.
We are a rescue team.
We're here to help. There's a psychic here, who's been calling out.
But we can get all of you out of here.

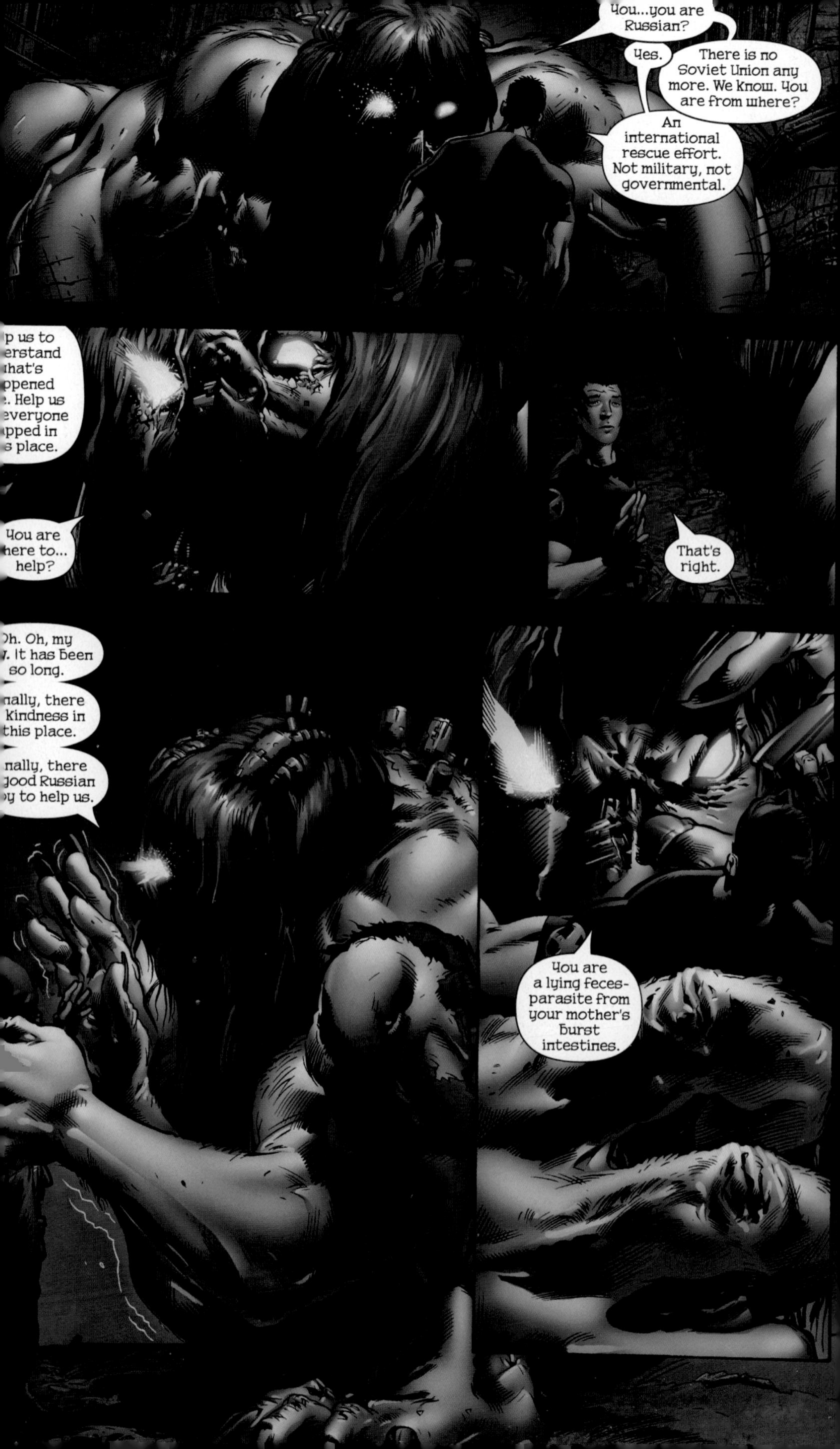
You...you are Russian?
Yes.
There is no Soviet Union any more. We know. You are from where?
An international rescue effort. Not military, not governmental.
p us to erstand hat's ppened . Help us everyone pped in s place.
You are here to... help?
That's right.
h. Oh, my . It has been so long.
nally, there kindness in this place.
nally, there good Russian y to help us.
You are a lying feces-parasite from your mother's burst intestines.

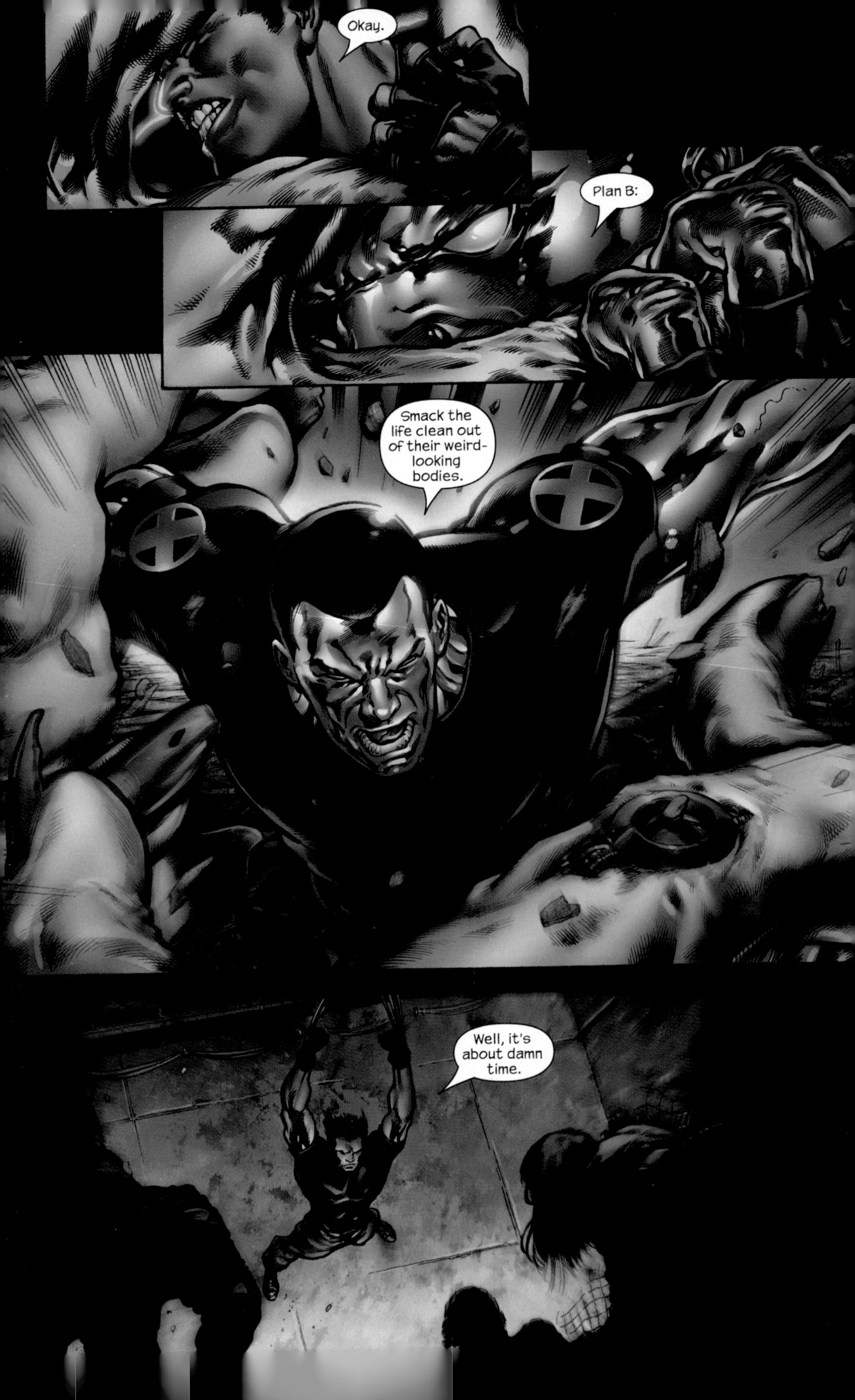
Okay.
Plan B:
Smack the life clean out of their weird-looking bodies.
Well, it's about damn time.

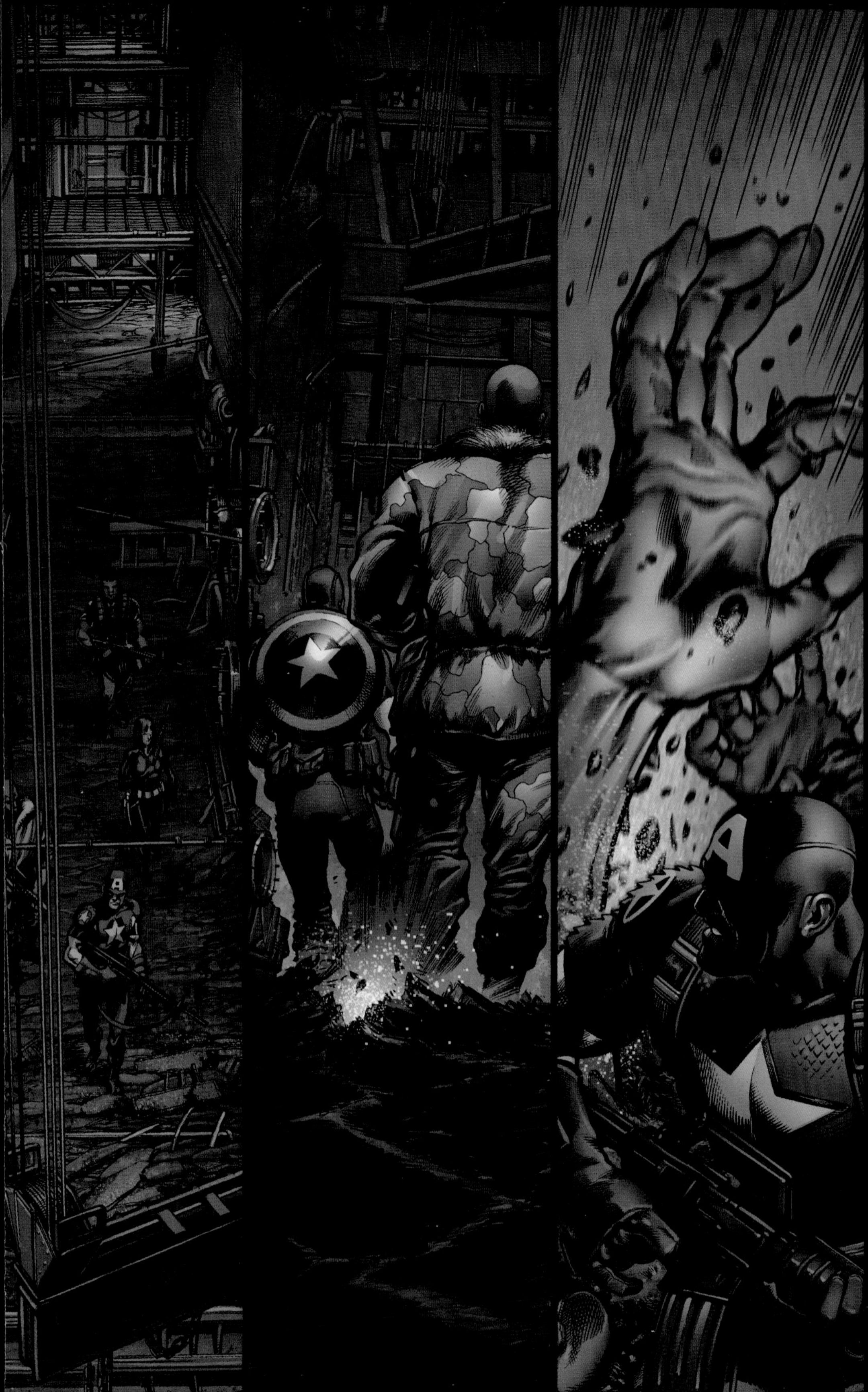

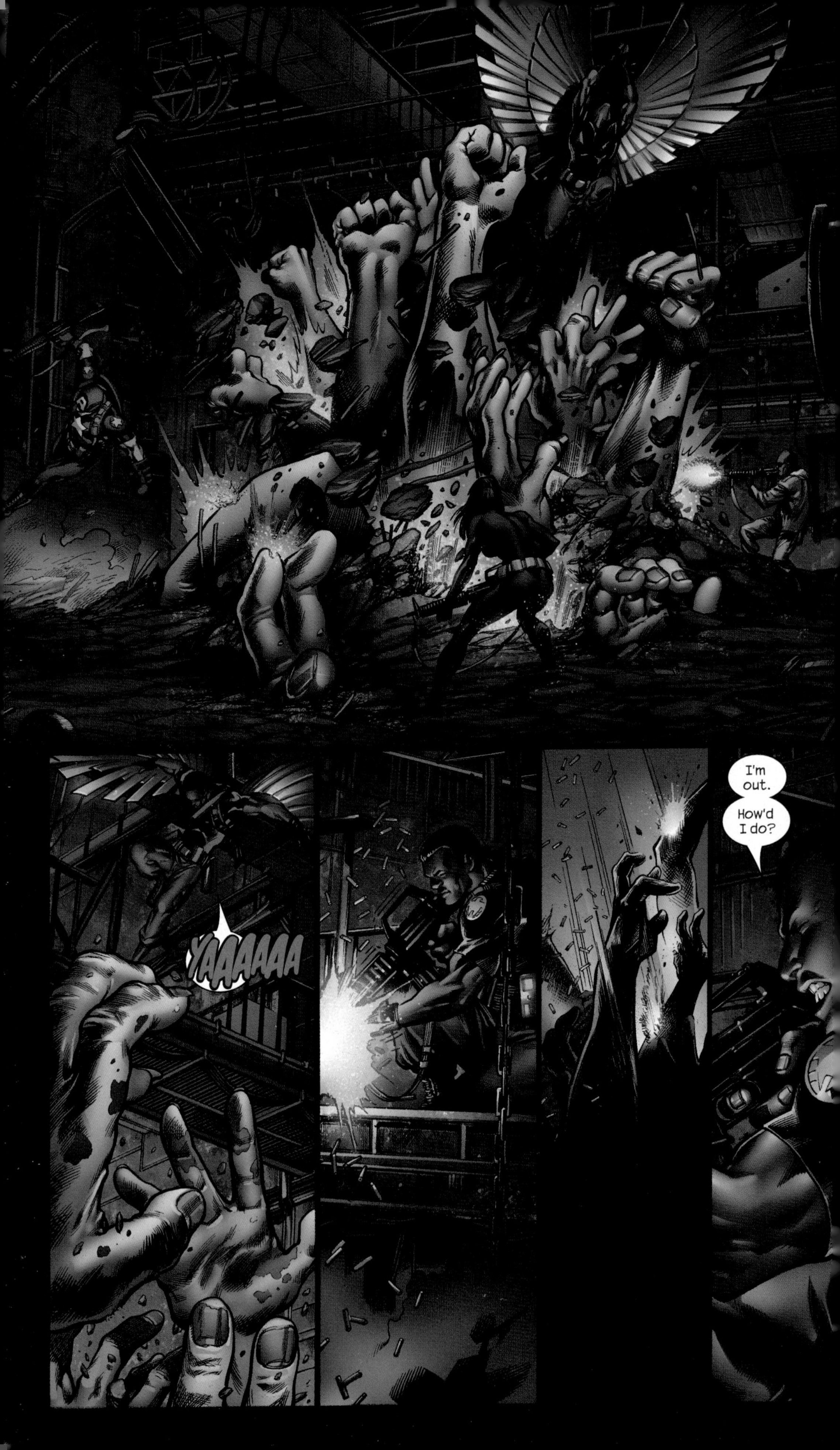

YAAAAAA
I'm out.
How'd I do?

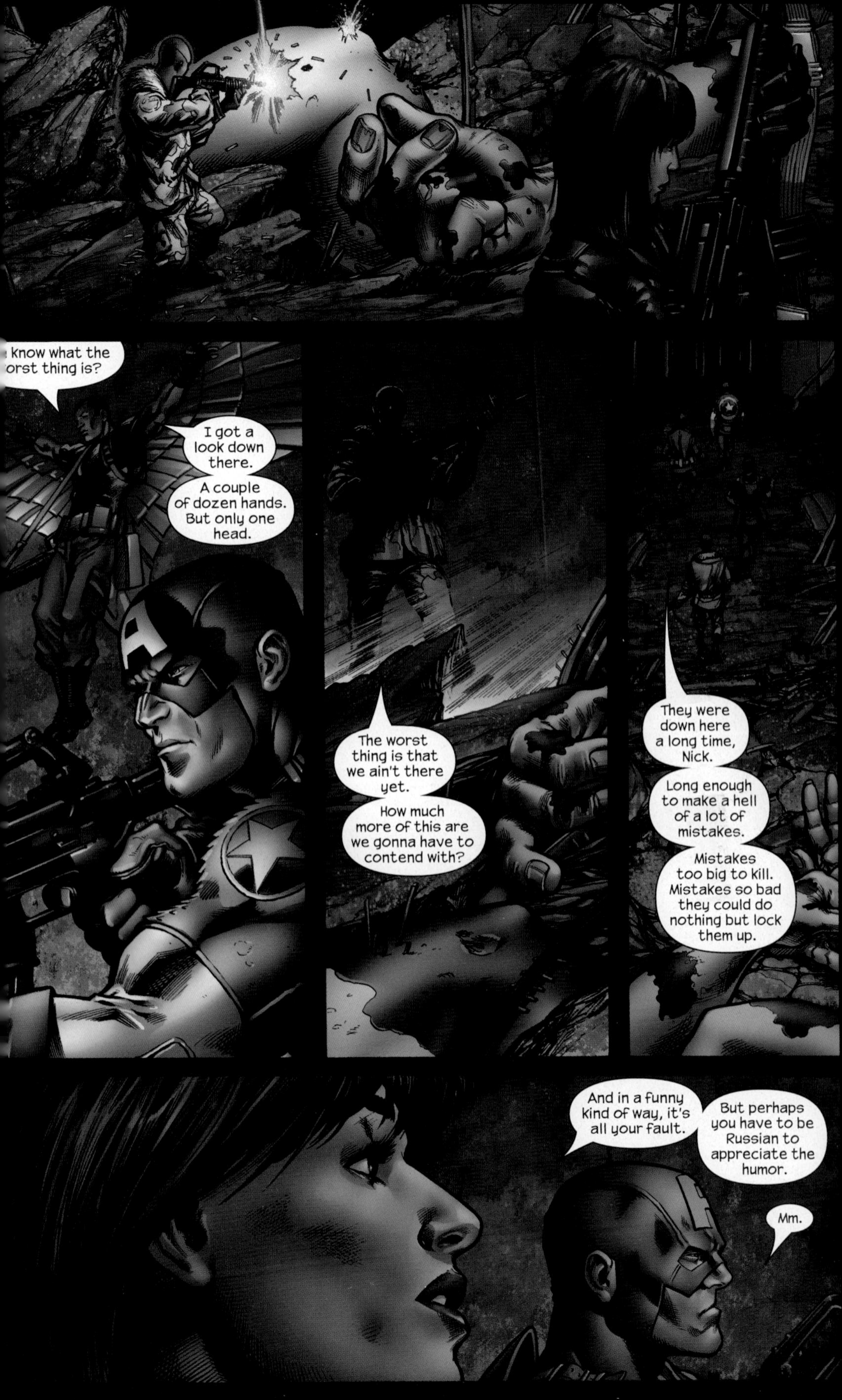
know what the
orst thing is?
I got a look down there.
A couple of dozen hands. But only one head.
The worst thing is that we ain't there yet.
How much more of this are we gonna have to contend with?
They were down here a long time, Nick.
Long enough to make a hell of a lot of mistakes.
Mistakes too big to kill. Mistakes so bad they could do nothing but lock them up.
And in a funny kind of way, it's all your fault.
But perhaps you have to be Russian to appreciate the humor.
Mm.

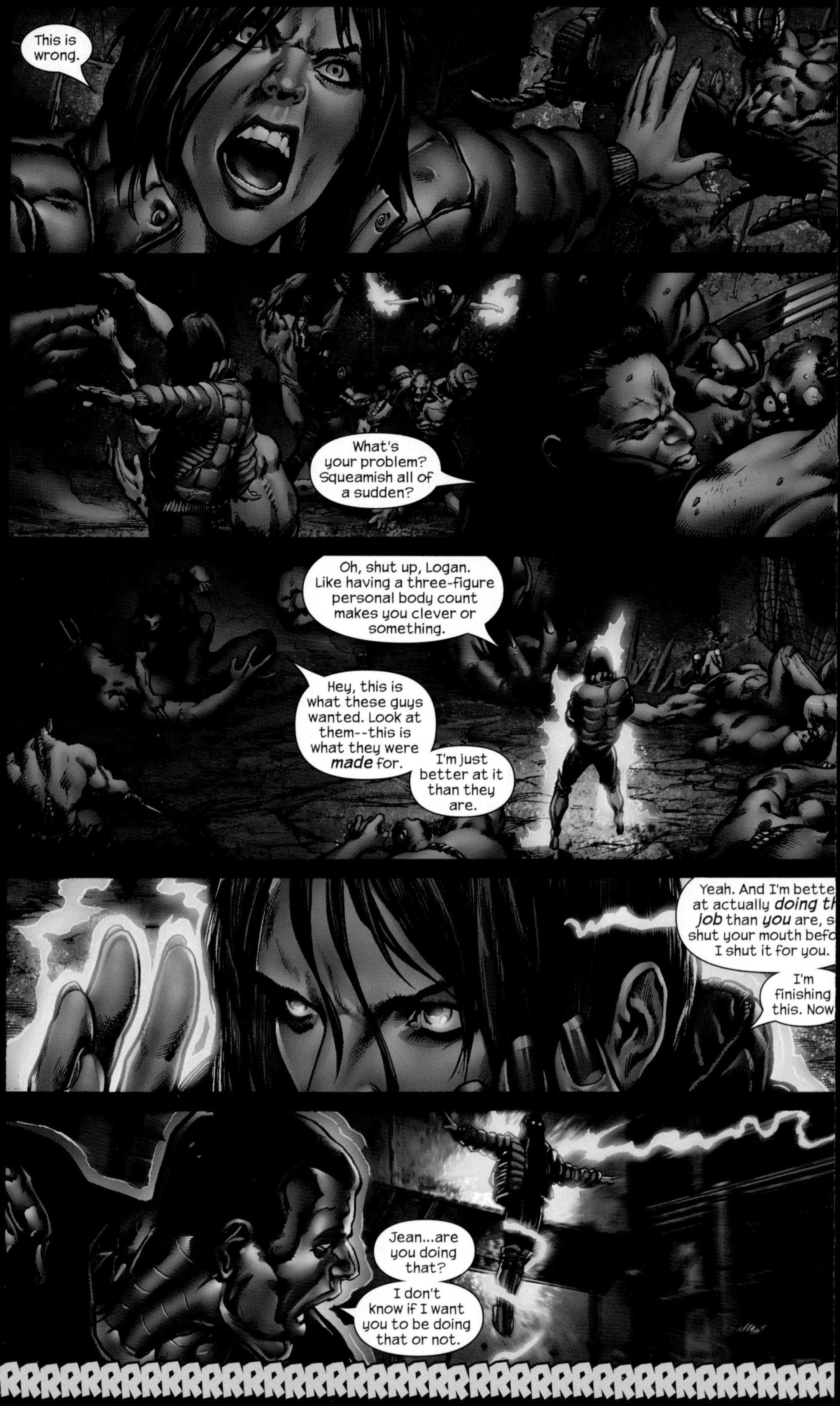

This is wrong.
What's your problem? Squeamish all of a sudden?
Oh, shut up, Logan. Like having a three-figure personal body count makes you clever or something.
Hey, this is what these guys wanted. Look at them--this is what they were *made* for.
I'm just better at it than they are.
Yeah. And I'm bette at actually *doing th* *job* than *you* are, s shut your mouth befo I shut it for you.
I'm finishing this. Now
Jean...are you doing that?
I don't know if I want you to be doing that or not.
RRRRRRRRRRRRRRRRRRRRRRRRRRRRRRRRRRRRRR

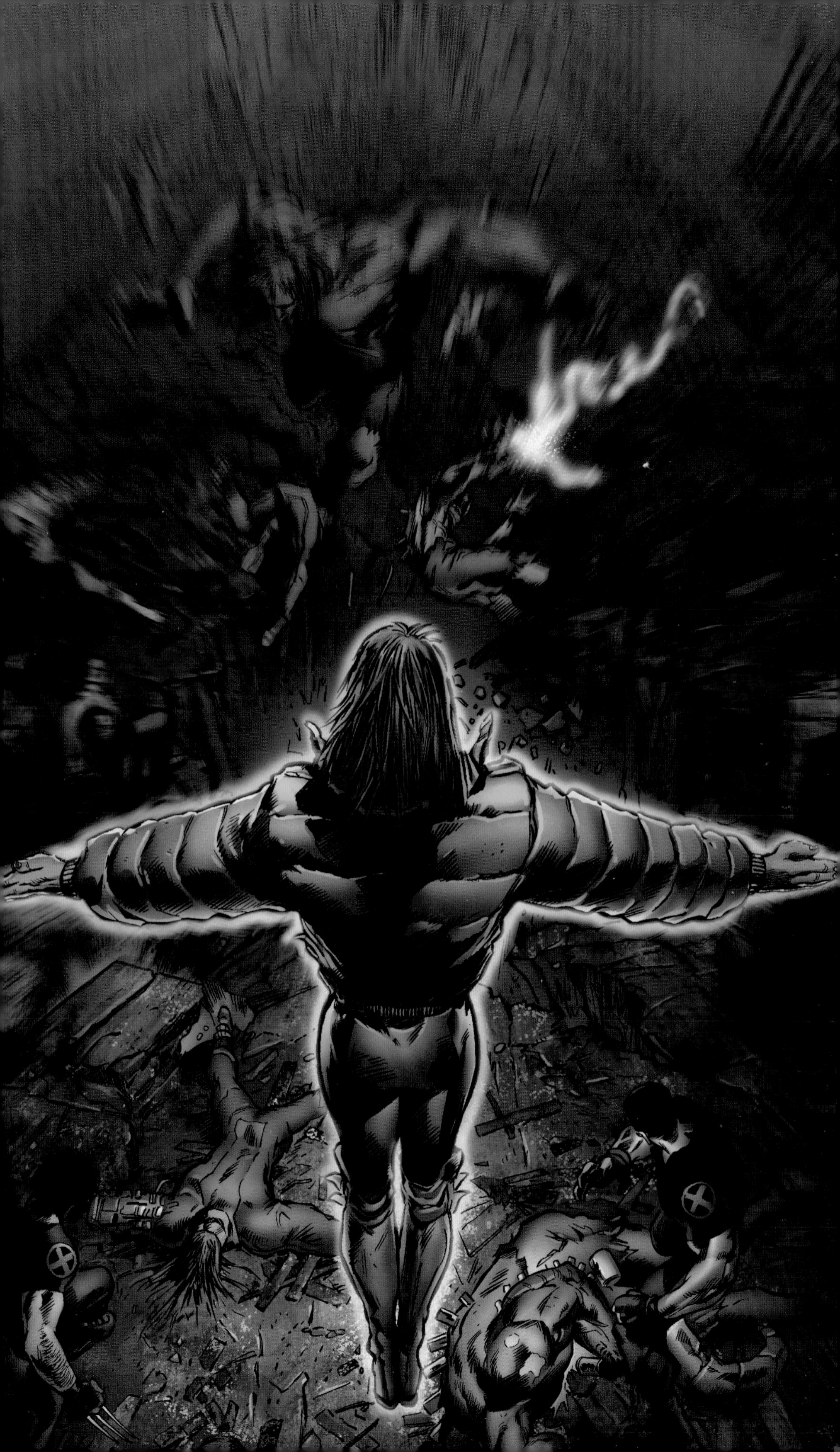

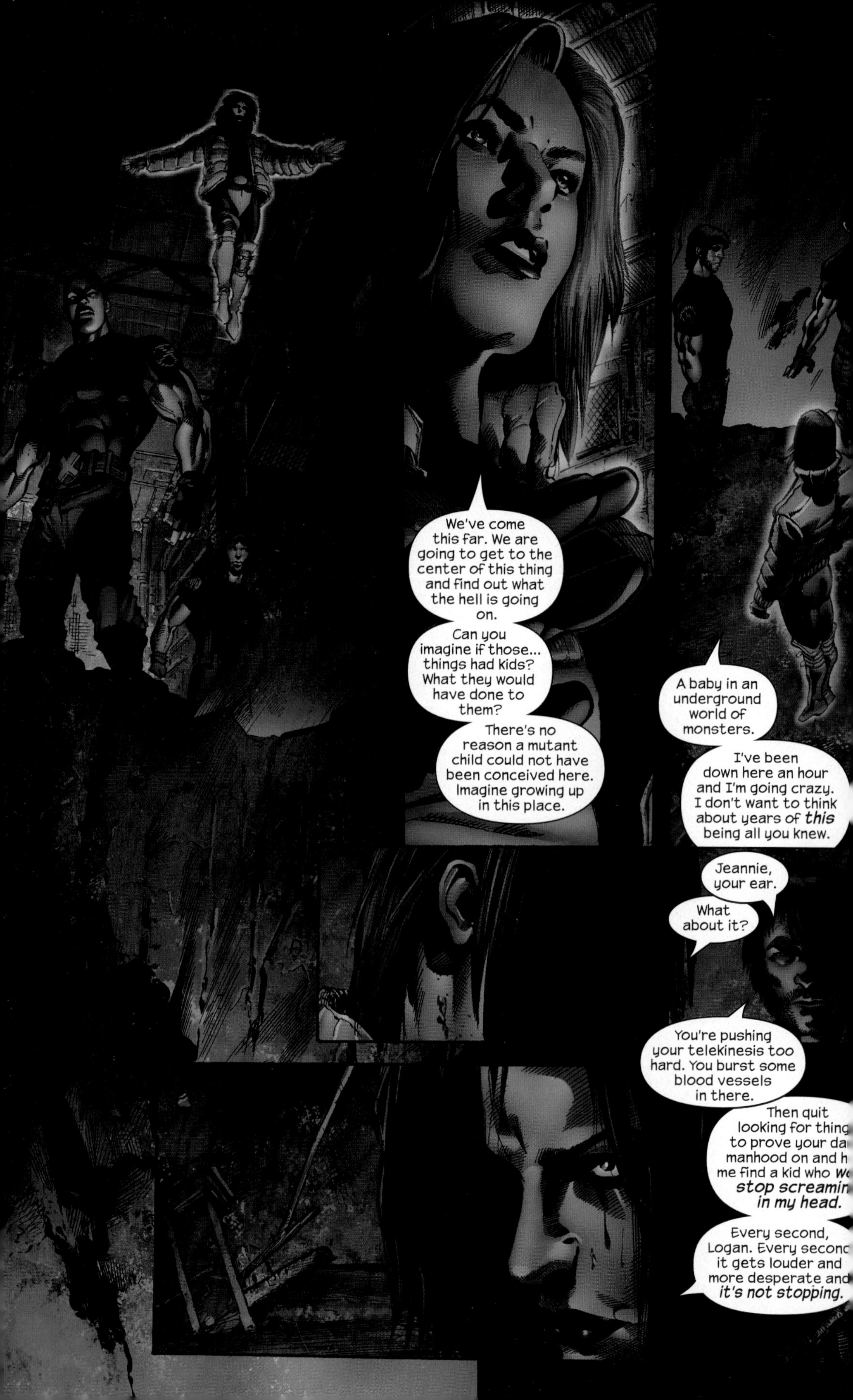

We've come this far. We are going to get to the center of this thing and find out what the hell is going on.
Can you imagine if those... things had kids? What they would have done to them?
There's no reason a mutant child could not have been conceived here. Imagine growing up in this place.
A baby in an underground world of monsters.
I've been down here an hour and I'm going crazy. I don't want to think about years of *this* being all you knew.
Jeannie, your ear.
What about it?
You're pushing your telekinesis too hard. You burst some blood vessels in there.
Every second, Logan. Every secon
it gets louder and more desperate and
it's not stopping.

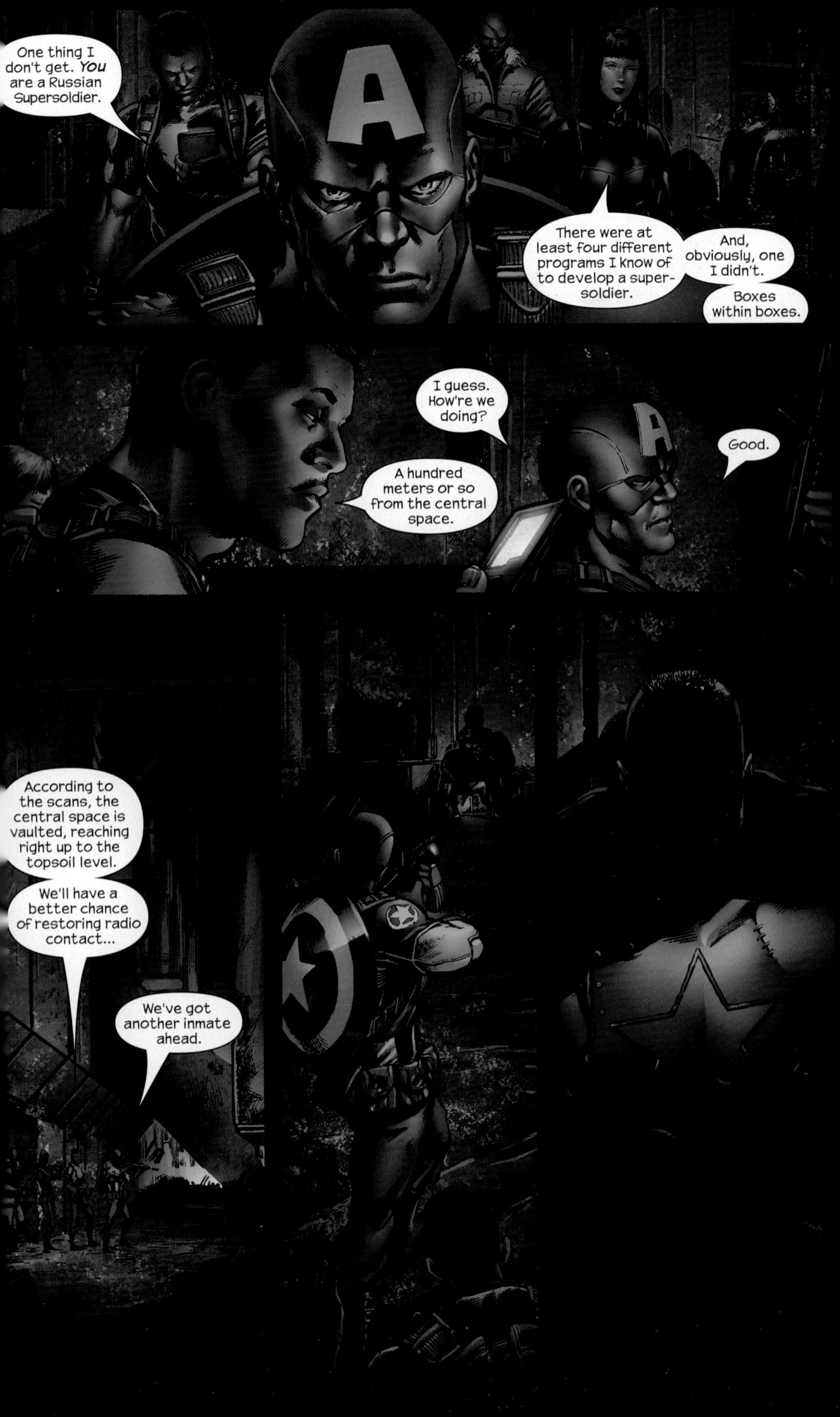
One thing I don't get. *You* are a Russian Supersoldier.
There were at least four different programs I know of to develop a super-soldier.
And, obviously, one I didn't.
Boxes within boxes.
I guess. How're we doing?
A hundred meters or so from the central space.
Good.
According to the scans, the central space is vaulted, reaching right up to the topsoil level.
We'll have a better chance of restoring radio contact...
We've got another inmate ahead.

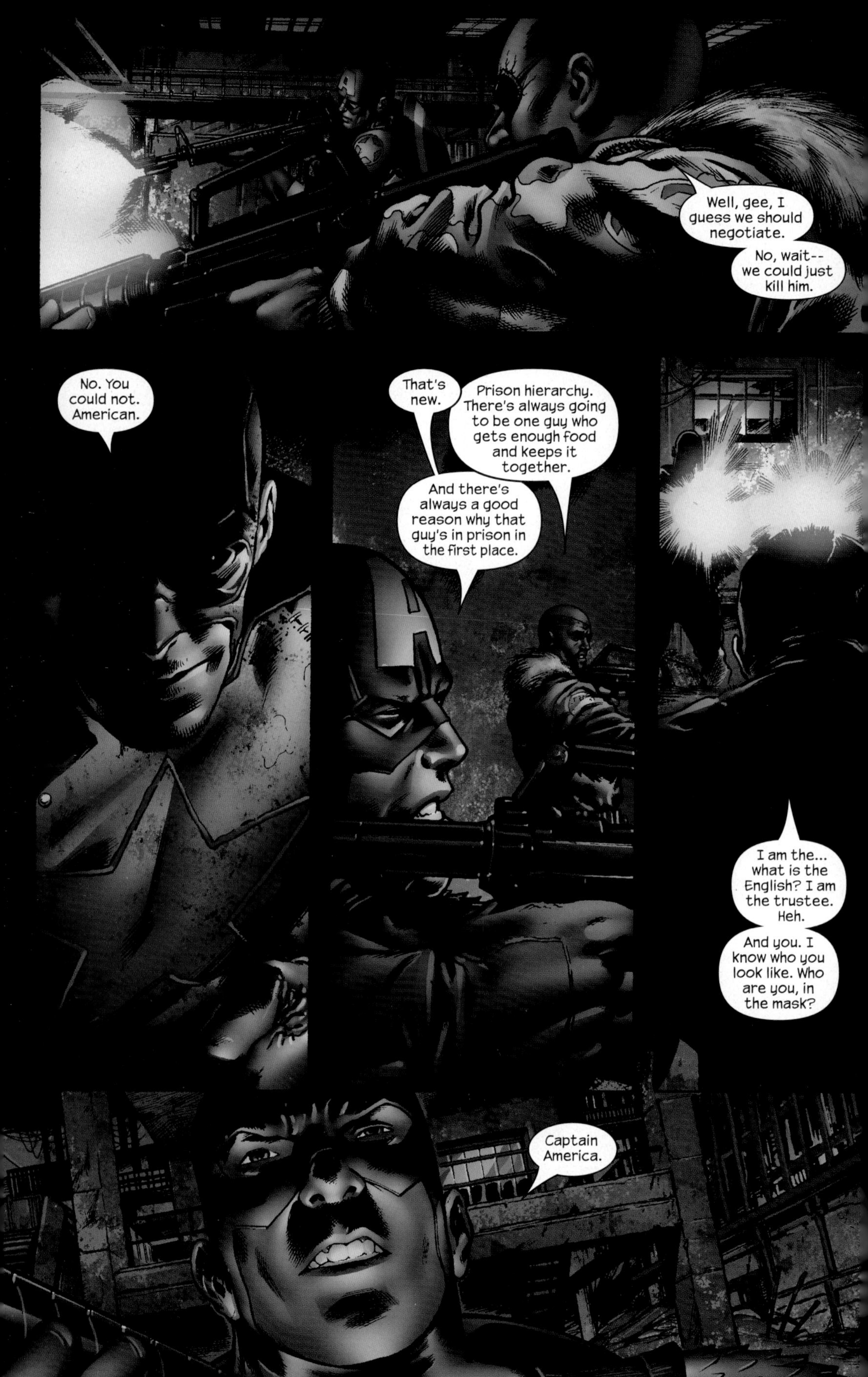

Well, gee, I guess we should negotiate.
No, wait-- we could just kill him.
No. You could not. American.
That's new.
Prison hierarchy. There's always going to be one guy who gets enough food and keeps it together.
And there's always a good reason why that guy's in prison in the first place.
I am the... what is the English? I am the trustee. Heh.
And you. I know who you look like. Who are you, in the mask?
Captain America.

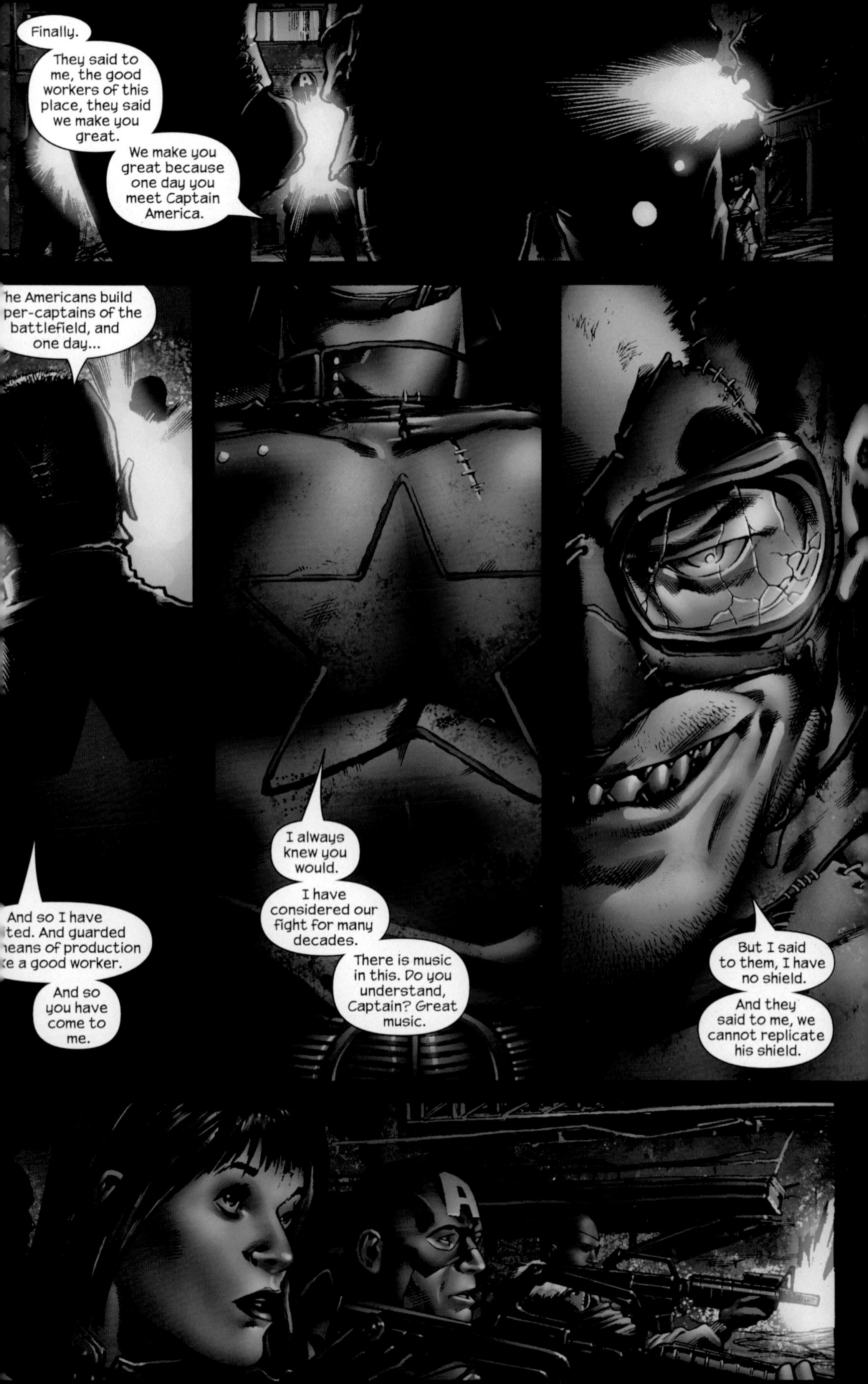
Finally.
They said to me, the good workers of this place, they said we make you great.
We make you great because one day you meet Captain America.
he Americans build per-captains of the battlefield, and one day...
I always knew you would.
I have considered our fight for many decades.
There is music in this. Do you understand, Captain? Great music.
But I said to them, I have no shield.
And they said to me, we cannot replicate his shield.
And so I have ted. And guarded eans of production e a good worker.
And so you have come to me.

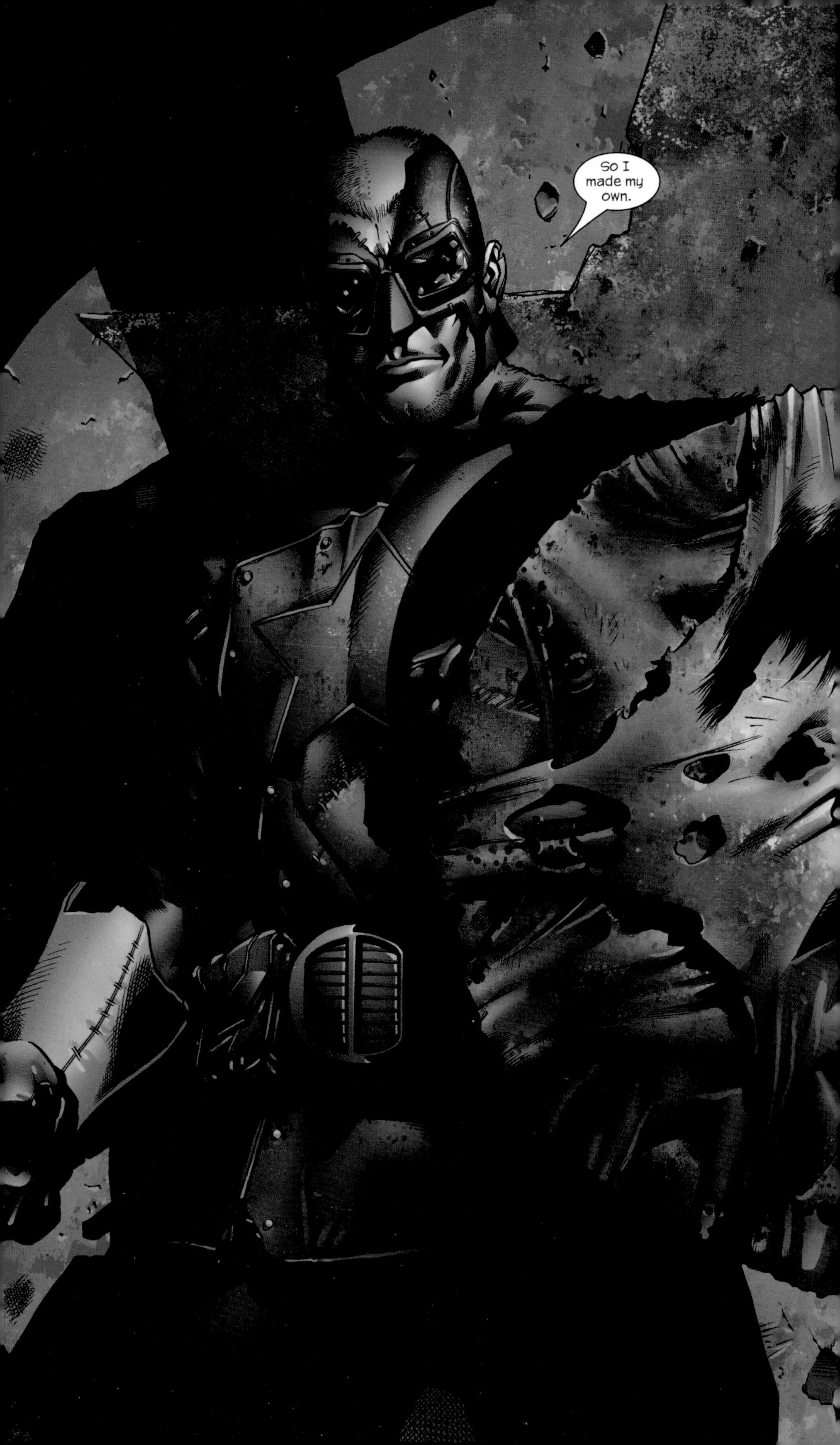
So I made my own.

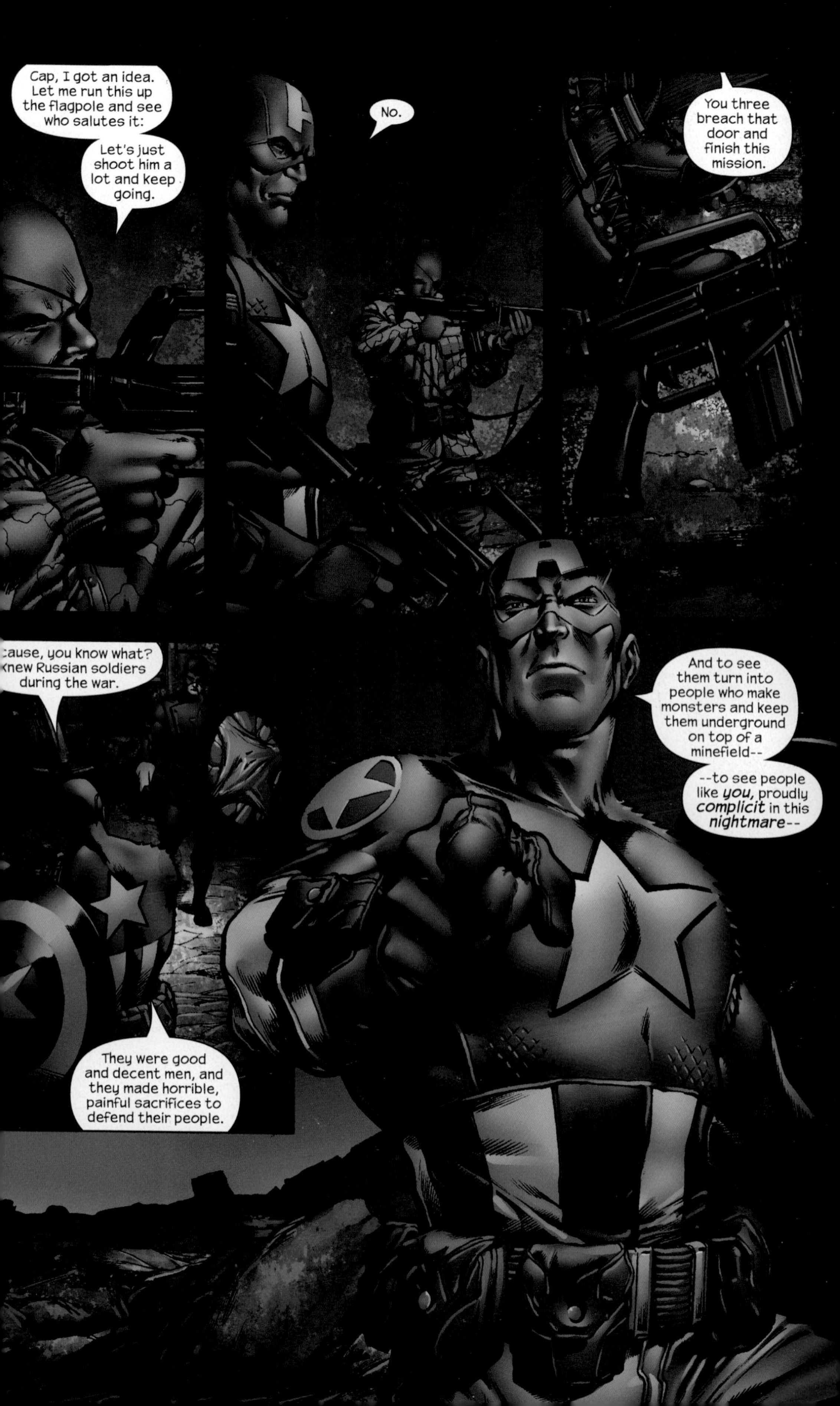

Cap, I got an idea. Let me run this up the flagpole and see who salutes it:
Let's just shoot him a lot and keep going.
No.
You three breach that door and finish this mission.
'cause, you know what? I knew Russian soldiers during the war.
They were good and decent men, and they made horrible, painful sacrifices to defend their people.
And to see them turn into people who make monsters and keep them underground on top of a minefield--
--to see people like *you,* proudly *complicit* in this *nightmare*--

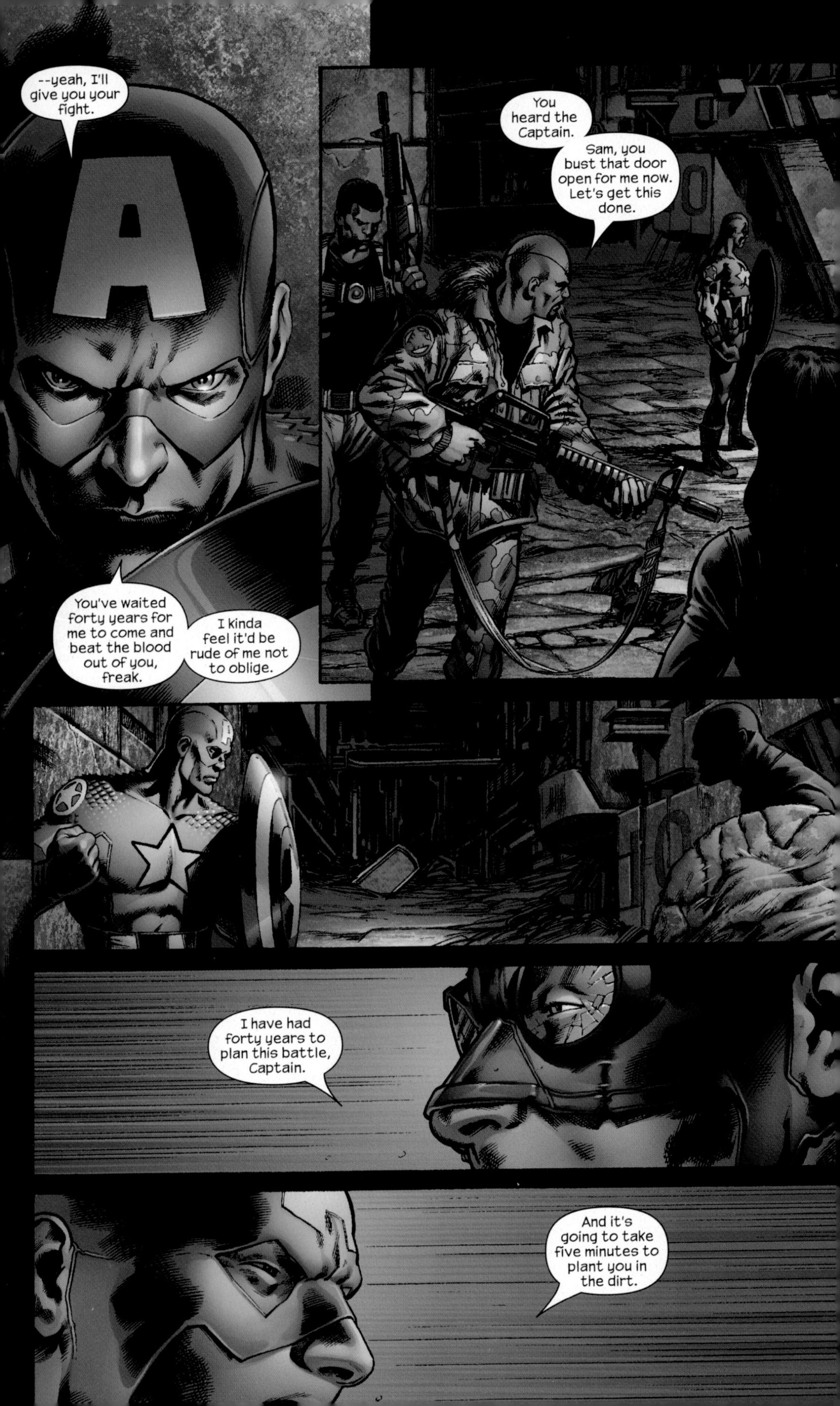
--yeah, I'll give you your fight.
You've waited forty years for me to come and beat the blood out of you, freak.
I kinda feel it'd be rude of me not to oblige.
You heard the Captain.
Sam, you bust that door open for me now. Let's get this done.
I have had forty years to plan this battle, Captain.
And it's going to take five minutes to plant you in the dirt.

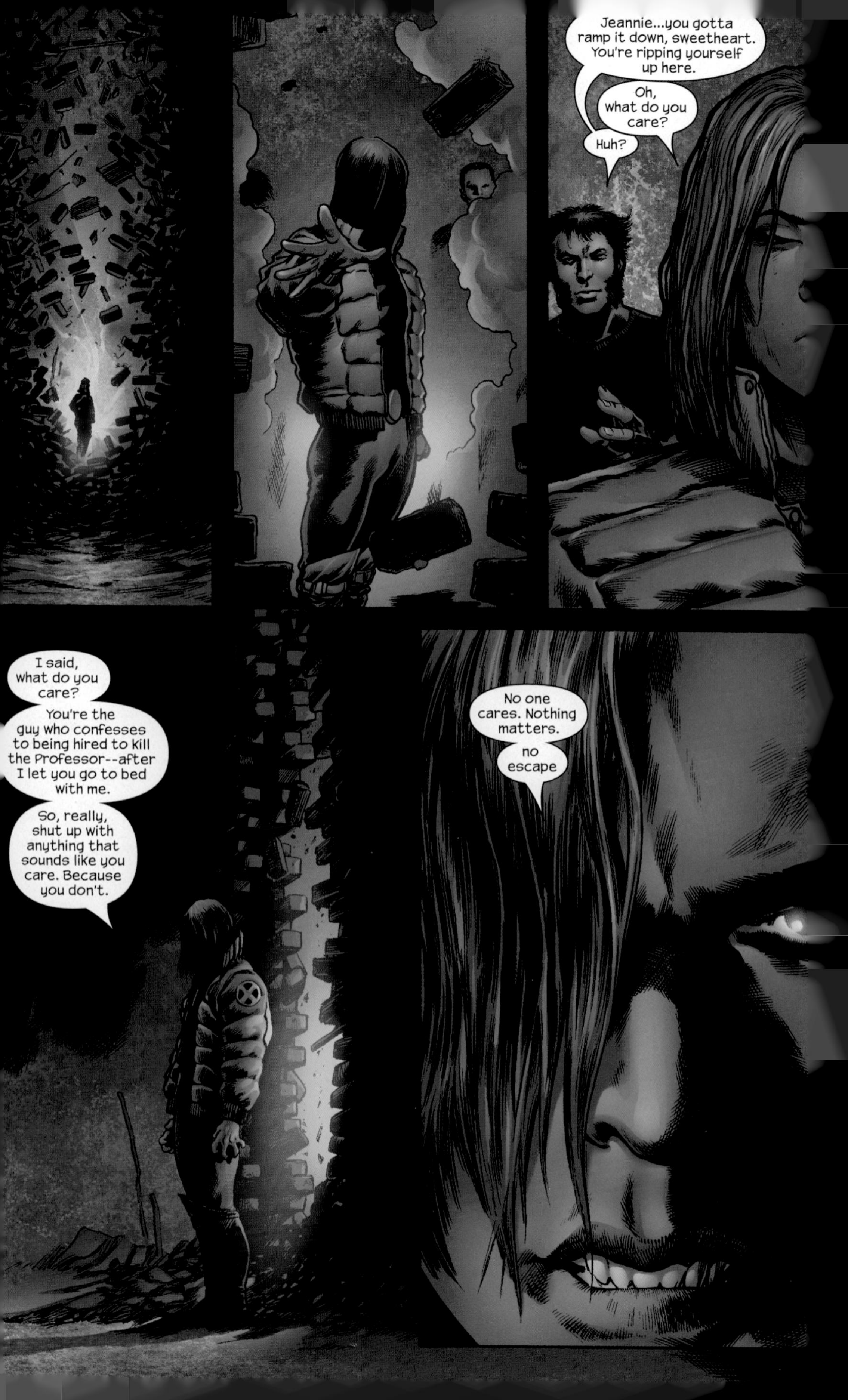
Jeannie...you gotta ramp it down, sweetheart. You're ripping yourself up here.
Oh, what do you care?
Huh?
I said, what do you care?
You're the guy who confesses to being hired to kill the Professor--after I let you go to bed with me.
So, really, shut up with anything that sounds like you care. Because you don't.
No one cares. Nothing matters.
no escape

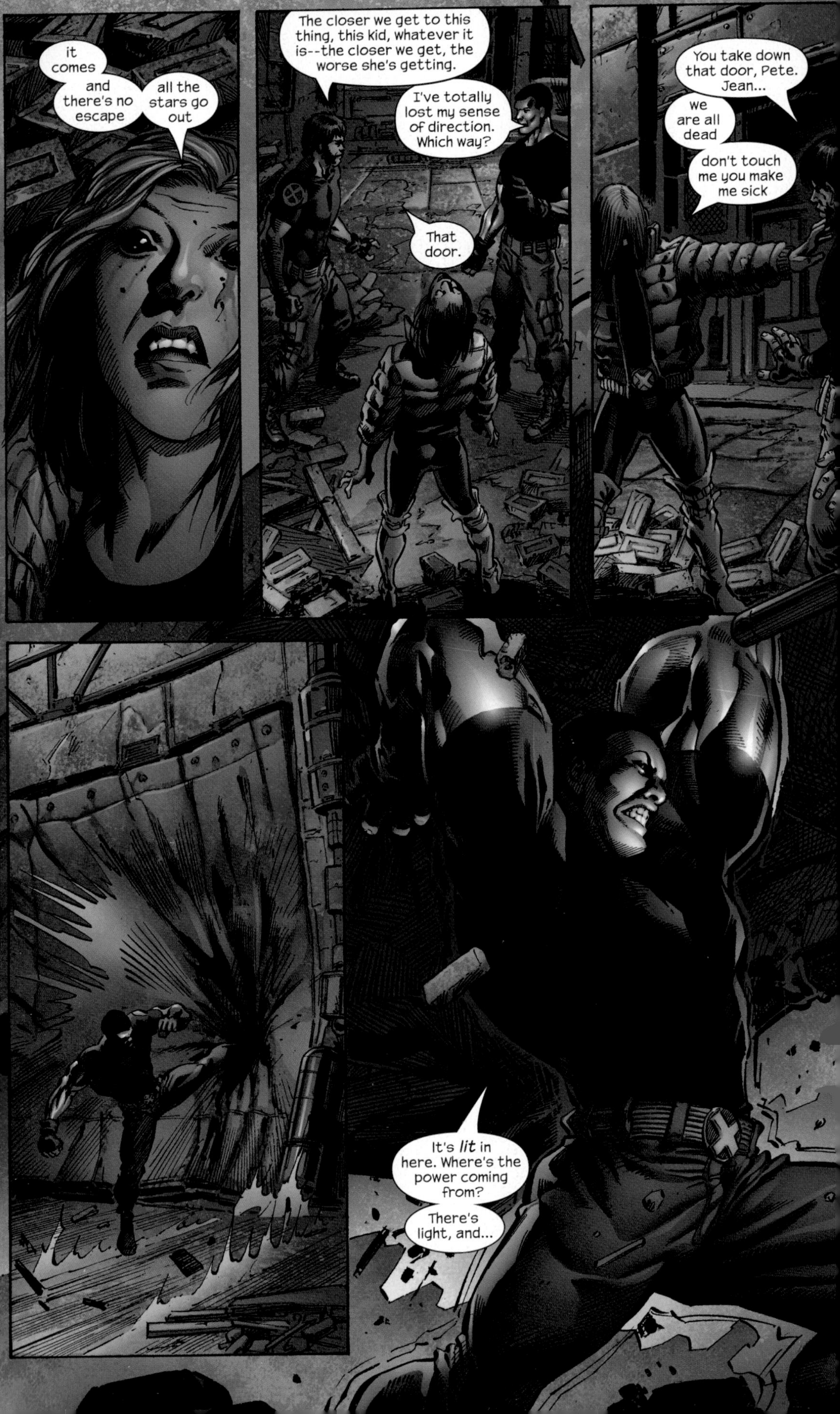

it comes
and there's no escape
all the stars go out
The closer we get to this thing, this kid, whatever it is--the closer we get, the worse she's getting.
I've totally lost my sense of direction. Which way?
That door.
You take down that door, Pete. Jean...
we are all dead
don't touch me you make me sick
It's *lit* in here. Where's the power coming from?
There's light, and...

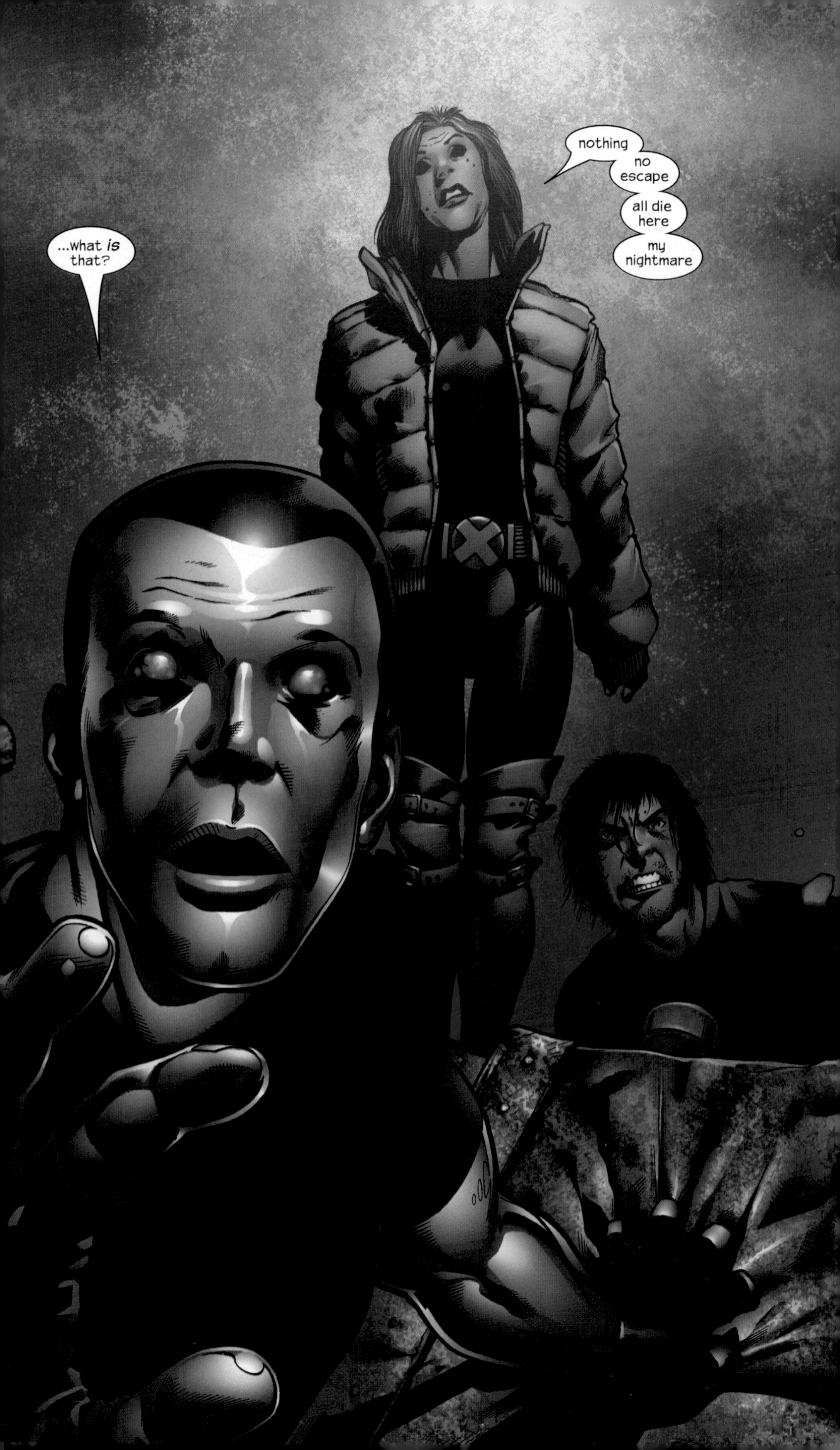
...what *is* that?
nothing
no escape
all die here
my nightmare

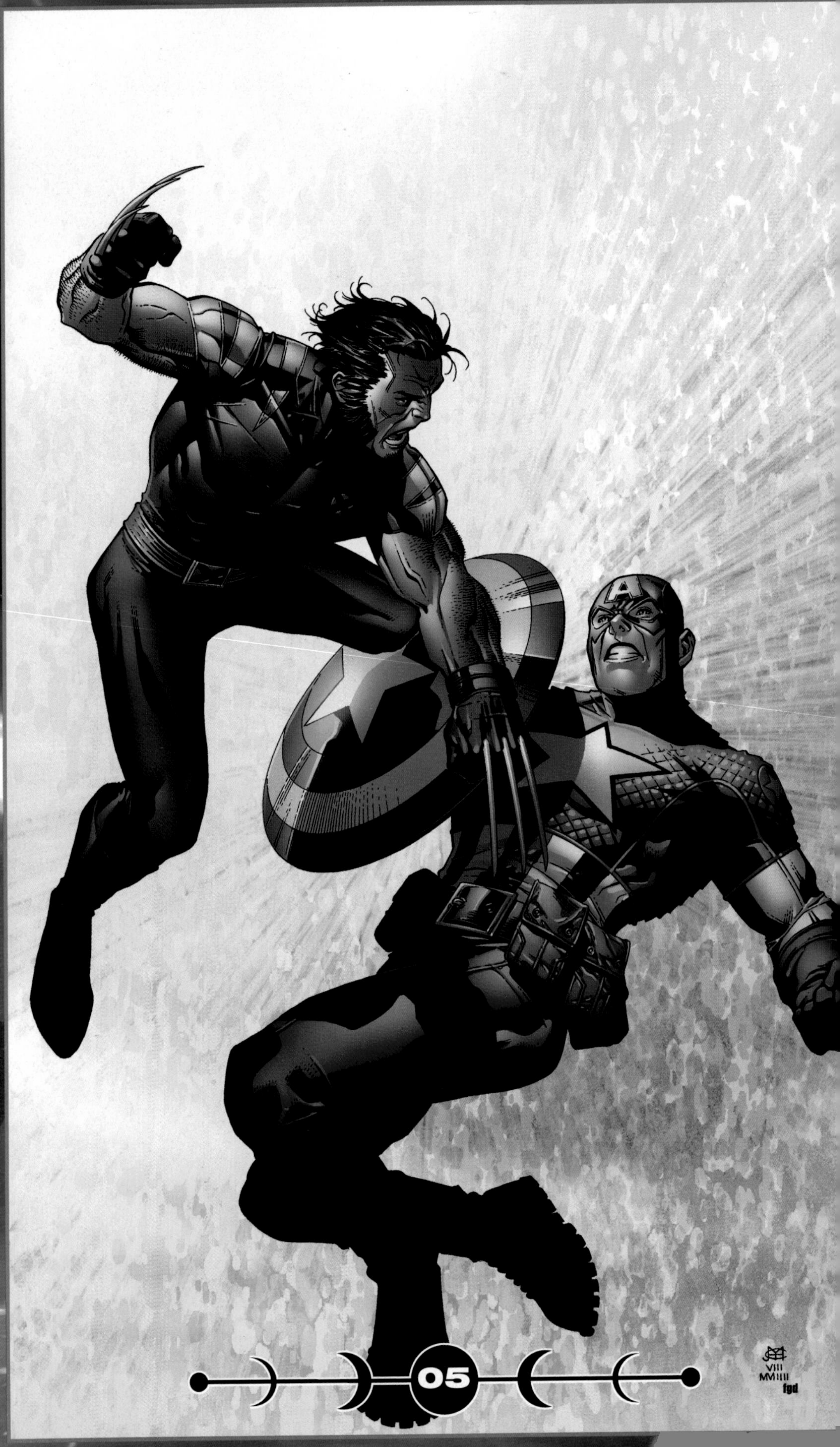
05

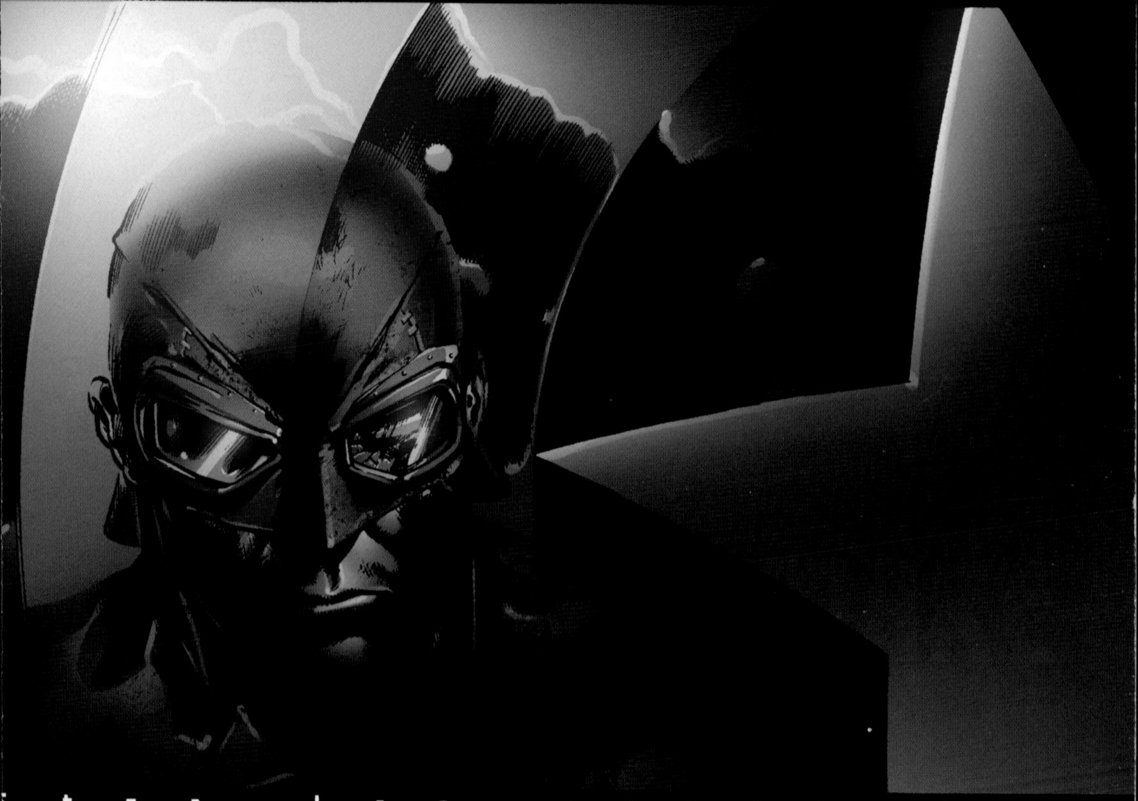

Stan Lee presents:

ULTIMATE NIGHTMARE

CHAPTER FIVE

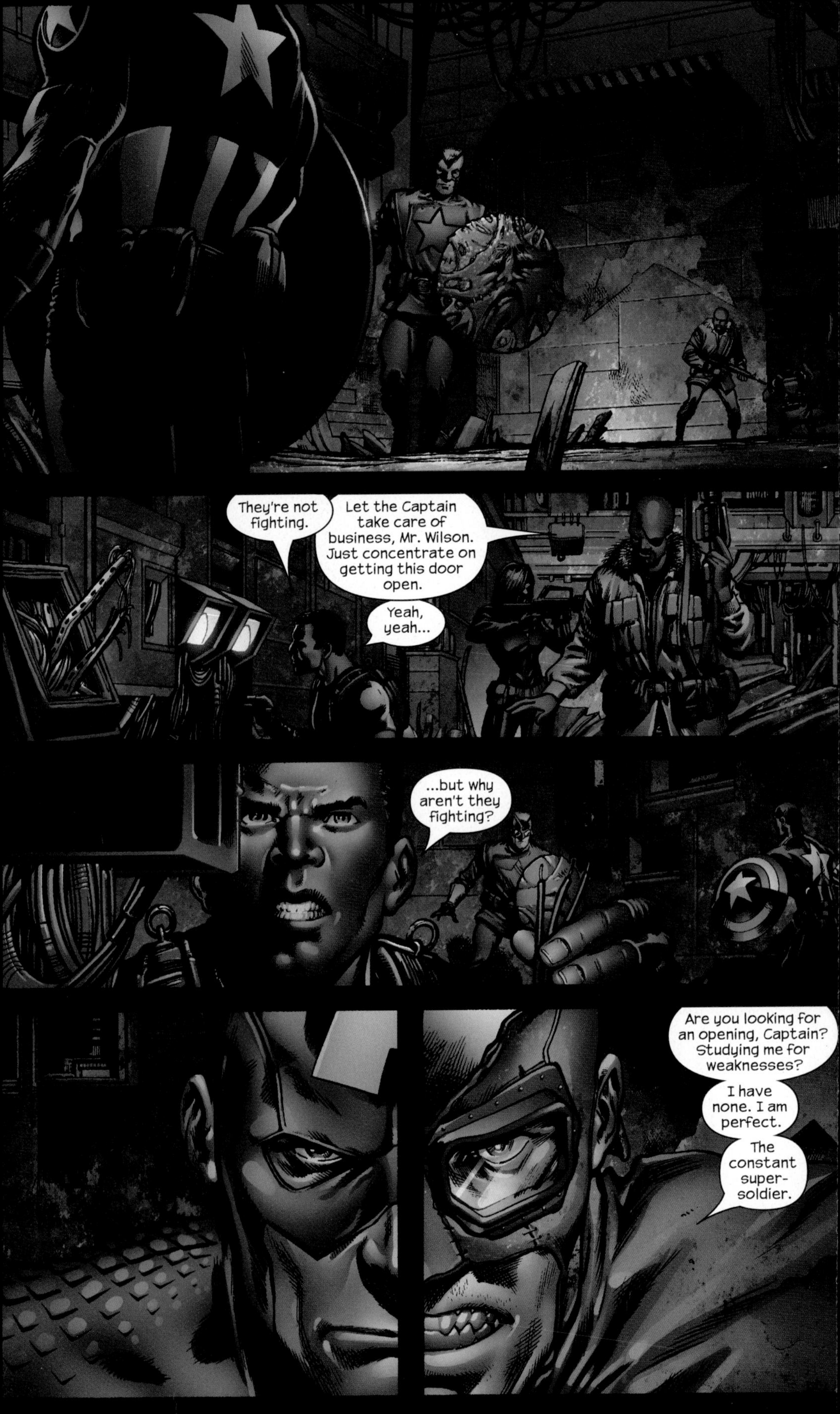
They're not fighting.
Let the Captain take care of business, Mr. Wilson. Just concentrate on getting this door open.
Yeah, yeah...
...but why aren't they fighting?
Are you looking for an opening, Captain? Studying me for weaknesses?
I have none. I am perfect.
The constant super-soldier.

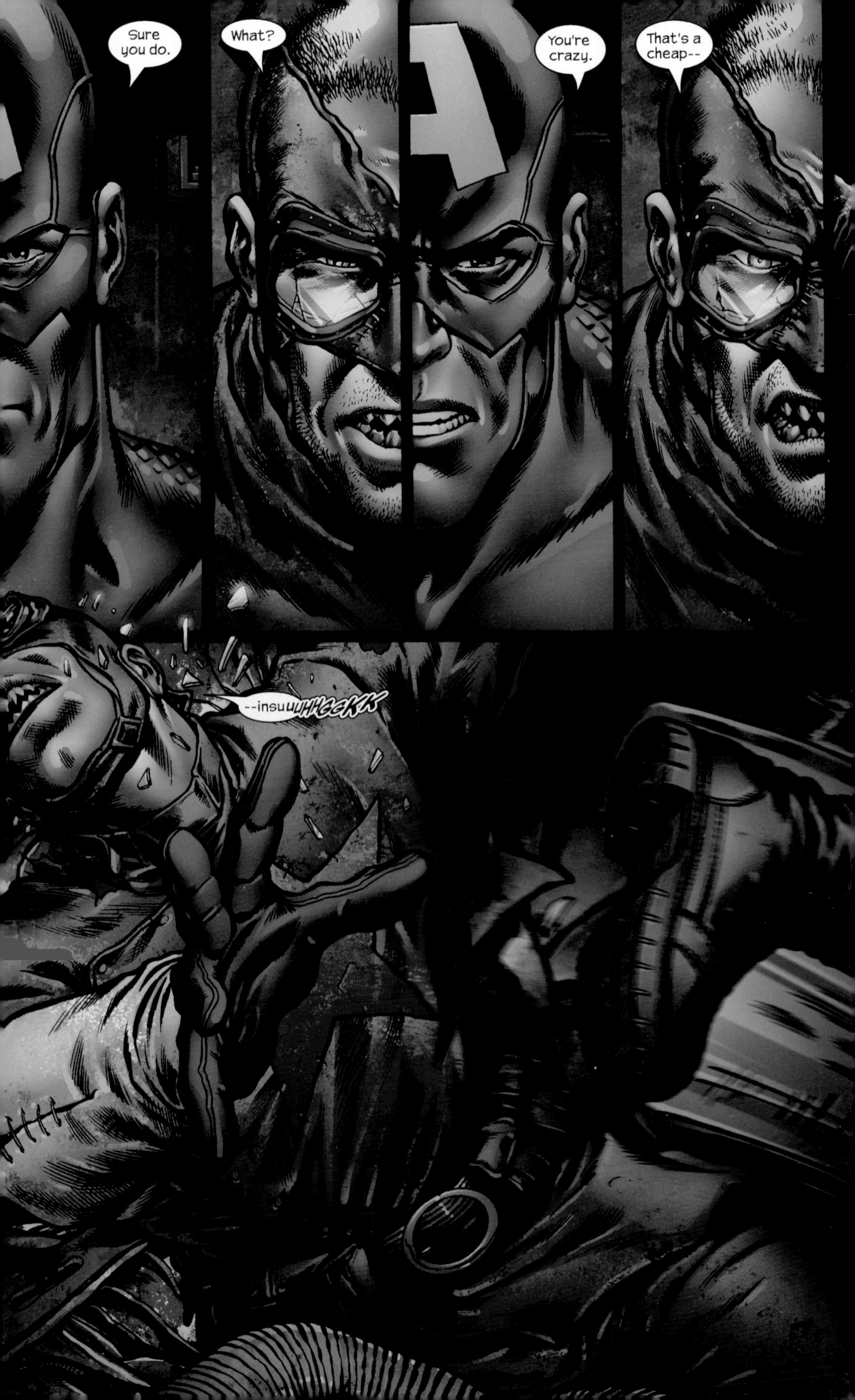
Sure you do.
What?
You're crazy.
That's a cheap--
--insuuuHHGGKK

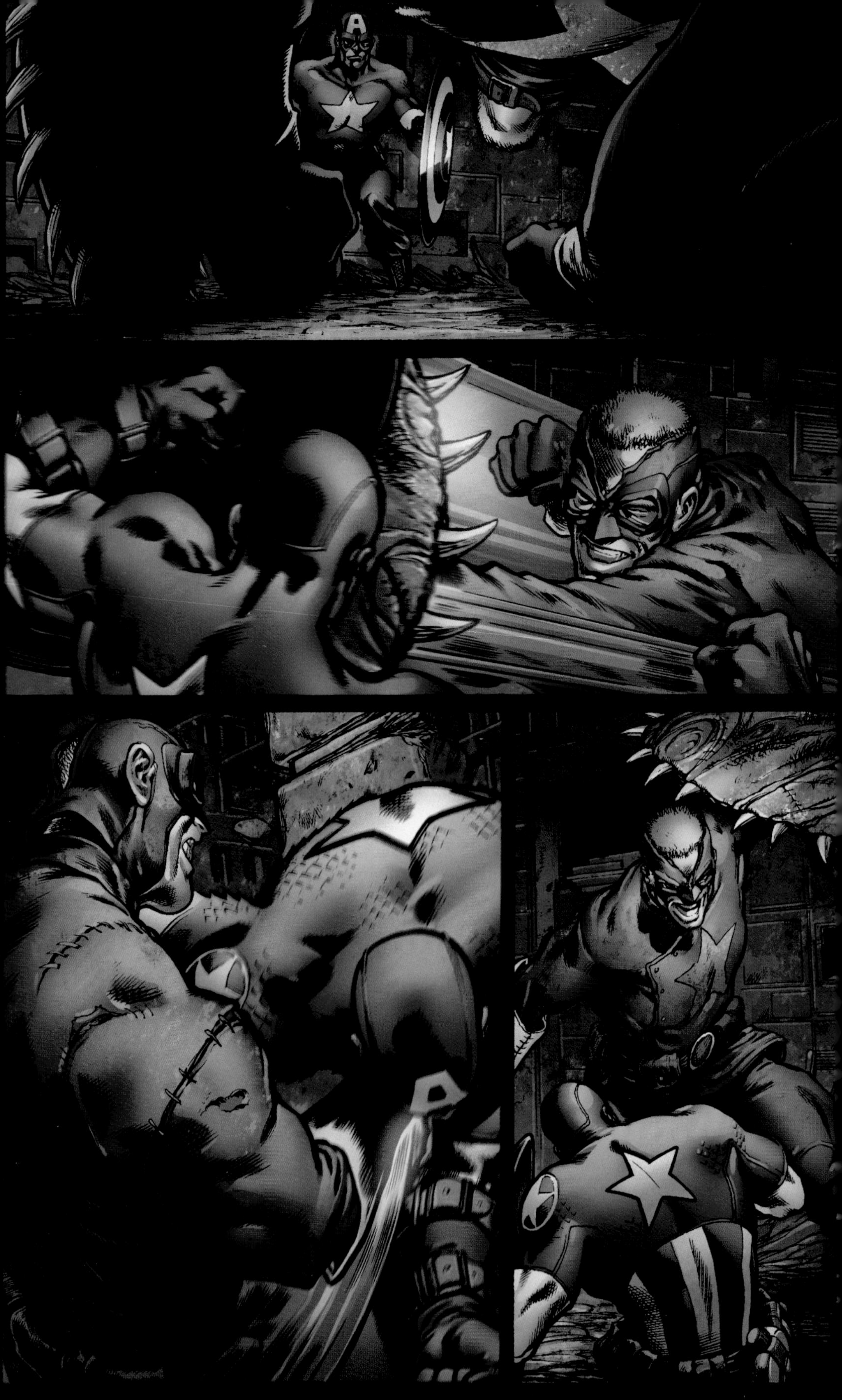

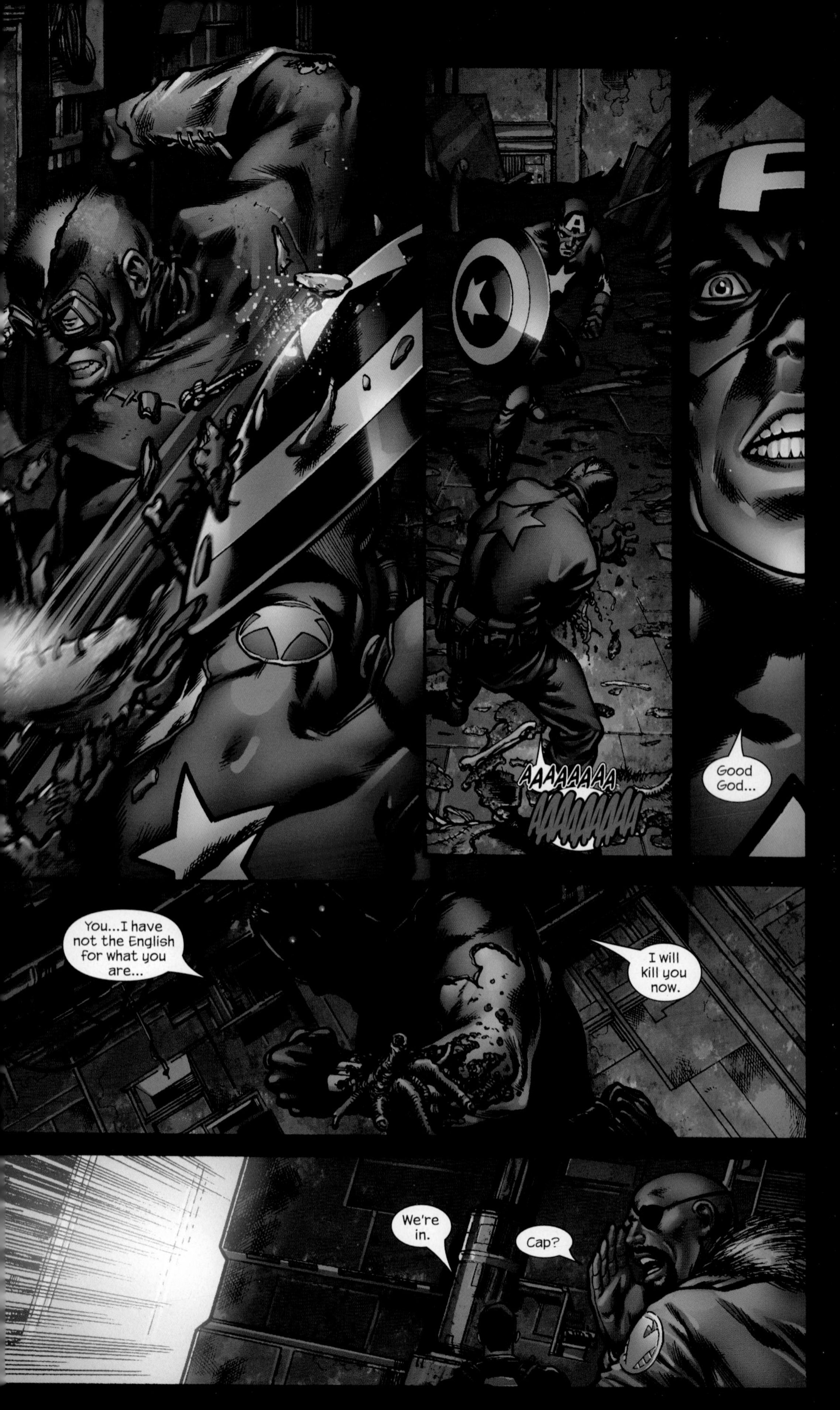
AAAAAAAA
AAAAAAAAAA
Good God...
You...I have not the English for what you are...
I will kill you now.
We're in.
Cap?

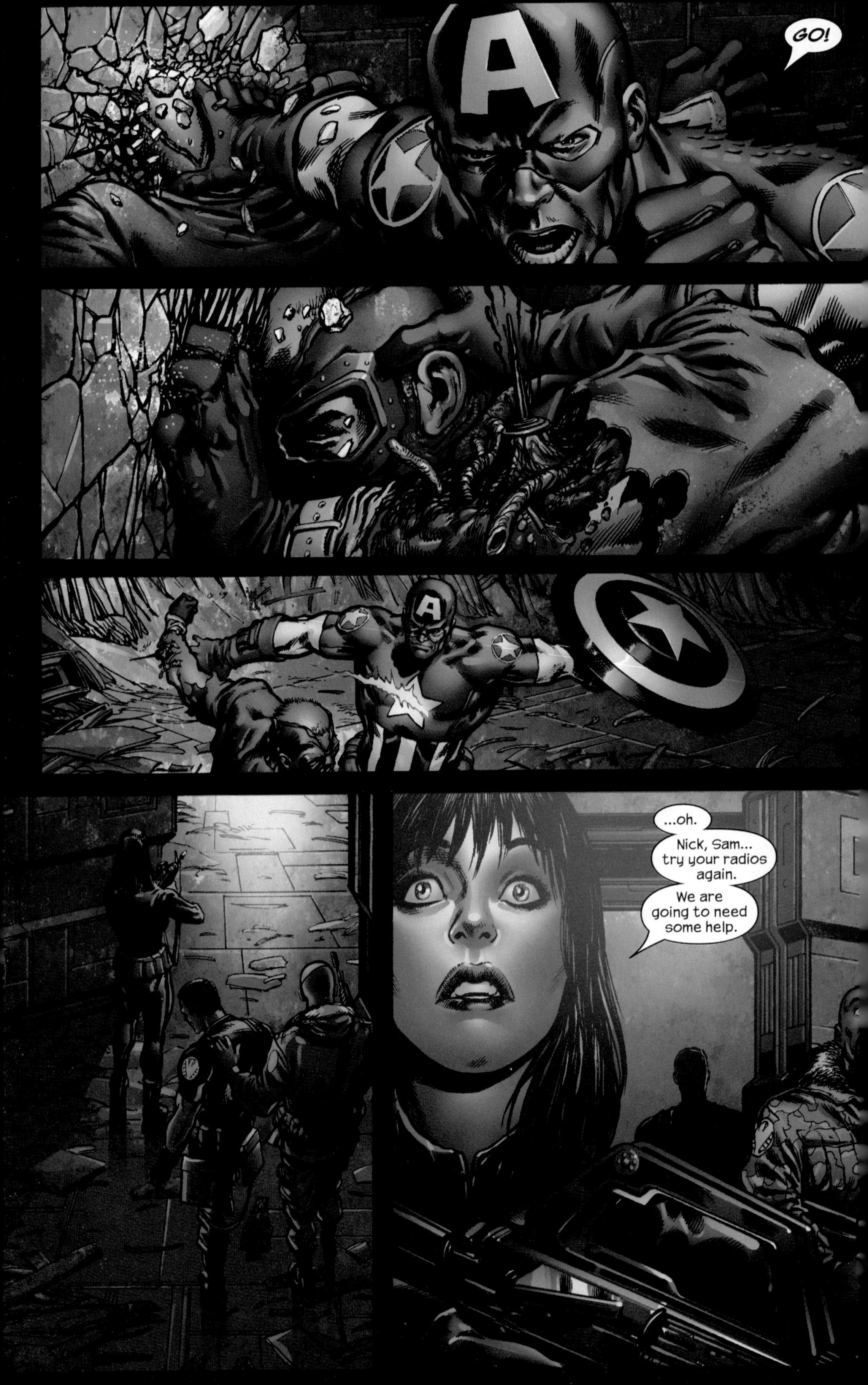
GO!
...oh.
Nick, Sam... try your radios again.
We are going to need some help.

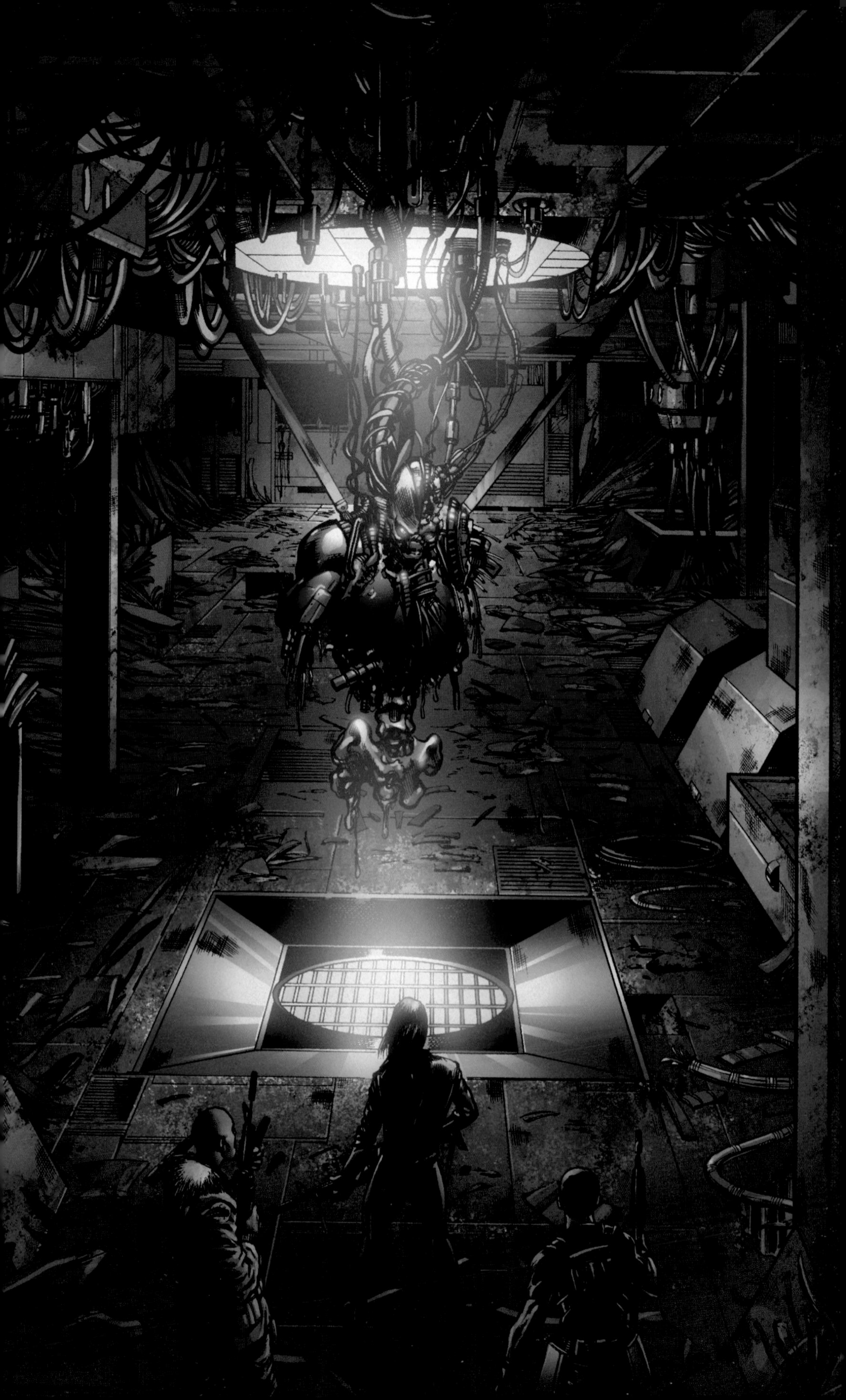

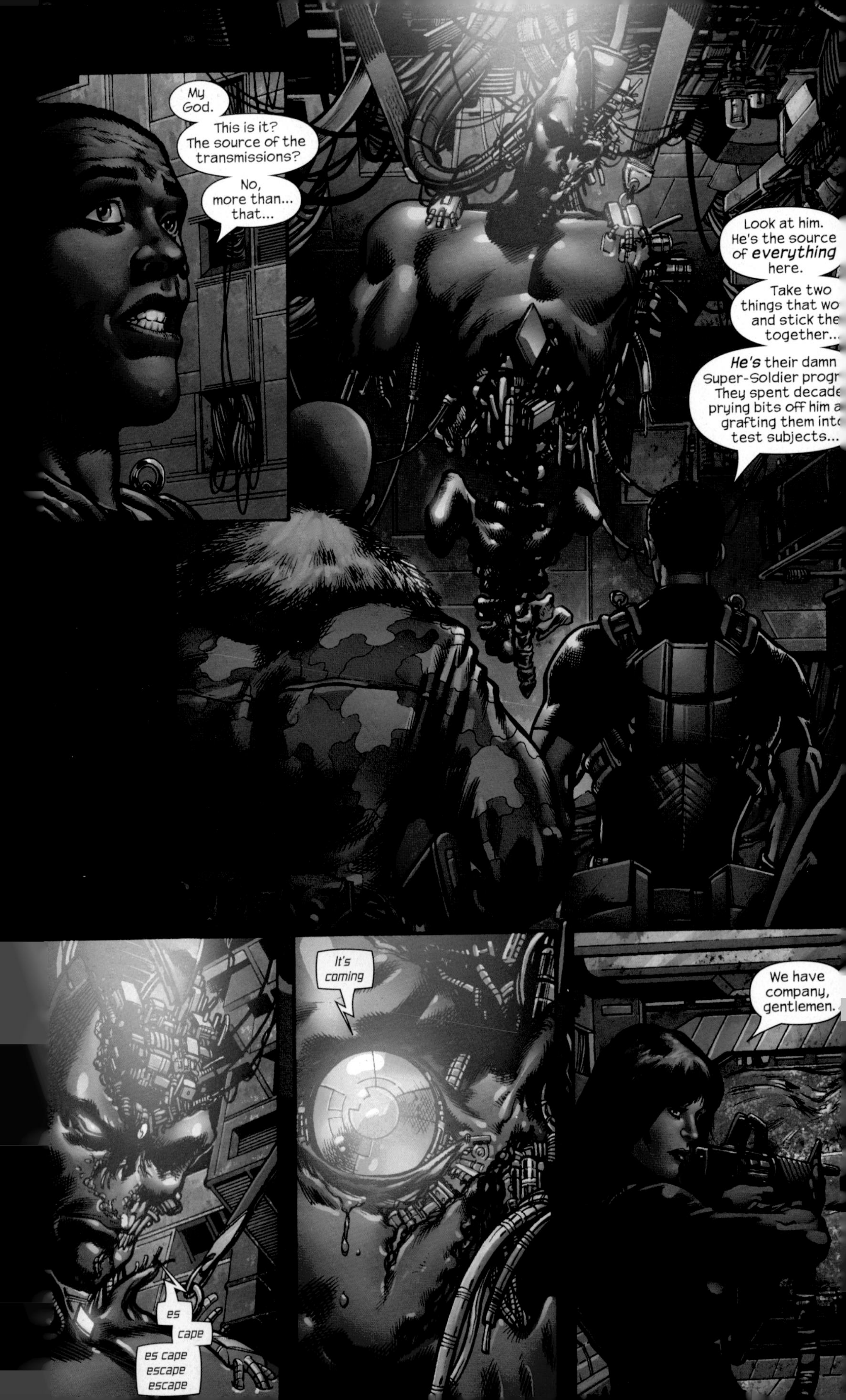
My God.
This is it? The source of the transmissions?
No, more than... that...
Look at him. He's the source of *everything* here.
Take two things that wo and stick the together...
He's their damn Super-Soldier progr They spent decade prying bits off him a grafting them int test subjects...
es
cape
es cape escape escape
It's coming
We have company, gentlemen.

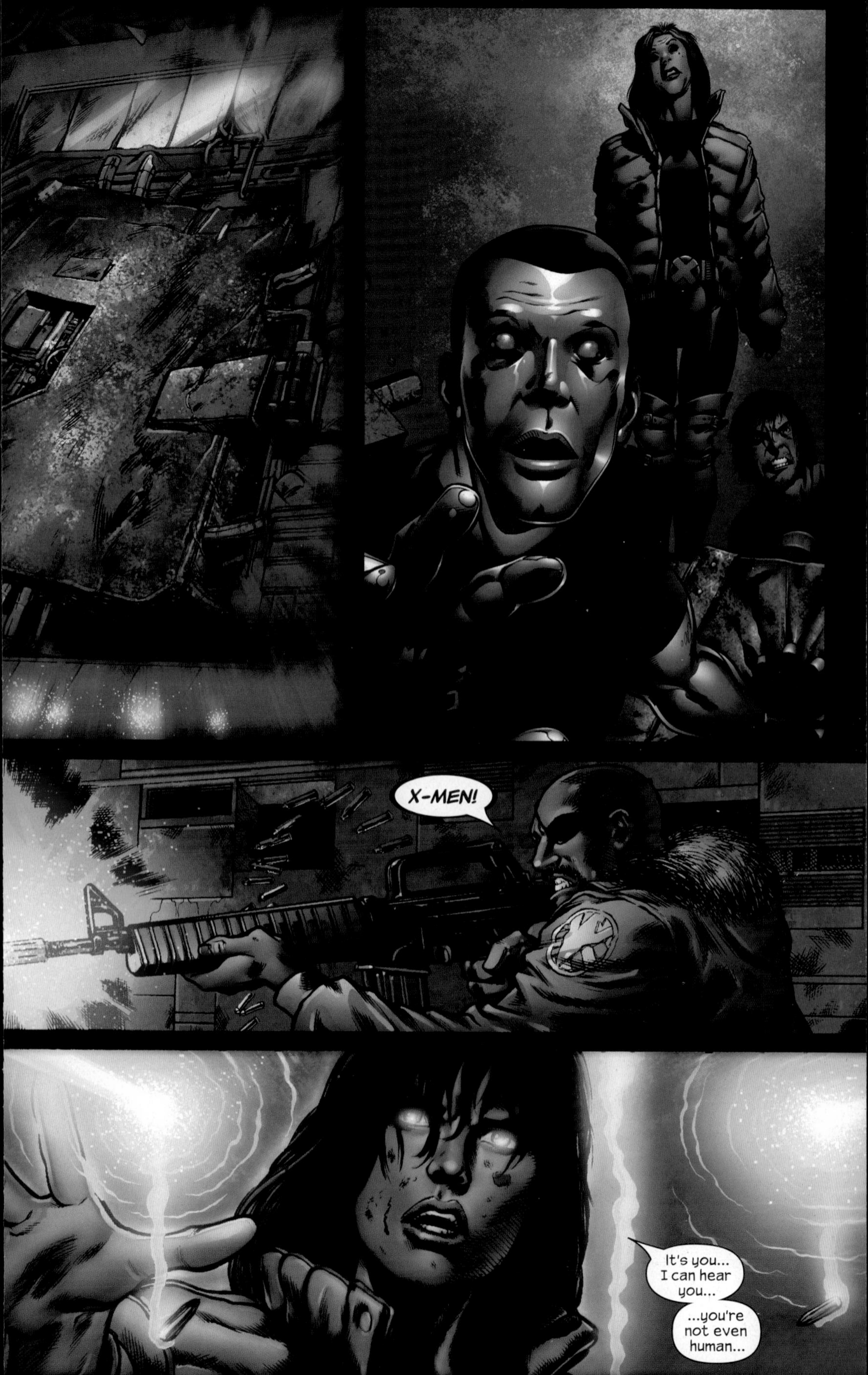
X-MEN!
It's you... I can hear you...
...you're not even human...

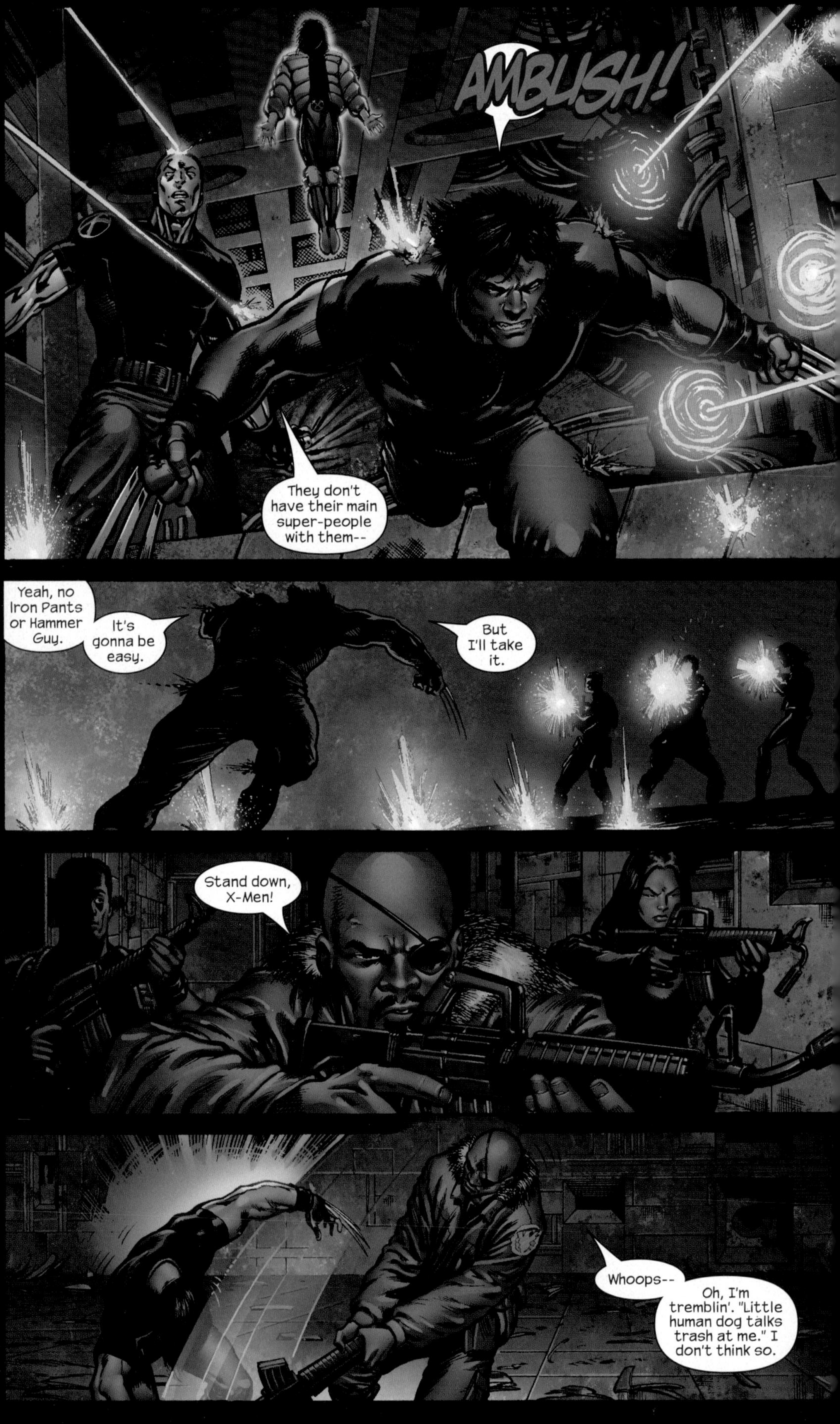
AMBUSH!
They don't have their main super-people with them--
Yeah, no Iron Pants or Hammer Guy.
It's gonna be easy.
But I'll take it.
Stand down, X-Men!
Whoops--
Oh, I'm tremblin'. "Little human dog talks trash at me." I don't think so.

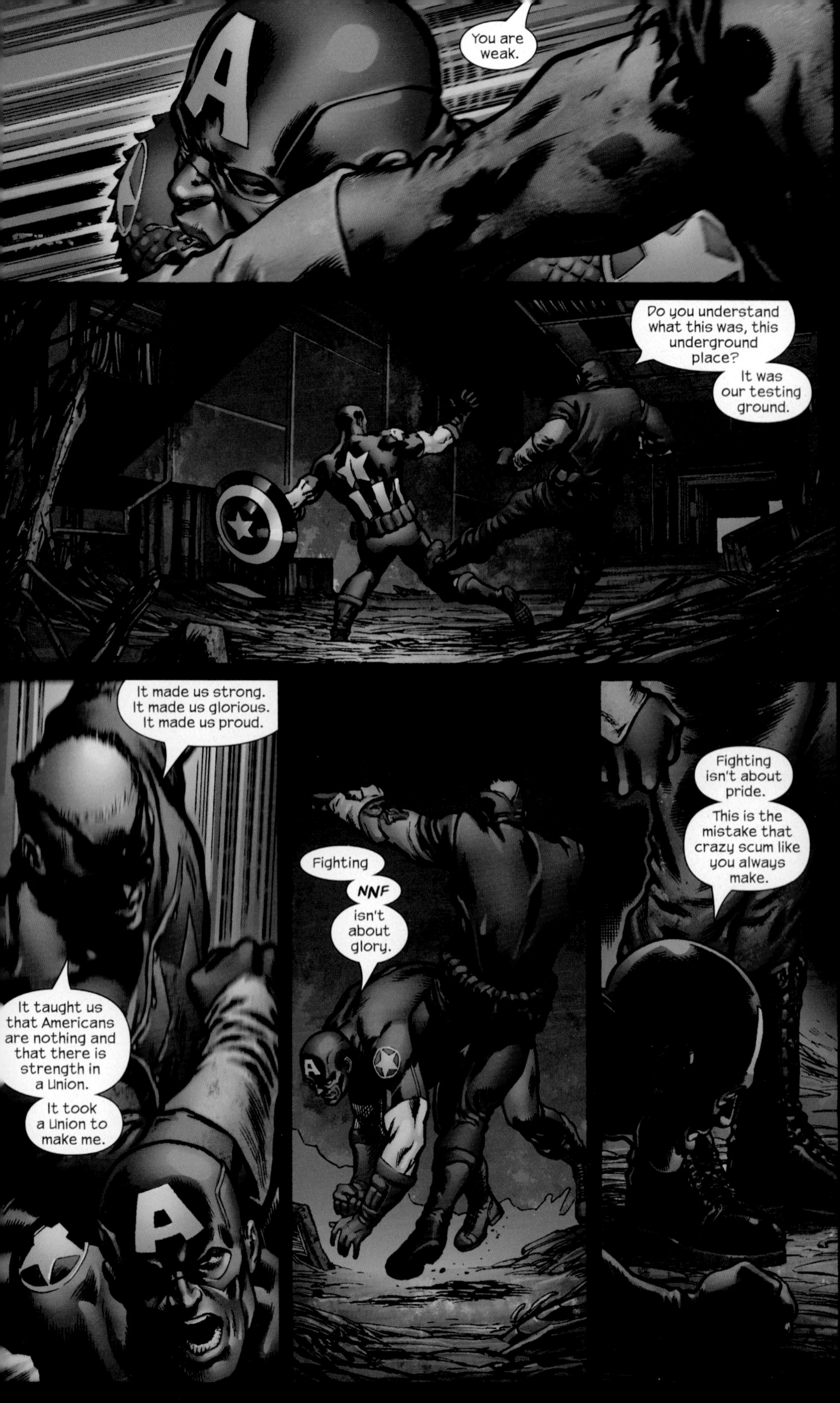

You are weak.
Do you understand what this was, this underground place?
It was our testing ground.
It made us strong. It made us glorious. It made us proud.
It taught us that Americans are nothing and that there is strength in a Union.
It took a Union to make me.
Fighting
NNF
isn't about glory.
Fighting isn't about pride.
This is the mistake that crazy scum like you always make.

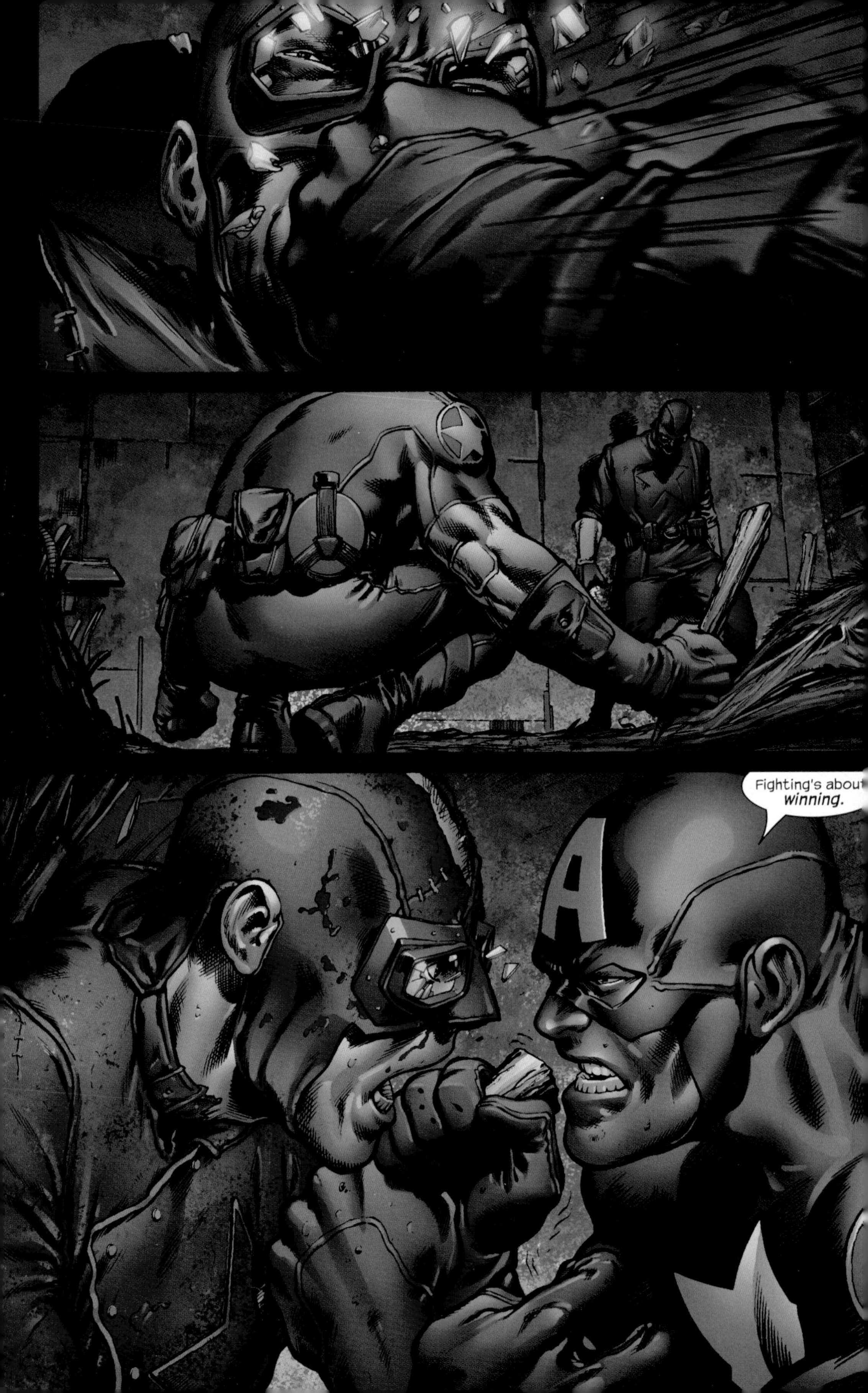
Fighting's about winning.

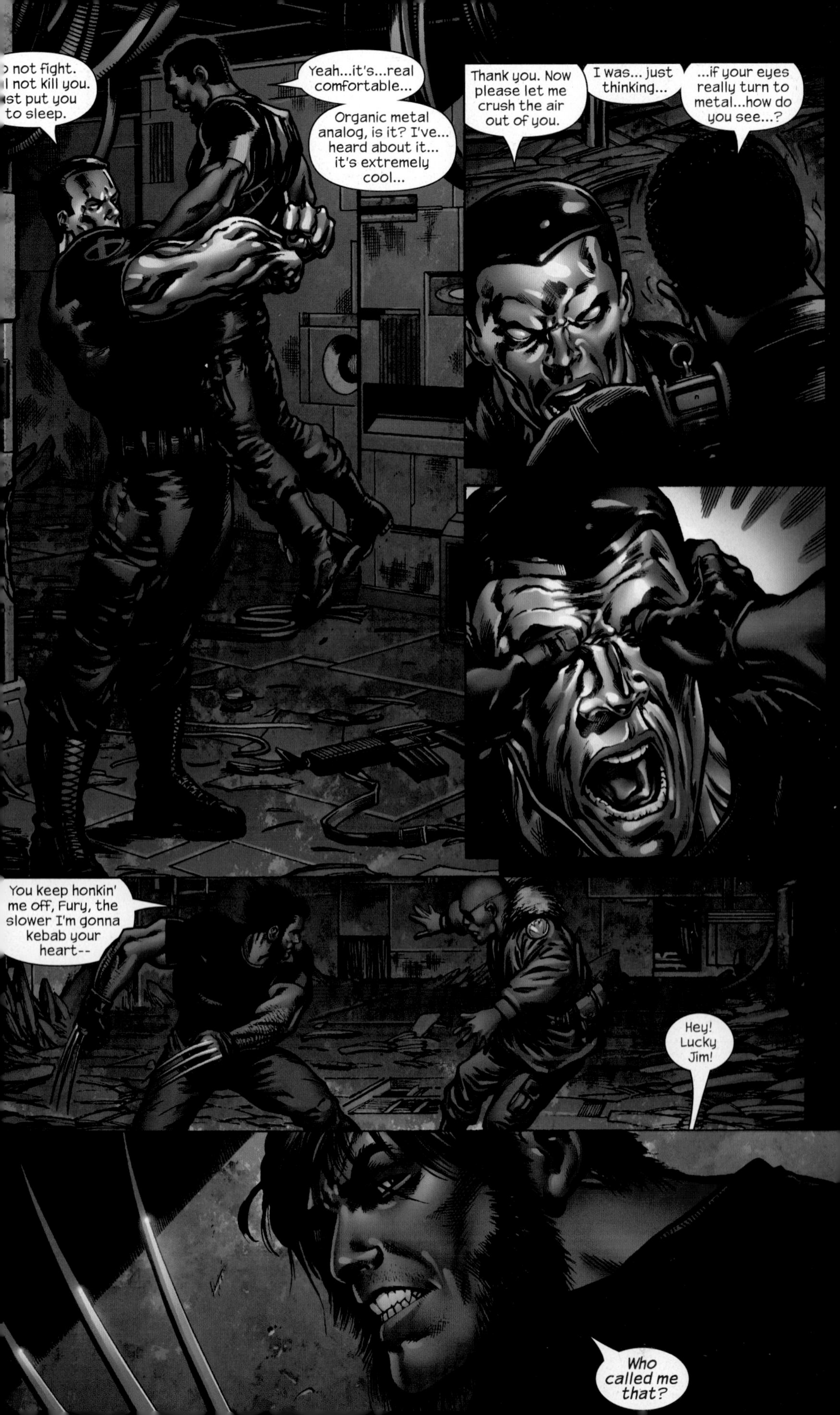

not fight. I not kill you. st put you to sleep.
Yeah...it's...real comfortable...
Organic metal analog, is it? I've... heard about it... it's extremely cool...
Thank you. Now please let me crush the air out of you.
I was... just thinking...
...if your eyes really turn to metal...how do you see...?
You keep honkin' me off, Fury, the slower I'm gonna kebab your heart--
Hey! Lucky Jim!
Who called me that?

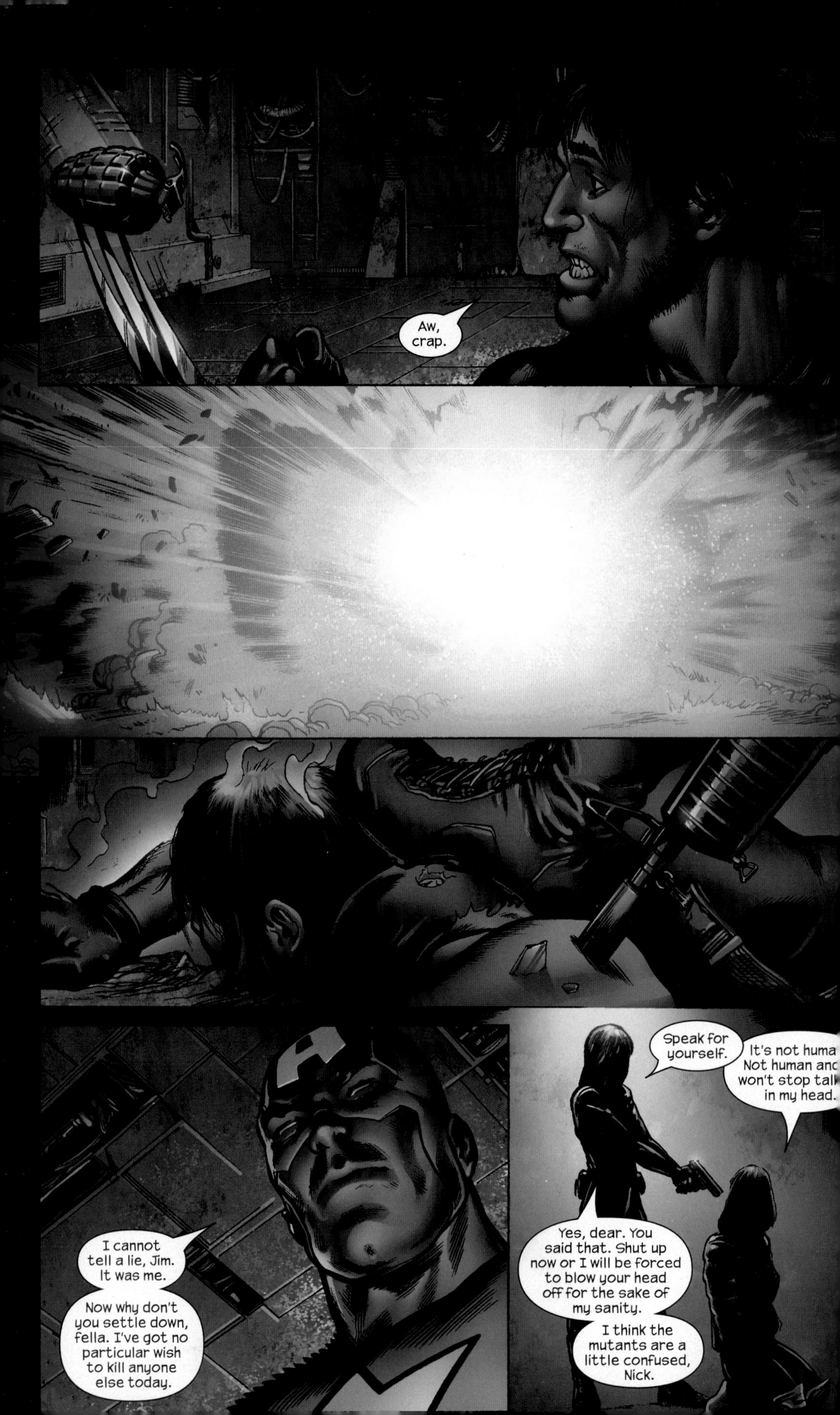
Aw, crap.
I cannot tell a lie, Jim. It was me.
Now why don't you settle down, fella. I've got no particular wish to kill anyone else today.
Speak for yourself.
It's not huma Not human anc won't stop tal in my head.
Yes, dear. You said that. Shut up now or I will be forced to blow your head off for the sake of my sanity.
I think the mutants are a little confused, Nick.

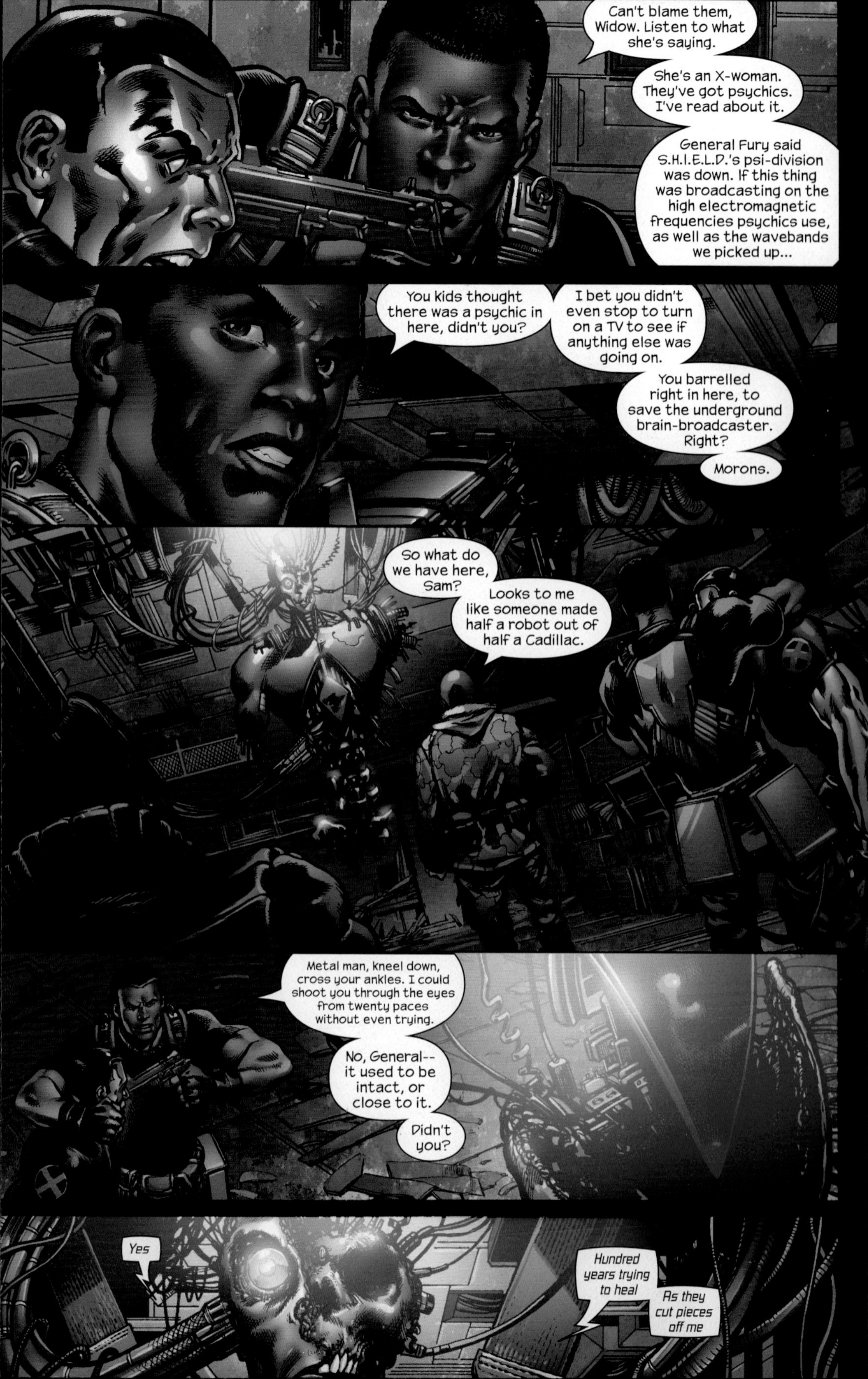

Can't blame them, Widow. Listen to what she's saying.
She's an X-woman. They've got psychics. I've read about it.
General Fury said S.H.I.E.L.D.'s psi-division was down. If this thing was broadcasting on the high electromagnetic frequencies psychics use, as well as the wavebands we picked up...
You kids thought there was a psychic in here, didn't you?
I bet you didn't even stop to turn on a TV to see if anything else was going on.
You barrelled right in here, to save the underground brain-broadcaster. Right?
Morons.
So what do we have here, Sam?
Looks to me like someone made half a robot out of half a Cadillac.
Metal man, kneel down, cross your ankles. I could shoot you through the eyes from twenty paces without even trying.
No, General-- it used to be intact, or close to it.
Didn't you?
Yes
Hundred years trying to heal
As they cut pieces off me

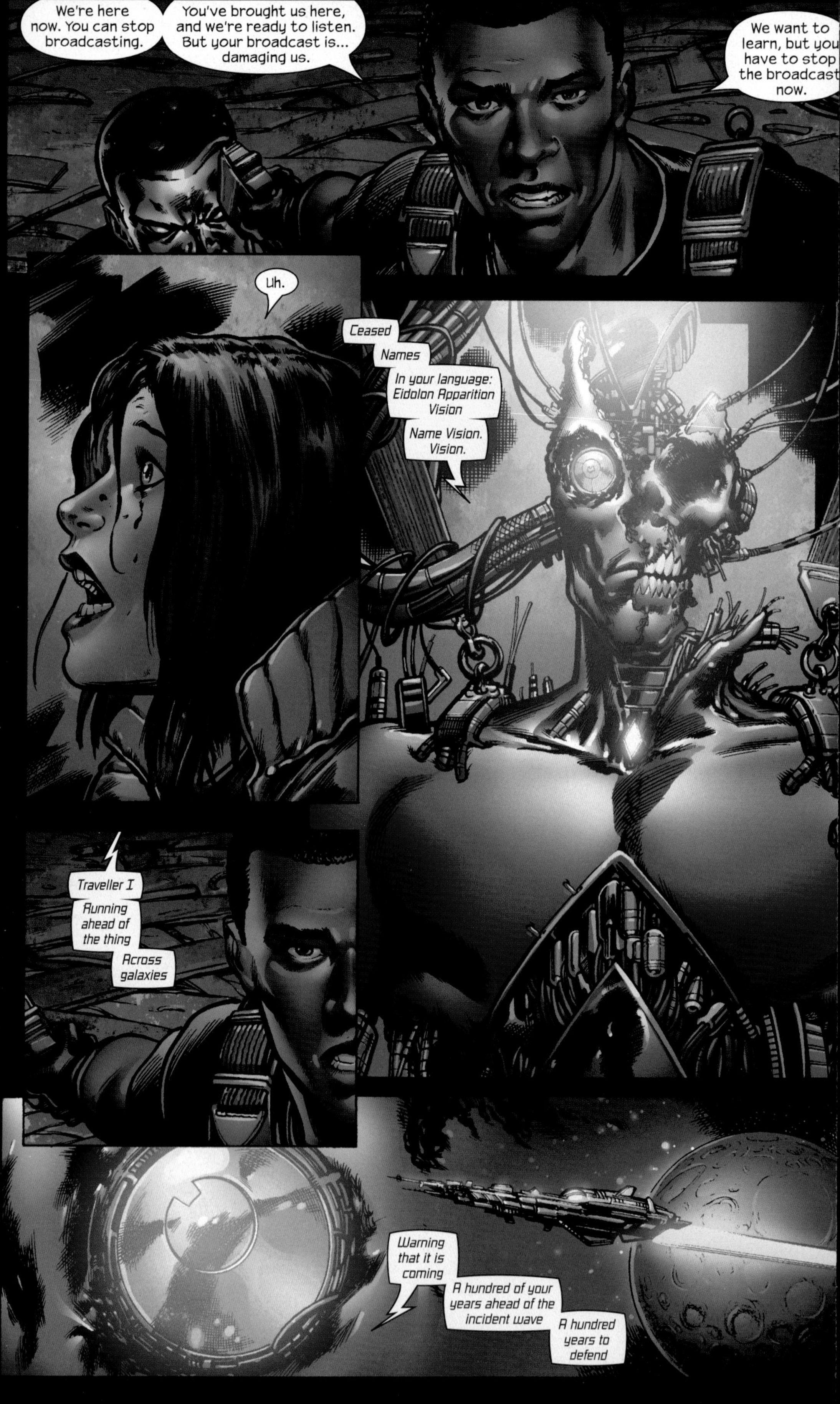
We're here now. You can stop broadcasting.
You've brought us here, and we're ready to listen. But your broadcast is... damaging us.
We want to learn, but you have to stop the broadcast now.
Uh.
Ceased
Names
In your language: Eidolon Apparition Vision
Name Vision. Vision.
Traveller I
Running ahead of the thing
Across galaxies
Warning that it is coming
A hundred of your years ahead of the incident wave
A hundred years to defend

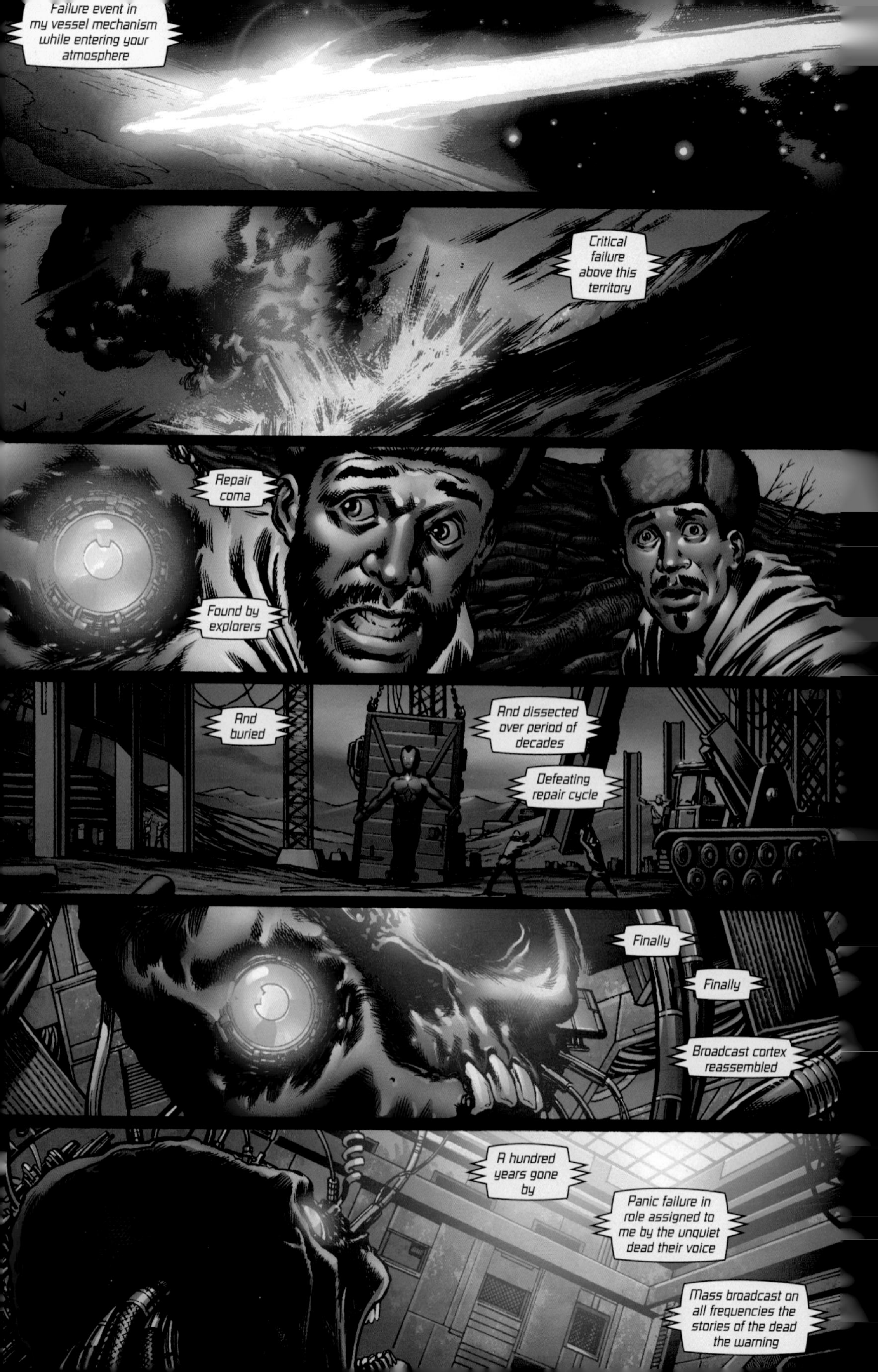
Failure event in my vessel mechanism while entering your atmosphere
Critical failure above this territory
Repair coma
Found by explorers
And buried
And dissected over period of decades
Defeating repair cycle
Finally
Finally
Broadcast cortex reassembled
A hundred years gone by
Panic failure in role assigned to me by the unquiet dead their voice
Mass broadcast on all frequencies the stories of the dead the warning

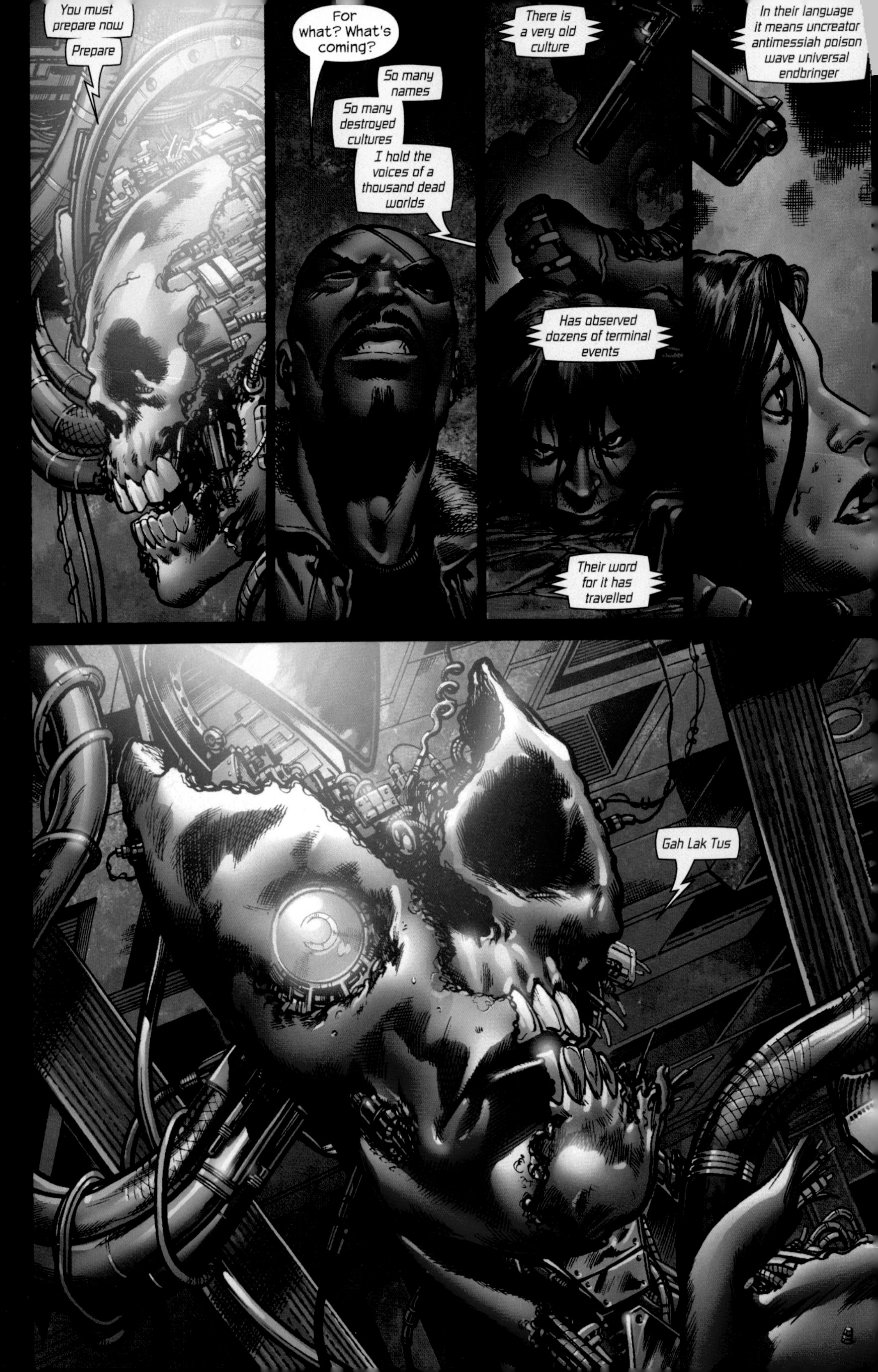

You must prepare now
Prepare
For what? What's coming?
So many names
So many destroyed cultures
I hold the voices of a thousand dead worlds
There is a very old culture
Has observed dozens of terminal events
Their word for it has travelled
In their language it means uncreator antimessiah poison wave universal endbringer
Gah Lak Tus

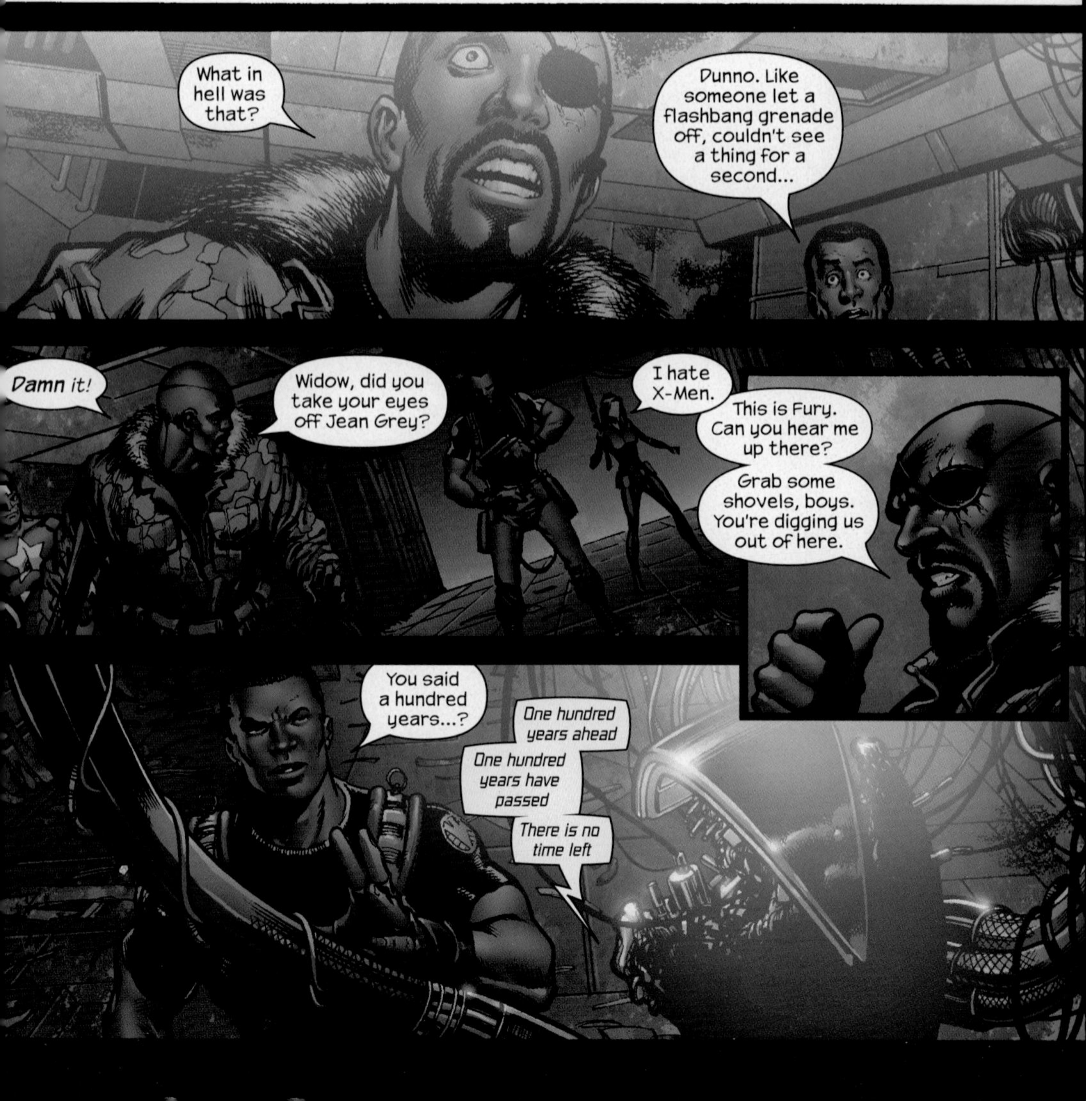
What in hell was that?
Dunno. Like someone let a flashbang grenade off, couldn't see a thing for a second...
Damn it!
Widow, did you take your eyes off Jean Grey?
I hate X-Men.
This is Fury. Can you hear me up there?
Grab some shovels, boys. You're digging us out of here.
You said a hundred years...?
One hundred years ahead
One hundred years have passed
There is no time left

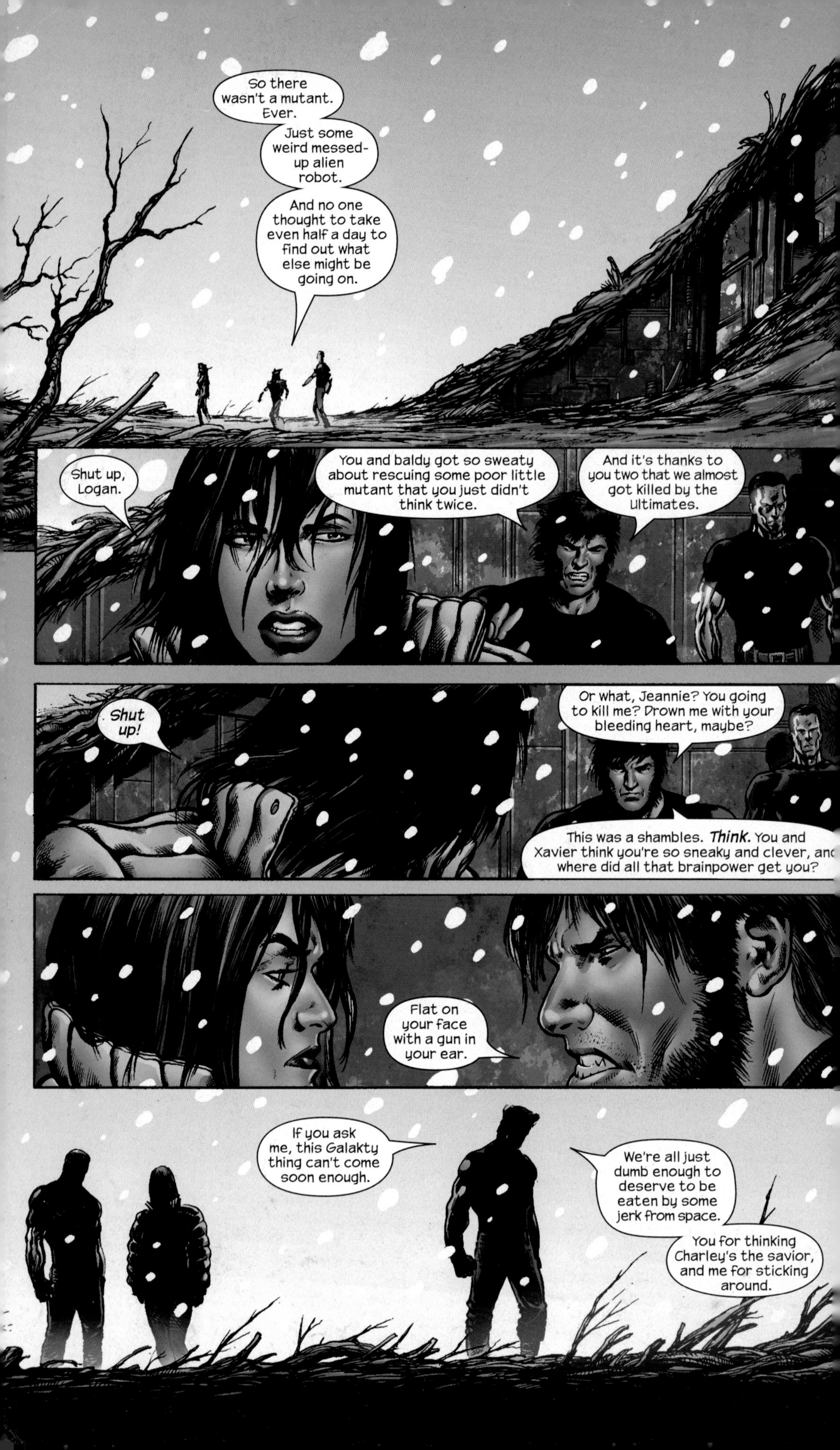
So there wasn't a mutant. Ever.
Just some weird messed-up alien robot.
And no one thought to take even half a day to find out what else might be going on.
Shut up, Logan.
You and baldy got so sweaty about rescuing some poor little mutant that you just didn't think twice.
And it's thanks to you two that we almost got killed by the Ultimates.
Shut up!
Or what, Jeannie? You going to kill me? Drown me with your bleeding heart, maybe?
This was a shambles. Think. You and Xavier think you're so sneaky and clever, and where did all that brainpower get you?
Flat on your face with a gun in your ear.
If you ask me, this Galakty thing can't come soon enough.
We're all just dumb enough to deserve to be eaten by some jerk from space.
You for thinking Charley's the savior, and me for sticking around.

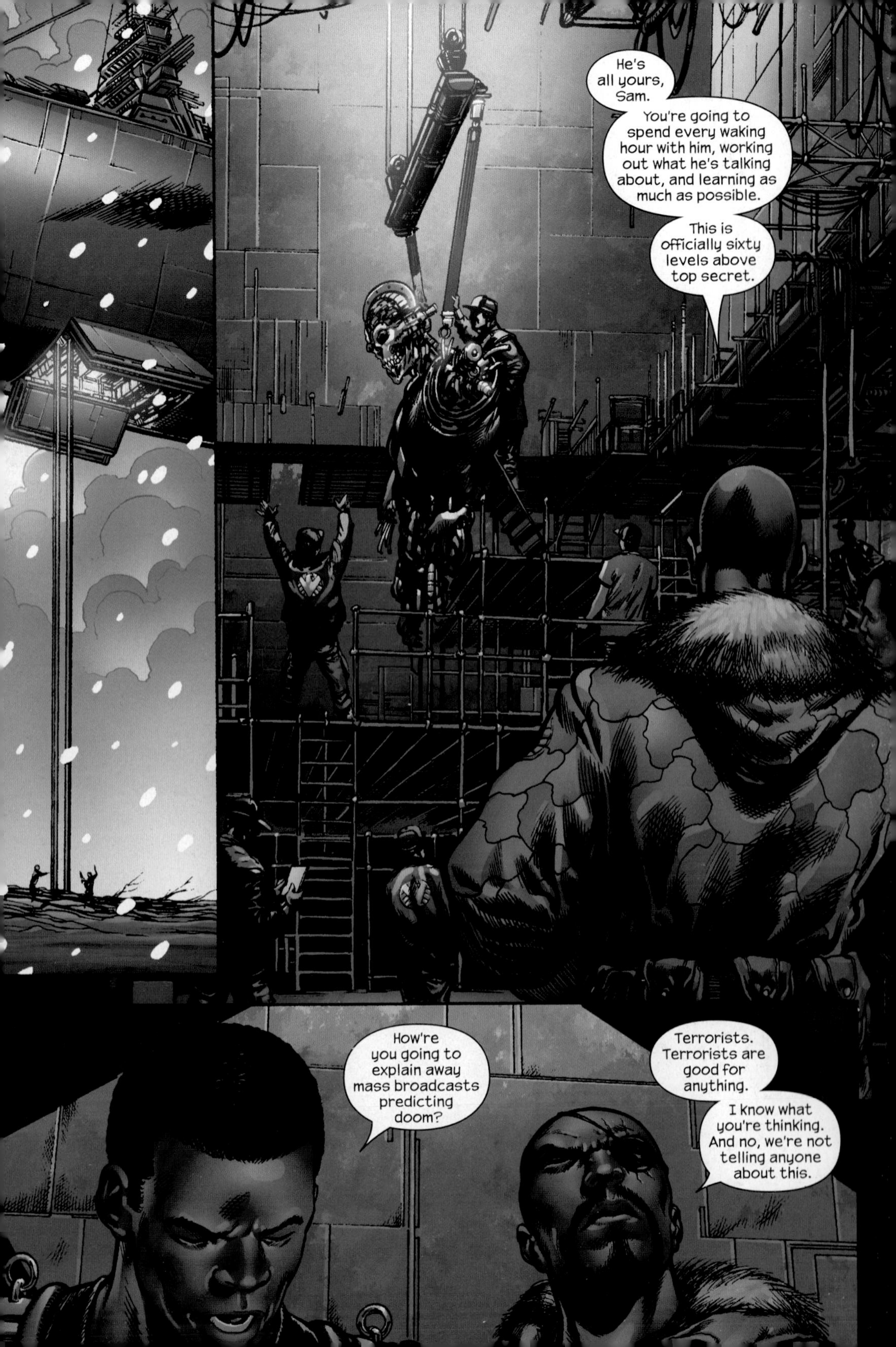
He's all yours, Sam.
You're going to spend every waking hour with him, working out what he's talking about, and learning as much as possible.
This is officially sixty levels above top secret.
How're you going to explain away mass broadcasts predicting doom?
Terrorists. Terrorists are good for anything.
I know what you're thinking. And no, we're not telling anyone about this.

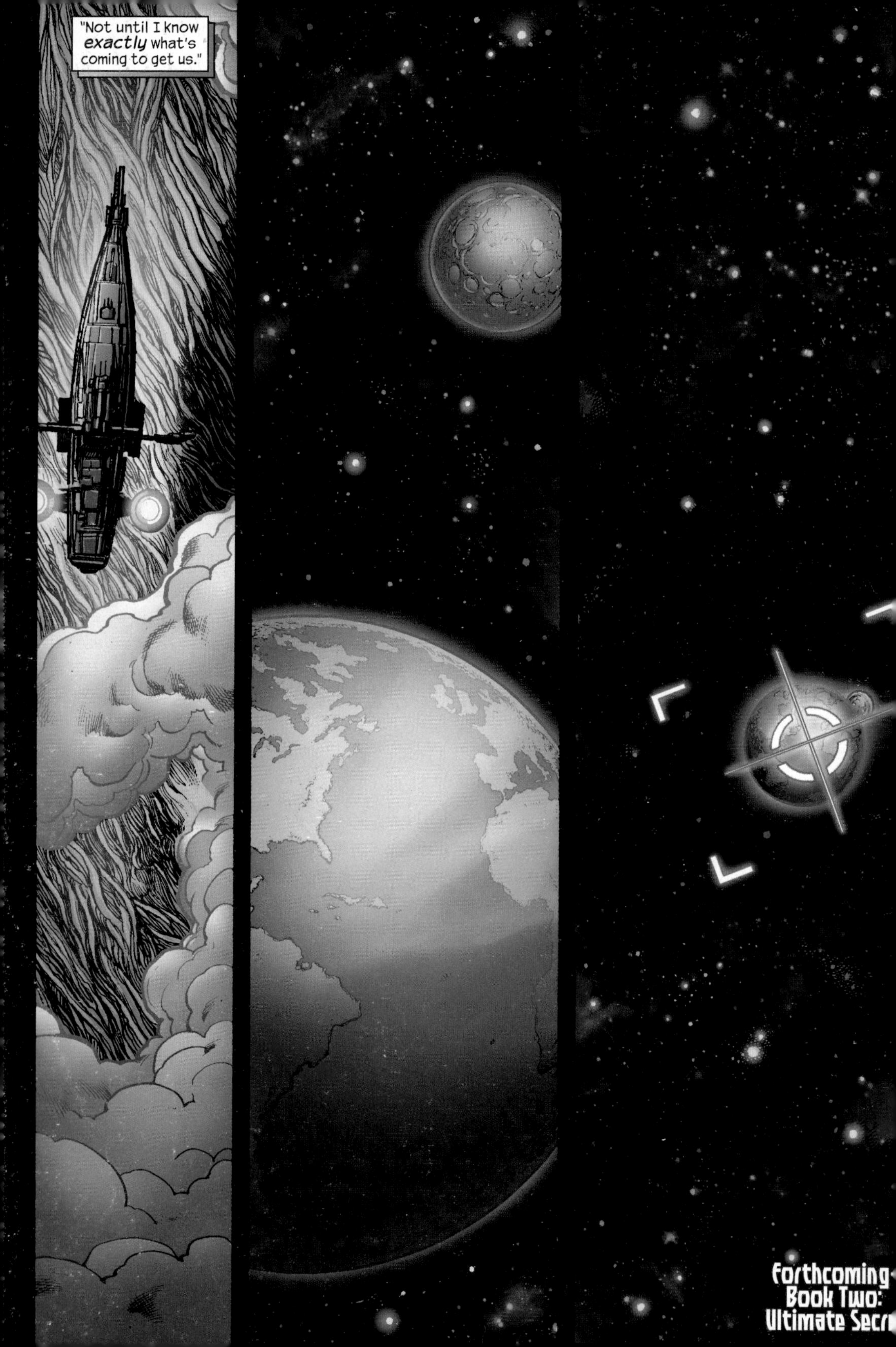
"Not until I know *exactly* what's coming to get us."
Forthcoming
Book Two:
Ultimate Secr